BIBLE

touchPOINTS™
for women

BIBLE

touchPOINTS™
for women

TYNDALE HOUSE PUBLISHERS, INC.
CAROL STREAM, ILLINOIS

Visit Tyndale online at www.tyndale.com.

TYNDALE, Tyndale's quill logo, *New Living Translation*, *NLT*, the New Living Translation logo, and *LeatherLike* are registered trademarks of Tyndale House Publishers, Inc.

TouchPoints is a trademark of Tyndale House Publishers, Inc.

Bible TouchPoints for Women

Previously published as *TouchPoints for Women* (Regular Edition) under ISBN 978-0-8423-3306-1 in 1998 and as *TouchPonts for Women—Gift Edition* under ISBN 978-1-4143-2020-5 in 2010.

General editors: Ronald A. Beers, V. Gilbert Beers, Amy Mason

Contributing writers: V. Gilbert Beers, Rebecca Beers, Brian R. Coffey, Jonathan Farrar, Jonathan Gray, Sean A. Harrison, Sandy Hull, Amy E. Mason, Rhonda K. O'Brien, Douglas J. Rumford, Linda Taylor

Designed by Jennifer Ghionzoli

ISBN 978-1-4964-0259-2

Printed in China

20 19 18 17 16 15 14
7   6   5   4   3   2   1

CONTENTS

ABANDONMENT

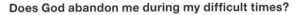

Does God abandon me during my difficult times?

PSALM 9:10 | *Those who know your name trust in you, for you, O LORD, do not abandon those who search for you.*

PSALM 27:10 | *Even if my father and mother abandon me, the LORD will hold me close.*

JOHN 14:16 | *[Jesus said,] "I will ask the Father, and he will give you another Advocate, who will never leave you."*

2 CORINTHIANS 4:9 | *We are hunted down, but never abandoned by God. We get knocked down, but we are not destroyed.*

God is always pursuing you, trying to get his attention. Are you aware of him? If you are sincerely looking for him, you are sure to find him because God will never abandon anyone who wants a relationship with him. In your difficult times some of your closest friends might neglect or even desert you, but God never will. In fact, your difficulties can become the means to help you look more intently for God—and you will see him right by your side.

Are there some things I must abandon in order to have a closer relationship with God?

PHILIPPIANS 3:8, 10 | *[Paul said,] "I have discarded everything else. . . . I want to know Christ and experience the mighty power that raised him from the dead. I want to suffer with him, sharing in his death."*

Abandoning those things that keep you from God is the best way to assure that you will not abandon him. If there is something in your life that is coming between you and God, work hard to get rid of it so you can have a closer relationship with him. Clinging to a sinful habit causes you to fall further and further away from God.

Promise from God HEBREWS 13:5 | *God has said, "I will never fail you. I will never abandon you."*

ABILITIES

Does God give me talents and abilities for a reason?

EXODUS 31:1-5 | *The LORD said to Moses, "Look, I have specifically chosen Bezalel. . . . I have filled him with the Spirit of God, giving him great wisdom, ability, and expertise in all kinds of crafts. He is a master craftsman, expert in working with gold, silver, and bronze. He is skilled in engraving and mounting gemstones and in carving wood."*

1 CORINTHIANS 12:6 | *God works in different ways, but it is the same God who does the work in all of us.*

Your talents and abilities are not random or accidental; they are part of the way God has uniquely designed you. God gave Bezalel talent as a craftsman and commissioned him to create beautiful objects for the Tabernacle. God does his work on earth through people, so he gives each person special gifts and talents.

Every ability you have is useful to God, so use each one for him. These abilities may become your full-time job, or

they may simply be hobbies. Either way, God can use them to accomplish his purposes. It is exciting and deeply satisfying to do the things you enjoy for God's service.

I'm really good at certain things. Can God use those abilities to serve him?

MATTHEW 25:21 | *Well done, my good and faithful servant. You have been faithful in handling this small amount, so now I will give you many more responsibilities.*

LUKE 12:48 | *When someone has been given much, much will be required in return; and when someone has been entrusted with much, even more will be required.*

1 CORINTHIANS 10:31 | *Whatever you do, do it all for the glory of God.*

The abilities you have are gifts from God, and with them comes the responsibility of using them well. You may be gifted in the area of cooking, entertaining, managing a business, sewing, handling money, playing an instrument, or some other gift. Use whatever gifts you have been given to bring honor and glory to God.

How can my God-given abilities have the most impact?

PHILIPPIANS 2:5-7 | *You must have the same attitude that Christ Jesus had. Though he was God, he did not think of equality with God as something to cling to. Instead, he gave up his divine privileges; he took the humble position of a slave.*

1 PETER 4:10 | *God has given each of you a gift from his great variety of spiritual gifts. Use them well to serve one another.*

God has given you specific abilities and strengths. Sometimes you might neglect to use those abilities or get in the rut of using them only for yourself. When you see your abilities as

gifts from almighty God, you will be humbled to think that he would value you enough to put these gifts in your care. Use them for your personal enjoyment, but use them also to serve others, for that is where they have the greatest impact.

Promise from God MATTHEW 25:29 | *To those who use well what they are given, even more will be given, and they will have an abundance.*

ABORTION

When does life begin?

PSALM 51:5 | *I was born a sinner—yes, from the moment my mother conceived me.*

The Bible points to the moment of conception as the beginning of human life.

What is the value of an unborn child?

PSALM 139:13-16 | *You made all the delicate, inner parts of my body and knit me together in my mother's womb. Thank you for making me so wonderfully complex! Your workmanship is marvelous—how well I know it. You watched me as I was being formed in utter seclusion, as I was woven together in the dark of the womb. You saw me before I was born. Every day of my life was recorded in your book. Every moment was laid out before a single day had passed.*

JEREMIAH 1:5 | *[The Lord said,] "I knew you before I formed you in your mother's womb. Before you were born I set you apart and appointed you as my prophet to the nations."*

God is present continuously during the nine months of pregnancy—forming, watching, creating, and even scheduling each day of the unborn baby's life. Before a baby is born, God knows him or her personally and intimately and he has already established a purpose for the baby. The value of an unborn child is priceless because he or she is already a friend of God.

Is abortion absolutely wrong?

EXODUS 20:13 | *You must not murder.*

One of God's Ten Commandments is a prohibition against murder. In the abortion debate, the issue becomes this: Is an unborn child really a person yet? If the unborn child is a person, then aborting that child becomes murder. Murder carries grave consequences because it ends a human life that held so much potential, and it puts authority over human life into the hands of human beings rather than leaving it in God's hands. The Bible is clear that life begins at conception, not birth. Therefore, aborting an unborn child is terminating the life of that child and is absolutely wrong.

The abortion issue has nothing to do with me. Why worry about it?

PROVERBS 24:11-12 | *Rescue those who are unjustly sentenced to die; save them as they stagger to their death. Don't excuse yourself by saying, "Look, we didn't know." For God understands all hearts, and he sees you. He who guards your soul knows you knew. He will repay all people as their actions deserve.*

Every child needs a champion, especially the unborn child. Perhaps God is calling you to be a voice for the unborn or to support a cause that helps the unborn. Maybe he wants you to adopt a baby or to help a new mother cope with her new child. Pray and ask God how he might want you to help the unborn.

Can I be forgiven if I have had an abortion or encouraged someone else to have one?

PSALM 103:3 | *[The Lord] forgives all my sins and heals all my diseases.*

ISAIAH 1:18 | *"Come now, let's settle this," says the LORD. "Though your sins are like scarlet, I will make them as white as snow. Though they are red like crimson, I will make them as white as wool."*

1 JOHN 1:9 | *If we confess our sins to him, he is faithful and just to forgive us our sins and to cleanse us from all wickedness.*

If you have had an abortion or encouraged someone to have one, you must clearly understand that it was wrong. But you must also clearly understand the wonder of God's grace and mercy to anyone who sincerely asks him for forgiveness. No matter how great your sin, God's forgiveness is even greater.

Promise from God JEREMIAH 1:5 | *[The Lord said,] "I knew you before I formed you in your mother's womb."*

ACCEPTANCE

I feel so unworthy—does God really accept me?

GENESIS 1:27 | *God created human beings in his own image. In the image of God he created them; male and female he created them.*

ROMANS 5:8 | *God showed his great love for us by sending Christ to die for us while we were still sinners.*

EPHESIANS 1:4-5 | *Even before he made the world, God loved us and chose us in Christ to be holy and without fault in his eyes. God decided in advance to adopt us into his own family by bringing us to himself through Jesus Christ. This is what he wanted to do, and it gave him great pleasure.*

You are accepted by God because he made you and created you in his image. Nothing you can do will cause God to love you more, because he loves you completely. And nothing you do can cause God to love you less. In fact, God accepts you and loves you so much that he sent his own Son to die for you, to take on himself the punishment for sin you deserve. He died in your place so you can be accepted into eternity with him.

What makes me acceptable to God?

ROMANS 3:30 | *There is only one God, and he makes people right with himself only by faith, whether they are Jews or Gentiles.*

GALATIANS 2:16 | *We know that a person is made right with God by faith in Jesus Christ, not by obeying the law. And we have believed in Christ Jesus, so that we might be made right with God because of our faith in Christ, not because we have obeyed the law. For no one will ever be made right with God by obeying the law.*

Sin separates you from a holy and perfect God. But faith in Jesus removes your sin, making you holy and acceptable in God's sight. When you ask for his forgiveness, he looks at you as though you had never sinned.

How do I accept others, especially people I dislike?

MATTHEW 5:44 | *Love your enemies! Pray for those who persecute you!*

ROMANS 14:1, 3 | *Accept other believers who are weak in faith, and don't argue with them about what they think is right or wrong. . . . Those who feel free to eat anything must not look* down on those who don't. And those who don't eat certain foods must not condemn those who do, for God has accepted them.

Pray for those you dislike. Through prayer, God can help you see people through his eyes. Then, don't be so quick to make up your mind about who they really are and what they should or shouldn't do. Judging others is better left to God because it is so easy for us to misjudge people. He sets the standard for accepting others.

Promise from God ROMANS 15:7 | *Accept each other just as Christ has accepted you so that God will be given glory.*

ADOPTION

Is adopting a child right for me and my family? How can I know for sure?

PSALM 138:8 | *The LORD will work out his plans for my life— for your faithful love, O LORD, endures forever. Don't abandon me, for you made me.*

JEREMIAH 1:5 | *[The Lord said,] "I knew you before I formed you in your mother's womb. Before you were born I set you apart and appointed you."*

MATTHEW 18:5 | *[Jesus said,] "Anyone who welcomes a little child like this on my behalf is welcoming me."*

There are some things in life you can't know for sure, but the Bible is clear on this: God puts a high priority on loving children. If you adopt a child and welcome him or her into your heart and life, you are demonstrating the kind of love Christ showed for you.

How has God adopted me? Why would he want to do that?

JOHN 1:12 | *To all who believed [the Father's one and only Son] and accepted him, he gave the right to become children of God.*

GALATIANS 3:26 | *You are all children of God through faith in Christ Jesus.*

GALATIANS 4:4-5 | *God sent his Son, born of a woman, subject to the law. God sent him to buy freedom for us who were slaves to the law, so that he could adopt us as his very own children.*

When you accept Jesus Christ as your Savior, God adopts you into his family.

1 JOHN 3:1 | *See how very much our Father loves us, for he calls us his children, and that is what we are!*

God's love for you makes him want to adopt you.

EPHESIANS 1:5 | *God decided in advance to adopt us into his own family by bringing us to himself through Jesus Christ. This is what he wanted to do, and it gave him great pleasure.*

Adopting you as his child has been part of God's plan since the beginning of time.

PHILIPPIANS 2:15 | *Live clean, innocent lives as children of God, shining like bright lights in a world full of crooked and perverse people.*

1 PETER 2:9 | *You are a chosen people. You are royal priests, a holy nation, God's very own possession. As a result, you can show others the goodness of God, for he called you out of the darkness into his wonderful light.*

God has adopted you to be an example to others of his goodness.

Promise from God EPHESIANS 1:4-6 | *Even before he made the world, God loved us and chose us in Christ to be holy and without fault in his eyes. God decided in advance to adopt us into his own family by bringing us to himself through Jesus Christ. This is what he wanted to do, and it gave him great pleasure. So we praise God for the glorious grace he has poured out on us who belong to his dear Son.*

AFFECTION

Where should I focus my affections?

PSALM 42:1-2 | *As the deer longs for streams of water, so I long for you, O God. I thirst for God, the living God. When can I go and stand before him?*

MARK 12:30 | *You must love the LORD your God with all your heart, all your soul, all your mind, and all your strength.*

If your greatest affection is for God, your priorities are in the right place.

PSALM 27:4 | *The one thing I ask of the LORD—the thing I seek most—is to live in the house of the LORD all the days of my life.*

PSALM 69:9 | *Passion for your house has consumed me.*

Develop a love for God's house, the church, for that is where you can worship him in a special way.

MATTHEW 5:44 | *Love your enemies! Pray for those who persecute you!*

JOHN 13:34 | *[Jesus said,] "I am giving you a new commandment: Love each other. Just as I have loved you, you should love each other."*

1 JOHN 4:7 | *Let us continue to love one another, for love comes from God. Anyone who loves is a child of God and knows God.*

Love others, even your enemies. Loving one another is how God's people show the world who God is, because God is love.

How does God express his affection for me?

1 JOHN 4:9-10 | *God showed how much he loved us by sending his one and only Son into the world so that we might have eternal life through him. This is real love—not that we loved God, but that he loved us and sent his Son as a sacrifice to take away our sins.*

Sacrificing one's life so that another can live—that is real love. Jesus, as an expression of his love for you, suffered and then died for your sins so that you can live forever.

PSALM 136:1 | *Give thanks to the LORD, for he is good! His faithful love endures forever.*

1 CORINTHIANS 2:9 | *No eye has seen, no ear has heard, and no mind has imagined what God has prepared for those who love him.*

God has a love for you that will never change or end. You will be utterly amazed at what he has prepared for you.

How can I express my affection for God?

PSALM 63:1 | *O God, you are my God; I earnestly search for you. My soul thirsts for you; my whole body longs for you.*

Your longing for God is evidence of your affection for him.

PSALM 119:40, 131 | *I long to obey your commandments! Renew my life with your goodness. . . . I pant with expectation, longing for your commands.*

ISAIAH 26:8 | *LORD, we show our trust in you by obeying your laws; our heart's desire is to glorify your name.*

Obedience to God and his Word is evidence of a deep affection for him. Obeying God is an important expression of love, for it demonstrates the desire to honor him.

MATTHEW 12:34-35 | *Whatever is in your heart determines what you say. A good person produces good things from the treasury of a good heart, and an evil person produces evil things from the treasury of an evil heart.*

Your words are evidence of your affection for God. So show your affection for God by telling him how great and awesome he is, and avoid saying anything that would displease him.

Promise from God 1 PETER 4:8 | *Most important of all, continue to show deep love for each other, for love covers a multitude of sins.*

AFFIRMATION

How does God affirm me?

GENESIS 1:27 | *God created human beings in his own image. In the image of God he created them; male and female he created them.*

1 CORINTHIANS 15:3 | *[Paul said,] "I passed on to you what was most important and what had also been passed on to me. Christ died for our sins, just as the Scriptures said."*

1 PETER 2:5 | *You are living stones that God is building into his spiritual temple. What's more, you are his holy priests. Through*

the mediation of Jesus Christ, you offer spiritual sacrifices that please God.

God affirmed you when he created you like himself. He values you so much that he was willing to send his Son to die for you because he wants you to live with him forever.

PSALM 5:12 | *You bless the godly, O LORD; you surround them with your shield of love.*

PSALM 67:1 | *May God be merciful and bless us. May his face smile with favor on us.*

JOHN 10:28-29 | *[Jesus said,] "I give them eternal life, and they will never perish. No one can snatch them away from me, for my Father has given them to me, and he is more powerful than anyone else. No one can snatch them from the Father's hand."*

COLOSSIANS 2:13 | *You were dead because of your sins and because your sinful nature was not yet cut away. Then God made you alive with Christ, for he forgave all our sins.*

God affirms you through his love, his blessings, his mercy, his forgiveness, and his gift of salvation. What greater affirmation is there than to be affirmed by the Creator of the universe?

How can I affirm others? Why is it so important?

ROMANS 14:19 | *Let us aim for harmony in the church and try to build each other up.*

1 CORINTHIANS 14:26 | *Well, my brothers and sisters, let's summarize. When you meet together, one will sing, another will teach, another will tell some special revelation God has given, one will speak in tongues, and another will interpret what is said. But everything that is done must strengthen all of you.*

1 THESSALONIANS 5:11, 13 | *Encourage each other and build each other up, just as you are already doing. . . . Show them great respect and wholehearted love because of their work. And live peacefully with each other.*

Affirm others by encouraging them, praising them, and building them up. .

Promise from God ISAIAH 54:10 | *"The mountains may move and the hills disappear, but even then my faithful love for you will remain. My covenant of blessing will never be broken," says the LORD, who has mercy on you.*

ANGER

Is God angry with me?

EXODUS 34:6-7 | *The LORD passed in front of Moses, calling out, "Yahweh! The LORD! The God of compassion and mercy! I am slow to anger and filled with unfailing love and faithfulness. I lavish unfailing love to a thousand generations. I forgive iniquity, rebellion, and sin. But I do not excuse the guilty."*

PSALM 18:26-27 | *To the pure you show yourself pure, but to the wicked you show yourself hostile. You rescue the humble, but you humiliate the proud.*

God cannot tolerate sin and rebellion against himself; therefore any kind of sin or evil angers him. But he is ready to forgive because he is kind and merciful. When you humbly confess your sin and turn to him in faith, you will receive God's abundant love and mercy instead of his anger.

PSALM 30:5 | *[The Lord's] anger lasts only a moment, but his favor lasts a lifetime! Weeping may last through the night, but joy comes with the morning.*

PSALM 145:8 | *The LORD is merciful and compassionate, slow to get angry and filled with unfailing love.*

1 THESSALONIANS 5:9 | *God chose to save us through our Lord Jesus Christ, not to pour out his anger on us.*

The Bible promises that God is kind and merciful and that he is always ready to receive you, and all his children, with love. The "always-angry God" is one of the worst caricatures ever attributed to God. His anger toward us is conveyed with gentle discipline and is an expression of his love in action.

How should I deal with my own anger in relationships?

EPHESIANS 4:26 | *"Don't sin by letting anger control you." Don't let the sun go down while you are still angry.*

EPHESIANS 4:31-32 | *Get rid of all bitterness, rage, anger. . . . Instead, be kind to each other, tenderhearted, forgiving one another, just as God through Christ has forgiven you.*

Anger must be dealt with quickly, before it becomes bitter, hateful, or vengeful. As hard as forgiveness might sound, it is most effective in melting anger away.

What is the best way to deal with an angry person?

PROVERBS 15:1 | *A gentle answer deflects anger, but harsh words make tempers flare.*

PROVERBS 29:8 | *Mockers can get a whole town agitated, but the wise will calm anger.*

Reacting to anger with anger almost always intensifies the problem. Responding with wisdom and gentleness almost always calms an angry person.

When is it okay to be angry?

MARK 3:2-5 | *Since it was the Sabbath, Jesus' enemies watched him closely. If he healed the man's hand, they planned to accuse him of working on the Sabbath. Jesus said to the man with the deformed hand, "Come and stand in front of everyone." Then he turned to his critics and asked, "Does the law permit good deeds on the Sabbath, or is it a day for doing evil? Is this a day to save life or to destroy it?" But they wouldn't answer him. He looked around at them angrily and was deeply saddened by their hard hearts. Then he said to the man, "Hold out your hand." So the man held out his hand, and it was restored!*

JOHN 2:15-17 | *Jesus made a whip from some ropes and chased them all out of the Temple. He drove out the sheep and cattle, scattered the money changers' coins over the floor, and turned over their tables. Then, going over to the people who sold doves, he told them, "Get these things out of here. Stop turning my Father's house into a marketplace!" Then his disciples remembered this prophecy from the Scriptures: "Passion for God's house will consume me."*

Anger at sin is not only appropriate but necessary. Jesus' righteous anger arose from his devotion to God and compassion for others. It led to good deeds, not bad ones.

Promise from God PSALM 103:8 | *The LORD is compassionate and merciful, slow to get angry and filled with unfailing love.*

APATHY

Why am I not always on fire for God?

GENESIS 3:6 | *The woman was convinced. She saw that the tree was beautiful and its fruit looked delicious, and she wanted the wisdom it would give her. So she took some of the fruit and ate it. Then she gave some to her husband, who was with her, and he ate it, too.*

Temptation takes your focus off God and makes thinking about something else more exciting. When this happens, it's not that you really want to move away from God, but something else has suddenly got your attention! It's interesting and enticing. If what you're excited about is not what God wants for you, your passion for God will quickly die.

1 KINGS 11:1-3 | *King Solomon loved many foreign women. . . . He married women from Moab, Ammon, Edom, Sidon. . . . The LORD had clearly instructed the people of Israel, "You must not marry them, because they will turn your hearts to their gods." Yet Solomon insisted on loving them anyway. . . . And in fact, they did turn his heart away from the LORD.*

When sin takes a foothold in your life, it always leads you away from God and substitutes an apathetic attitude toward him. Satan will use all his power to keep you from getting excited about following God.

MARK 14:32, 34-35, 37-38 | *[Jesus and the disciples] went to the olive grove called Gethsemane, and Jesus said, ". . . Stay here and keep watch with me." He went on a little farther and fell to the ground. He prayed. . . . Then he returned and found the disciples asleep. He said to Peter, "Simon, are you asleep? Couldn't you watch with me even one hour? Keep watch and pray, so that you will not give in to temptation. For the spirit is willing, but the body is weak."*

Sometimes you're simply too tired or don't see the significance of what is going on around you. Peter thought this was just another night out. If he'd had his spiritual antenna

up, he might have sensed how significant this night was
going to be.

MALACHI 1:13 | *"You say, 'It's too hard to serve the LORD,' and
you turn up your noses at my commands," says the LORD of
Heaven's Armies.*

COLOSSIANS 1:22-23 | *You are holy and blameless as you stand
before [God] without a single fault. But you must continue to
believe this truth and stand firmly in it. Don't drift away from
the assurance you received when you heard the Good News.*

REVELATION 2:4 | *[God said,] "I have this complaint against you.
You don't love me or each other as you did at first!"*

Like all relationships, your relationship with God takes effort
and energy. God continues to be fully committed to you. In
order for your relationship to continue to be exciting, you
must be fully committed to him—diligent in your efforts to
know him better. A lack of effort and energy shows apathy.

What can I do when I am feeling apathetic?

LUKE 21:34 | *[Jesus said,] "Watch out! Don't let your hearts be
dulled by carousing and drunkenness, and by the worries of this
life. Don't let [the day of my return] catch you unaware."*

Jesus warns his followers to be alert to spiritual apathy. You
don't want to be caught at the end of life having neglected
your relationship with God because you were too focused
on living the good life. Always make your relationship with
God a priority.

PSALM 119:83 | *I am shriveled like a wineskin in the smoke,
but I have not forgotten to obey your decrees.*

Obey God's commands even when you don't feel like it.
This takes tremendous effort, but it's hard to be apathetic

when you're focused on something. Whatever takes great effort is stimulating and engaging. This will help keep you close to God.

ACTS 16:25 | *Around midnight Paul and Silas were praying and singing hymns to God, and the other prisoners were listening.*

Instead of sinking into apathy when adversity strikes, worship God through prayer and song and stay connected with Christian friends. Even when you don't feel like doing these things, choose to do them anyway and your efforts will be rewarded. Prayer and praise to God are sure cures for apathy.

PHILIPPIANS 2:4 | *Don't look out only for your own interests, but take an interest in others, too.*

HEBREWS 6:10-12 | *God is not unjust. He will not forget how hard you have worked for him and how you have shown your love to him by caring for other believers, as you still do. Our great desire is that you will keep on loving others as long as life lasts, in order to make certain that what you hope for will come true. Then you will not become spiritually dull and indifferent.*

The more interested you are in something, the less apathy you will experience. The more interested you become in the lives of those around you, the more you'll care about them. Getting involved in the lives of others not only keeps you from becoming dull and indifferent but also challenges you to think about ways to reflect the love of Jesus to them.

PROVERBS 13:4 | *Lazy people want much but get little, but those who work hard will prosper.*

ROMANS 12:11 | *Never be lazy, but work hard and serve the Lord enthusiastically.*

2 THESSALONIANS 3:11 | *We hear that some of you are living idle lives, refusing to work and meddling in other people's business.*

One of the best cures for apathy is hard work! When you work hard, you become productive. The more productive you are, the more satisfied and fulfilled you will be. Moreover, when your hard work is an act of service to God, you gain more energy as you see God working through you to bless others.

JEREMIAH 1:4-5 | *The LORD gave me this message: "I knew you before I formed you in your mother's womb. Before you were born I set you apart and appointed you."*

You can stimulate your passion for life by realizing that God has a purpose for you. God created you specifically to make a difference for his Kingdom! Purpose stirs passion, and passion drives apathy away.

Promise from God EZEKIEL 11:19 | *[The Lord said,] "I will give [my people] singleness of heart and put a new spirit within them. I will take away their stony, stubborn heart and give them a tender, responsive heart."*

APPEARANCE

How much does appearance matter?

1 SAMUEL 16:7 | *The LORD doesn't see things the way you see them. People judge by outward appearance, but the LORD looks at the heart.*

PROVERBS 31:30 | *Charm is deceptive, and beauty does not last; but a woman who fears the LORD will be greatly praised.*

ROMANS 8:10 | *Christ lives within you.*

EPHESIANS 5:8-9 | *Once you were full of darkness, but now you have light from the Lord. . . . This light within you produces only what is good and right and true.*

1 PETER 3:3-4 | *Don't be concerned about the outward beauty of fancy hairstyles, expensive jewelry, or beautiful clothes. You should clothe yourselves instead with the beauty that comes from within, the unfading beauty of a gentle and quiet spirit, which is so precious to God.*

Appearance does matter; just make sure you're focusing on the right things. Your body, which is in a constant process of aging and decay, and your hair, makeup, and clothes are only your outward shell. Your soul and character are your inner being, which is ageless and eternal and communicates who you really are. Walking with God causes you to reflect his beauty. There's nothing wrong with paying attention to your physical appearance, but not to the neglect of your spiritual appearance. What an impact you can have on others when they miss what's on your outside because they can't take their eyes off what's on the inside—God himself shining through.

How can I see beyond appearances?

MATTHEW 7:16-17, 20 | *You can identify [false prophets] by their fruit, that is, by the way they act. . . . A good tree produces good fruit, and a bad tree produces bad fruit. . . . Yes, just as you can identify a tree by its fruit, so you can identify people by their actions.*

1 JOHN 4:1 | *Do not believe everyone who claims to speak by the Spirit. You must test them to see if the spirit they have comes from God.*

All God's people must be "fruit inspectors," looking beyond appearances and words to the actual fruit of a person's behavior and character. Obedience to the Bible is an essential test of authentic faith in Jesus Christ. Good works alone are not sufficient. There must be a match between words and works, character and conduct.

Is there any value to maintaining a good appearance?

ECCLESIASTES 9:7-8; 11:9-10; 12:13 | *Eat your food with joy, and drink your wine with a happy heart, for God approves of this! Wear fine clothes, with a splash of cologne! . . . But remember that you must give an account to God for everything you do. So refuse to worry, and keep your body healthy. . . . Fear God and obey his commands, for this is everyone's duty.*

MATTHEW 6:17 | *When you fast, comb your hair and wash your face.*

1 CORINTHIANS 6:19-20 | *Don't you realize that your body is the temple of the Holy Spirit, who lives in you and was given to you by God? You do not belong to yourself, for God bought you with a high price. So you must honor God with your body.*

You should not be obsessed with your physical appearance, but neither should you ignore it. How you present yourself is in part a reflection of who you are, and it plays a role in your ability to interact with others. Your body is the house in which the Holy Spirit dwells, so you should keep up the place in which he lives. The more you keep up your body, the more energy you have to serve him. Keeping your body clean and healthy allows more opportunities to become involved in others' lives and influence them with the good news of Jesus. How you present yourself can help you in the way you represent Christ.

Promise from God 1 SAMUEL 16:7 | *People judge by outward appearance, but the LORD looks at the heart.*

ASSUMPTIONS

What are some assumptions I should avoid?

JUDGES 6:13-14 | *"Sir," Gideon replied, "if the LORD is with us, why has all this happened to us? And where are all the miracles our ancestors told us about? Didn't they say, 'The LORD brought us up out of Egypt'? But now the LORD has abandoned us and handed us over to the Midianites." Then the LORD turned to him and said, "Go with the strength you have, and rescue Israel from the Midianites. I am sending you!"*

Don't assume God won't help you or doesn't want to help you, for he has already done so in more ways than you know, and he will continue to do so. And don't assume you know better than God the best way through your problems.

MALACHI 2:17 | *You have wearied the LORD with your words. "How have we wearied him?" you ask. You have wearied him by saying that all who do evil are good in the LORD's sight, and he is pleased with them. You have wearied him by asking, "Where is the God of justice?"*

Don't assume that God will not address good and evil; his plan includes justice for everyone.

JOHN 14:6 | *Jesus [said], "I am the way, the truth, and the life. No one can come to the Father except through me."*

Don't just assume you will go to heaven. The Bible says the only way to heaven is by accepting Jesus Christ as Savior and Lord.

ACTS 9:13, 15 | *"But Lord," exclaimed Ananias, "I've heard many people talk about the terrible things this man has done to the believers in Jerusalem! . . . But the Lord said, "Go, for Saul is my chosen instrument to take my message to the Gentiles and to kings, as well as to the people of Israel."*

Don't assume people can't change; you may miss out when they want to give their best to you. Like Paul (previously known as Saul), even the worst sinner in God's eyes can become the mightiest Christian leader.

JOHN 3:8 | *Just as you can hear the wind but can't tell where it comes from or where it is going, so you can't explain how people are born of the Spirit.*

ACTS 10:34-35 | *God shows no favoritism. In every nation he accepts those who fear him and do what is right.*

ACTS 16:27-30 | *The jailer woke up to see the prison doors wide open. He assumed the prisoners had escaped, so he drew his sword to kill himself. But Paul shouted to him, "Stop! Don't kill yourself! We are all here!" The jailer called for lights and ran to the dungeon and fell down trembling before Paul and Silas. Then he brought them out and asked, "Sirs, what must I do to be saved?"*

Don't assume that someone won't respond to the gospel. In God's hands, people can be transformed into godly heroes.

Promise from God 1 CORINTHIANS 4:5 | *Don't make judgments about anyone ahead of time—before the Lord returns. For he will bring our darkest secrets to light and will reveal our private motives. Then God will give to each one whatever praise is due.*

BEAUTY

What does God consider beautiful?

1 SAMUEL 16:7 | *People judge by outward appearance, but the LORD looks at the heart.*

1 PETER 3:3-4 | *Don't be concerned about the outward beauty of fancy hairstyles, expensive jewelry, or beautiful clothes. You should clothe yourselves instead with the beauty that comes from within, the unfading beauty of a gentle and quiet spirit, which is so precious to God.*

People tend to look at physical appearance only. God sees through physical appearance into the heart. Society too often believes that an ugly face with a beautiful heart makes an unattractive person. To God, real beauty comes from who a person is, not what he or she looks like.

1 CORINTHIANS 15:41 | *The sun has one kind of glory, while the moon and stars each have another kind. And even the stars differ from each other in their glory.*

Beauty comes in assorted sizes, shapes, appearance, and actions. There is no one model for beauty. In a very real sense each of us, as we strive to reflect God's beauty, creates a unique model for the beauty we exhibit to others.

How can my words be beautiful?

PROVERBS 15:26 | *The LORD detests evil plans, but he delights in pure words.*

PROVERBS 25:11 | *Timely advice is lovely, like golden apples in a silver basket.*

LUKE 6:45 | *What you say flows from what is in your heart.*

Beautiful words are a fruit of godly thoughts and character. When you spend most of your time thinking about what is right and good (see Philippians 4:8), your words will be mostly right and good.

How can my actions be beautiful?

1 TIMOTHY 2:10 | *Women who claim to be devoted to God should make themselves attractive by the good things they do.*

Beautiful conduct is also a fruit of godly thoughts and character. When you spend most of your time thinking about what is right and good, your actions will be mostly right and good.

How can my worship be beautiful?

PSALM 33:1 | *Let the godly sing for joy to the LORD; it is fitting for the pure to praise him.*

Beautiful worship is a fruit of a beautiful relationship with God. When you spend most of your time focused on the beauty and majesty of God, your life will be an example of worship and celebration of God's beauty and majesty.

Who is our role model for beauty?

2 CORINTHIANS 3:18 | *All of us who [believe in Christ] can see and reflect the glory of the Lord. And the Lord—who is the Spirit—makes us more and more like him as we are changed into his glorious image.*

The more you reflect God and his character, the more you radiate his beauty. What could be more beautiful than a perfect God?

Promise from God PROVERBS 31:30 | *Charm is deceptive, and beauty does not last; but a woman who fears the LORD will be greatly praised.*

BELONGING

Why is it important to feel like I belong somewhere—to a family, a spouse, a church?

DEUTERONOMY 33:27 | *The eternal God is your refuge, and his everlasting arms are under you.*

PSALM 73:23-24 | *I still belong to you; you hold my right hand. You guide me with your counsel, leading me to a glorious destiny.*

ROMANS 1:6 | *You are included among those . . . who have been called to belong to Jesus Christ.*

ROMANS 8:1 | *There is no condemnation for those who belong to Christ Jesus.*

We all need a sense of belonging, for in belonging is security and acceptance. Feeling accepted gives you confidence to share your deepest feelings without worry of rejection. And when you belong to God, that security and acceptance can never be taken away—they last for eternity.

What are the privileges of belonging to God?

ROMANS 8:1 | *There is no condemnation for those who belong to Christ Jesus.*

GALATIANS 3:29 | *Now that you belong to Christ, you are the true children of Abraham. You are his heirs, and God's promise to Abraham belongs to you.*

GALATIANS 4:7 | *You are no longer a slave but God's own child. And since you are his child, God has made you his heir.*

EPHESIANS 1:3 | *All praise to God, the Father of our Lord Jesus Christ, who has blessed us with every spiritual blessing in the heavenly realms because we are united with Christ.*

Belonging to God means you are no longer a slave to sin nor guilty before God. Now you can receive all the blessings he freely gives to his children—you inherit the family privileges of the Almighty.

ISAIAH 26:19 | *Those who die in the LORD will live; their bodies will rise again! Those who sleep in the earth will rise up and sing for joy! For your life-giving light will fall like dew on your people in the place of the dead!*

When you belong to God, you are assured of eternal life. Belonging to God is an eternal relationship: not merely for this world, but for the world to come. The grave is not the last chapter, merely the transitional one.

How can I be sure I belong to God?

1 JOHN 2:3-5 | *We can be sure that we know him if we obey his commandments. If someone claims, "I know God," but doesn't obey God's commandments, that person is a liar and is not living in the truth. But those who obey God's word truly show how completely they love him. That is how we know we are living in him.*

1 JOHN 3:10 | *We can tell who are children of God and who are children of the devil. Anyone who does not live righteously and does not love other believers does not belong to God.*

Obedience to God is a reflection of love for him and belief in him. Since you are human, you will not obey God perfectly all the time. But what God looks for is a desire to please and obey him, as well as a commitment to make your best effort to do so every day.

Promise from God ROMANS 8:1 | *There is no condemnation for those who belong to Christ Jesus.*

BIBLE

How can a book written so long ago be relevant for me today?

ISAIAH 40:8 | *The grass withers and the flowers fade, but the word of our God stands forever.*

2 TIMOTHY 3:16-17 | *All Scripture is inspired by God and is useful to teach us what is true and to make us realize what is wrong in our lives. It corrects us when we are wrong and teaches us to do what is right. God uses it to prepare and equip his people to do every good work.*

HEBREWS 4:12 | *The word of God is alive and powerful. It is sharper than the sharpest two-edged sword, cutting between soul and spirit, between joint and marrow. It exposes our innermost thoughts and desires.*

Because the Bible is the Word of God, it is the only document that is "living"; in other words, it is relevant for all people in all places in any time period. It is as contemporary as the heart of God and as relevant as your most urgent need.

How can the Bible give me guidance?

PSALM 73:24 | *You guide me with your counsel, leading me to a glorious destiny.*

PSALM 119:24 | *Your laws please me; they give me wise advice.*

PSALM 119:105 | *Your word is a lamp to guide my feet and a light for my path.*

The Word of God is from the mind and heart of God, who loves you unconditionally and is all-wise, all-powerful, and ever-present. As you read the Bible, you find that God is personally guiding you and giving you his wisdom.

How can the Bible give me comfort?

PSALM 119:49-50, 52, 54 | *Remember your promise to me; it is my only hope. . . . It comforts me in all my troubles. . . . I meditate on your age-old regulations; O LORD, they comfort me. . . . Your decrees have been the theme of my songs wherever I have lived.*

PROVERBS 30:5 | *Every word of God proves true. He is a shield to all who come to him for protection.*

ROMANS 15:4 | *The Scriptures give us hope and encouragement as we wait patiently for God's promises to be fulfilled.*

The Bible is filled with God's promises, which give you comfort and encouragement in this life as well as the confident assurance that you will one day live forever in peace and security with him.

What is promised to me when I read the Bible? Why is it so important to read the Bible regularly?

JEREMIAH 15:16 | *When I discovered your words, I devoured them. They are my joy and my heart's delight, for I bear your name, O LORD God of Heaven's Armies.*

God's Word shapes your heart, mind, and soul. It brings true joy and purpose to life. And it inspires you to live a life that reflects God's character and leaves a lasting spiritual legacy. As you read the Bible regularly, these promises come true in your life.

JOHN 8:32 | *You will know the truth, and the truth will set you free.*

JOHN 12:50 | *I know his commands lead to eternal life.*

Reading the Bible tells you how to be set free forever from sin.

ACTS 17:11 | *The people of Berea were more open-minded than those in Thessalonica, and they listened eagerly to Paul's message. They searched the Scriptures day after day to see if Paul and Silas were teaching the truth.*

Reading the Bible helps you recognize what is true about life and what is not.

DEUTERONOMY 17:20 | *This regular reading will prevent [the king] from becoming proud and acting as if he is above his fellow citizens.*

Reading the Bible regularly helps you keep a right attitude toward God and others.

Promise from God PSALM 119:89 | *Your eternal word, O LORD, stands firm in heaven.*

BITTERNESS

Why do I sometimes feel bitter?

GENESIS 27:41 | *Esau hated Jacob because their father had given Jacob the blessing. And Esau began to scheme: . . . "I will kill my brother, Jacob."*

ESTHER 5:9 | *Haman was a happy man as he left the banquet! But when he saw Mordecai sitting at the palace gate, not standing up or trembling nervously before him, Haman became furious.*

Bitterness comes when you allow anger to control you.

1 SAMUEL 30:6 | *David was now in great danger because all his men were very bitter about losing their sons and daughters, and they began to talk of stoning him. But David found strength in the LORD his God.*

2 CORINTHIANS 2:7 | *It is time to forgive and comfort him. Otherwise he may be overcome by discouragement.*

COLOSSIANS 3:13 | *Make allowance for each other's faults, and forgive anyone who offends you. Remember, the Lord forgave you, so you must forgive others.*

Bitterness comes when others hurt you and you refuse to forgive. Never stop forgiving and forgetting. Remember that God has forgiven you despite your continual tendency to sin.

HEBREWS 12:15 | *Look after each other so that none of you fails to receive the grace of God. Watch out that no poisonous root of bitterness grows up to trouble you, corrupting many.*

Bitterness comes when you forget God's grace, which is showered on you each day.

What is the result of unresolved bitterness?

GENESIS 27:41-42 | *Esau hated Jacob because their father had given Jacob the blessing. And Esau began to scheme: . . . "I will kill my brother, Jacob." But Rebekah heard about Esau's plans. So she sent for Jacob and told him, "Listen, Esau is . . . plotting to kill you."*

JOB 5:2 | *Surely resentment destroys the fool, and jealousy kills the simple.*

Unresolved bitterness leads to hatred, anger, jealousy, and revenge. It can keep you from fellowship with God and others and blinds you from noticing God's blessings.

How do I deal with bitterness toward others?

MARK 11:25 | *When you are praying, first forgive anyone you are holding a grudge against, so that your Father in heaven will forgive your sins, too.*

ACTS 8:22-23 | *Repent of your wickedness and pray to the Lord. Perhaps he will forgive your evil thoughts, for . . . you are full of bitter jealousy and are held captive by sin.*

EPHESIANS 4:31-32 | *Get rid of all bitterness, rage, anger, harsh words, and slander. . . . Instead, be kind to each other, tenderhearted, forgiving one another, just as God through Christ has forgiven you.*

Forgiveness is the antidote to bitterness. It lifts burdens, cancels debts, and frees you from the chains of unresolved anger.

Promise from God COLOSSIAN 3:13 | *Remember, the Lord forgave you.*

BLESSINGS

How can I bring God's blessings?

PSALM 128:1 | *How joyful are those who fear the LORD—all who follow his ways!*

PSALM 146:5 | *Joyful are those who have the God of Israel as their helper, whose hope is in the LORD their God.*

JEREMIAH 17:7 | *Blessed are those who trust in the LORD and have made the LORD their hope and confidence.*

A life focused on trusting and obeying God brings him joy. His smile of favor sends forth many blessings to you. Blessings are not merely words spoken but grace that comes from a special relationship with God.

What kinds of blessings does God send my way?

NUMBERS 6:24-26 | *May the LORD bless you and protect you. May the LORD smile on you and be gracious to you. May the LORD show you his favor and give you his peace.*

PSALM 84:11 | *The LORD God is our sun and our shield. He gives us grace and glory. The LORD will withhold no good thing from those who do what is right.*

1 CORINTHIANS 15:57 | *Thank God! He gives us victory over sin and death through our Lord Jesus Christ.*

Success and prosperity are not the most common blessings from God. Rather peace, comfort, joy, fellowship with God, hope, and eternal life with him are the best blessings of all—and they have been promised to you.

ROMANS 1:11-12 | *[Paul said,] "I long to visit you so I can bring you some spiritual gift that will help you grow strong in the Lord. When we get together, I want to encourage you in your faith, but I also want to be encouraged by yours."*

2 CORINTHIANS 2:14 | *Thank God! He has made us his captives and continues to lead us along in Christ's triumphal procession. Now he uses us to spread the knowledge of Christ everywhere, like a sweet perfume.*

The ability to encourage others with God's good news is one of the most rewarding of his blessings. As you share the blessings God has poured on you, you bless others as well.

Why should I bless my enemies?

ROMANS 12:14 | *Bless those who persecute you. Don't curse them; pray that God will bless them.*

Jesus introduced a revolutionary new idea—blessing and forgiving enemies. The natural response is to seek revenge on enemies. Prayer for your enemies is a severe test of your devotion to Christ. Which is the greater blessing: to win over your enemies or to continue fighting with them?

Promise from God GALATIANS 6:9 | *Let's not get tired of doing what is good. At just the right time we will reap a harvest of blessing if we don't give up.*

BOREDOM

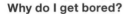

Why do I get bored?

HEBREWS 6:11-12 | *Keep on loving others as long as life lasts, in order to make certain that what you hope for will come true. Then you will not become spiritually dull and indifferent.*

Being a Christian can seem boring to many—"Don't do this"; "You can't do that." But those who grasp what the Christian life is all about find it full and exciting. When you realize that almighty God wants to work through you to accomplish some of his work in the world, you will be amazed to see the great things he could accomplish through you. Focus on using and developing your God-given gifts, as well as on the eternal rewards God promises to believers, and your life will be continually exciting. If you become bored in your Christian life, it is because you are not making yourself available to God and asking him to pour his blessings through you onto others.

What are some signs of boredom?

PROVERBS 26:14 | *As a door swings back and forth on its hinges, so the lazy person turns over in bed.*

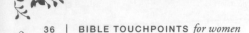

ECCLESIASTES 2:23 | *[Some people's] days of labor are filled with pain and grief; even at night their minds cannot rest. It is all meaningless.*

GALATIANS 6:9 | *Let's not get tired of doing what is good. At just the right time we will reap a harvest of blessing if we don't give up.*

Weariness with what is good, a sense of meaninglessness, laziness—these are all signs of boredom.

What eliminates boredom?

NEHEMIAH 8:10 | *The joy of the LORD is your strength!*

ROMANS 5:11 | *We can rejoice in our wonderful new relationship with God because our Lord Jesus Christ has made us friends of God.*

EPHESIANS 5:1-2 | *Imitate God, therefore, in everything you do. . . . Live a life filled with love, following the example of Christ.*

God has a plan for you (see Jeremiah 29:11). Boredom disappears when you recognize this purpose. When you really try to follow Christ's example every day and when you ask God to do his work through you, you will never be bored!

Promise from God HEBREWS 6:11-12 | *Keep on loving others as long as life lasts, in order to make certain that what you hope for will come true. Then you will not become spiritually dull and indifferent.*

BOUNDARIES

Why do I need boundaries?

PSALM 119:35 | *Make me walk along the path of your commands, for that is where my happiness is found.*

PSALM 119:133 | *Guide my steps by your word, so I will not be overcome by evil.*

If you've ever walked on a path in the woods, you need the path to be clearly marked; if it's not, you can stray off the path and become hopelessly lost. As darkness falls, things get dangerous and you become afraid. God's commands and laws act as boundaries to clearly mark life's path before you. They protect you from danger and fear.

GENESIS 3:4-7 | *"You won't die!" the serpent replied to the woman. "God knows that your eyes will be opened as soon as you eat it, and you will be like God, knowing both good and evil." The woman was convinced. . . . So she took some of the fruit and ate it. Then she gave some to her husband . . . and he ate it, too. At that moment their eyes were opened, and they suddenly felt shame.*

Temptation moves your focus away from God and toward your limitations. It causes you to think that stepping out of bounds might be better than obeying God. But just as Adam and Eve found out too late, giving in to temptation never gives you more freedom. It just messes up your life and cuts off the blessings from God that make your life worth living.

ECCLESIASTES 3:1 | *For everything there is a season, a time for every activity under heaven.*

God provides the boundaries of seasons and time. These provide certain parameters of predictability for your life, giving you confidence that you can trust in his reliability.

What are God's boundaries for me?

MICAH 6:8 | *O people, the LORD has told you what is good, and this is what he requires of you: to do what is right, to love mercy, and to walk humbly with your God.*

God's boundaries are his loving restraints—his commands—to keep you from falling away from him.

DEUTERONOMY 10:12-13 | *What does the LORD your God require of you? He requires only that you fear the LORD your God, and live in a way that pleases him, and love him and serve him with all your heart and soul. And you must always obey the LORD's commands and decrees that I am giving you today for your own good.*

These verses sum up God's general boundaries for his people, for you. Keep within these lines, and God promises your life will be far better than if you don't, because you will have purpose and direction, blessing and joy.

How can I set boundaries for myself?

ROMANS 12:2 | *Don't copy the behavior and customs of this world, but let God transform you into a new person by changing the way you think. Then you will learn to know God's will for you, which is good and pleasing and perfect.*

2 CORINTHIANS 10:13 | *We will not boast about things done outside our area of authority. We will boast only about what has happened within the boundaries of the work God has given us, which includes our working with you.*

Study God's Word to find out how to live as a believer and to discover what he wants you to do. Ask the Holy Spirit to transform your thinking to be more like his.

1 CORINTHIANS 7:35 | *[Paul said,] "I am saying this for your benefit, not to place restrictions on you. I want you to do whatever will help you serve the Lord best, with as few distractions as possible."*

Serving the Lord is a lifetime priority. Rather than restricting you, setting boundaries will eliminate the distractions that can keep you from accomplishing magnificent things for him.

1 CORINTHIANS 10:29, 33 | *It might not be a matter of conscience for you, but it is for the other person. . . . I, too, try to please everyone in everything I do. I don't just do what is best for me; I do what is best for others so that many may be saved.*

God's Word clearly states certain rules you must live by, such as the Ten Commandments. But God also asks you to refrain from doing things that could damage another person's conscience, even if you feel they are okay to do. You should consider others when setting your personal boundaries. Part of the reason we set up personal boundaries is to keep us from hurting others, particularly if that means causing them to stumble when considering belief in God.

PROVERBS 21:16 | *The person who strays from common sense will end up in the company of the dead.*

Common sense is necessary in establishing personal boundaries. You can so easily get into trouble when you make a decision based on impulse or emotion. When common sense screams for you to say "no," say "no"!

Promise from God PSALM 119:98 | *Your commands make me wiser than my enemies, for they are my constant guide.*

BUILDING UP OTHERS

How do I build up others?

ZECHARIAH 7:9 | *Judge fairly, and show mercy and kindness to one another.*

EPHESIANS 4:2 | *Always be humble and gentle. Be patient with each other, making allowance for each other's faults because of your love.*

You can build others up by treating them with honesty, mercy, humility, gentleness, and tenderness.

PROVERBS 15:30 | *A cheerful look brings joy to the heart; good news makes for good health.*

You can build others up by communicating approval and acceptance, sometimes simply by means of a look.

HEBREWS 10:24 | *Let us think of ways to motivate one another to acts of love and good works.*

You can build others up by offering regular, intentional encouragement. Encouragement is generous, spontaneous love in action.

1 THESSALONIANS 5:14 | *Encourage those who are timid. Take tender care of those who are weak. Be patient with everyone.*

You can build others up by meeting their needs, which is loving service in action.

2 CORINTHIANS 13:11 | *Be joyful. Grow to maturity. Encourage each other. Live in harmony and peace. Then the God of love and peace will be with you.*

You can build others up by living in harmony and peace, which affirms your love for them.

EPHESIANS 4:32 | *Be kind to each other, tenderhearted, forgiving one another, just as God through Christ has forgiven you.*

You can build others up by forgiving them.

1 SAMUEL 23:16 | *Jonathan went to find David and encouraged him to stay strong in his faith in God.*

ACTS 11:23 | *When [Barnabas] arrived and saw this evidence of God's blessing, he was filled with joy, and he encouraged the believers to stay true to the Lord.*

You can build others up by encouraging them in their relationship with God.

COLOSSIANS 3:16 | *Let the message about Christ, in all its richness, fill your lives. Teach and counsel each other with all the wisdom he gives. Sing psalms and hymns and spiritual songs to God with thankful hearts.*

You can build others up by sharing God's Word and by worshiping him together.

2 CHRONICLES 30:22 | *Hezekiah encouraged all the Levites regarding the skill they displayed as they served the LORD.*

You can build others up by acknowledging their quality service to the Lord.

ROMANS 12:10 | *Love each other with genuine affection, and take delight in honoring each other.*

ROMANS 13:7 | *Give to everyone what you owe them: Pay your taxes and government fees to those who collect them, and give respect and honor to those who are in authority.*

You can build others up by showing them honor and respect.

ROMANS 14:19 | *Let us aim for harmony in the church and try to build each other up.*

You can build others up by maintaining peaceful relationships with them.

Promise from God 2 CORINTHIANS 13:11 | *Encourage each other. Live in harmony and peace. Then the God of love and peace will be with you.*

BUSYNESS

What are the benefits of being busy?

PROVERBS 31:17, 27 | *[A virtuous and capable wife] is energetic and strong, a hard worker. . . . She carefully watches everything in her household and suffers nothing from laziness.*

ECCLESIASTES 11:6 | *Plant your seed in the morning and keep busy all afternoon, for you don't know if profit will come from one activity or another—or maybe both.*

Rich harvests come from energetic effort; hard work over a period of time will produce fruitfulness in your life.

What are the dangers of busyness?

PSALM 39:6 | *We are merely moving shadows, and all our busy rushing ends in nothing. We heap up wealth, not knowing who will spend it.*

PROVERBS 19:2 | *Enthusiasm without knowledge is no good; haste makes mistakes.*

Never confuse activity with accomplishment. A too-full schedule may reflect a lack of wise priorities and leave you no time to enjoy the fruits of your labor. Activity without purpose can leave you with nothing to show for your efforts.

How can I find rest from the busyness of life?

EXODUS 34:21 | *You have six days each week for your ordinary work, but on the seventh day you must stop working, even during the seasons of plowing and harvest.*

PSALM 23:2 | *He lets me rest in green meadows; he leads me beside peaceful streams.*

PSALM 91:1 | *Those who live in the shelter of the Most High will find rest in the shadow of the Almighty.*

God is both the model for and the source of rest. Just as God rested after Creation was finished, he encourages you to set aside a day of rest from your labors.

MARK 6:31 | *Jesus said, "Let's go off by ourselves to a quiet place and rest awhile." He said this because there were so many people coming and going that Jesus and his apostles didn't even have time to eat.*

Rest and renewal need to be planned into your busy schedule. You must be proactive about this, or else all the other demands of life will completely dictate your schedule. God planned for work, but he also planned for rest. Keep both in balance. One of life's greatest challenges is learning to use your time wisely.

MARK 1:36-38 | *Simon and the others went out to find [Jesus]. When they found him, they said, "Everyone is looking for you." But Jesus replied, "We must go on to other towns as well, and I will preach to them, too. That is why I came."*

Freeing yourself from the trap of incessant activity requires learning to say no—sometimes even to worthwhile activities.

Promise from God MATTHEW 11:28-29 | *Jesus said, "Come to me, all of you who are weary and carry heavy burdens, and*

I will give you rest. Take my yoke upon you. Let me teach you, because I am humble and gentle at heart, and you will find rest for your souls."

CARING

How does God show he cares for me?

PSALM 121:7-8 | *The LORD keeps you from all harm and watches over your life. The LORD keeps watch over you as you come and go, both now and forever.*

PSALM 145:18-20 | *The LORD is close to all who call on him, yes, to all who call on him in truth. He grants the desires of those who fear him; he hears their cries for help and rescues them. The LORD protects all those who love him, but he destroys the wicked.*

MATTHEW 6:30 | *If God cares so wonderfully for wildflowers that are here today and thrown into the fire tomorrow, he will certainly care for you. Why do you have so little faith?*

God is always close to you, ready to help in your time of need. God's presence surrounds you, protecting you from Satan's attacks far more than you realize. God sends opportunities your way to make your life more full and satisfying. He also sends blessings your way in a variety of forms. He promises to take your worries and cares upon himself. And he offers you eternal life in heaven, away from all hurt, pain, and sin. This is a God who is fulfilling his promise to be caring.

How can I show others I care?

MATTHEW 25:36 | *I was naked, and you gave me clothing. I was sick, and you cared for me. I was in prison, and you visited me.*

LUKE 10:34-35 | *The Samaritan soothed [the Jewish man's] wounds with olive oil and wine and bandaged them. Then he put the man on his own donkey and took him to an inn, where he took care of him. The next day he handed the innkeeper two silver coins, telling him, "Take care of this man. If his bill runs higher than this, I'll pay you the next time I'm here."*

1 CORINTHIANS 12:22, 24-25 | *Some parts of the body that seem weakest and least important are actually the most necessary. . . . God has put the body together such that extra honor and care are given to those parts that have less dignity. This makes for harmony among the members, so that all the members care for each other.*

Just as God cares for you by protecting you, providing for you, and preserving you, so you can show his care to others by doing the same for them. You can protect others by being kind, helpful, and willing to reach out. You can provide for others by giving of your time, possessions, and talents to those in need. You can preserve, maintaining harmony by your words and your actions.

Promise from God 1 PETER 5:7 | *Give all your worries and cares to God, for he cares about you.*

CELEBRATION

What causes God to celebrate?

ZEPHANIAH 3:17 | *The LORD your God . . . will take delight in you with gladness. . . . He will rejoice over you with joyful songs.*

MATTHEW 25:23 | *The master said, "Well done, my good and faithful servant. You have been faithful in handling this small amount, so now I will give you many more responsibilities. Let's celebrate together!"*

LUKE 15:10 | *In the same way, there is joy in the presence of God's angels when even one sinner repents.*

1 CORINTHIANS 15:57 | *Thank God! He gives us victory over sin and death through our Lord Jesus Christ.*

God celebrates the defeat of sin and evil, the salvation of the lost, and the daily joys and successes of his people. He celebrates when his people faithfully follow and obey his commands.

What is the importance of family in celebration?

EXODUS 12:26 | *Your children will ask, "What does this ceremony mean?"*

NEHEMIAH 12:43 | *Many sacrifices were offered on that joyous day, for God had given the people cause for great joy. The women and children also participated in the celebration, and the joy of the people of Jerusalem could be heard far away.*

ESTHER 9:28 | *[The Festival of Purim] would be remembered and kept from generation to generation and celebrated by every family throughout the provinces and cities of the empire.*

When you celebrate the Lord with your family, you model the Lord's presence in your life. This is the greatest inheritance you can give to your children and grandchildren; it is a treasure to be passed on to future generations.

Regardless of my personal circumstances, what can I always celebrate?

PSALM 135:3 | *Praise the LORD, for the LORD is good; celebrate his lovely name with music.*

ISAIAH 49:13 | *Sing for joy, O heavens! Rejoice, O earth! Burst into song, O mountains! For the LORD has comforted his people and will have compassion on them in their suffering.*

Sometimes you can celebrate the joy of good circumstances, but even during hard times, you can always celebrate the Lord himself!

Promise from God PSALM 5:11 | *Let all who take refuge in you rejoice; let them sing joyful praises forever. Spread your protection over them, that all who love your name may be filled with joy.*

CHANGE

How do I change the areas in my life that need to be changed?

ACTS 3:19 | *Repent of your sins and turn to God, so that your sins may be wiped away.*

If you haven't repented of your sins, this is the greatest change in your life you need to make. A personal encounter with Jesus Christ is the beginning of this most important change.

PSALM 51:10 | *Create in me a clean heart, O God. Renew a loyal spirit within me.*

ROMANS 12:2 | *Don't copy the behavior and customs of this world, but let God transform you into a new person by*

changing the way you think. Then you will learn to know
God's will for you, which is good and pleasing and perfect.

EPHESIANS 4:23-24 | *Let the Spirit renew your thoughts and*
attitudes. Put on your new nature, created to be like God—
truly righteous and holy.

For real and dynamic change to occur, God has to give you
a new way of thinking. He will help you focus on what is
true, good, and right. Then you will begin to see the new
you, a person who displays God's good, holy, and true spirit.

2 CORINTHIANS 5:17 | *This means that anyone who belongs to*
Christ has become a new person. The old life is gone; a new life
has begun!

PHILIPPIANS 1:6 | *God, who began the good work within you,*
will continue his work until it is finally finished on the day
when Christ Jesus returns.

COLOSSIANS 3:10 | *Put on your new nature, and be renewed as*
you learn to know your Creator and become like him.

A great work takes a long time to complete. Though you
become a believer in a moment of faith, the process of
transformation into being like Jesus takes a lifetime. While
it may appear slow to you, God's work in you is relentless,
certain, and positive.

Does God ever change?

LAMENTATIONS 5:19 | *LORD, you remain the same forever!*
Your throne continues from generation to generation.

MALACHI 3:6 | *I am the LORD, and I do not change.*

HEBREWS 13:8 | *Jesus Christ is the same yesterday, today,*
and forever.

JAMES 1:17 | *Whatever is good and perfect comes down to us from God our Father, who created all the lights in the heavens. He never changes or casts a shifting shadow.*

Not only does God live forever, but his character remains unchanged forever. He is the God of eternal consistency.

Promise from God ISAIAH 40:8 | *The grass withers and the flowers fade, but the word of our God stands forever.*

CHARACTER

What are the attributes of godly character?

EZEKIEL 18:5-9 | *Suppose a certain man is righteous and does what is just and right. He does not feast in the mountains before Israel's idols or worship them. He does not commit adultery. . . . He is a merciful creditor. . . . He does not rob the poor but instead gives food to the hungry and provides clothes for the needy. He grants loans without interest, stays away from injustice, is honest and fair when judging others, and faithfully obeys my decrees and regulations. Anyone who does these things is just and will surely live, says the Sovereign LORD.*

GALATIANS 5:22-23 | *The Holy Spirit produces this kind of fruit in our lives: love, joy, peace, patience, kindness, goodness, faithfulness, gentleness, and self-control.*

Much is said in the Bible about developing these godly fruits of the Spirit, which form our character.

Why is building character so hard?

ROMANS 5:4 | *Endurance develops strength of character, and character strengthens our confident hope of salvation.*

JAMES 1:2-4 | *When troubles come your way, consider it an opportunity for great joy. For you know that when your faith is tested, your endurance has a chance to grow. So let it grow, for when your endurance is fully developed, you will be perfect and complete, needing nothing.*

Developing character is a process that comes only through time and testing. It is trial and error. Pain, trials, and temptation refine you so that over time you will be better equipped and more experienced to deal with them.

Promise from God ROMANS 5:4 | *Endurance develops strength of character, and character strengthens our confident hope of salvation.*

CHILDREN

What childlike characteristics should an adult retain?

MATTHEW 18:3-4 | *[Jesus] said, "I tell you the truth, unless you turn from your sins and become like little children, you will never get into the Kingdom of Heaven. So anyone who becomes as humble as this little child is the greatest in the Kingdom of Heaven."*

MARK 10:14-15 | *[Jesus] said to [his disciples], "Let the children come to me. Don't stop them! For the Kingdom of God belongs to those who are like these children. I tell you the truth, anyone who doesn't receive the Kingdom of God like a child will never enter it."*

LUKE 10:21 | *[Jesus] said, "O Father, Lord of heaven and earth, thank you for hiding these things from those who think them-*

selves wise and clever, and for revealing them to the childlike. Yes, Father, it pleased you to do it this way."

Like a child, you must have simple faith and humility before the Lord.

What kind of relationship does God want between parents and children?

PROVERBS 22:6 | *Direct your children onto the right path, and when they are older, they will not leave it.*

EPHESIANS 6:1, 4 | *Children, obey your parents because you belong to the Lord, for this is the right thing to do. . . . Fathers, do not provoke your children to anger by the way you treat them. Rather, bring them up with the discipline and instruction that comes from the Lord.*

Parents are God's shepherds for their children, commissioned to guide them, nurture them, care for them, clothe them, feed them, and help them come to know the Lord. How can I most effectively teach my child about God and his ways?

EXODUS 10:1-2 | *The LORD said to Moses, . . . "I have made [Pharaoh] and his officials stubborn so I can display my miraculous signs among them. I've also done it so you can tell your children and grandchildren about how I made a mockery of the Egyptians and about the signs I displayed among them—and so you will know that I am the LORD."*

DEUTERONOMY 11:18-19 | *Commit yourselves wholeheartedly to these words of mine. Tie them to your hands and wear them on your forehead as reminders. Teach them to your children. Talk about them when you are at home and when you are on the road, when you are going to bed and when you are getting up.*

PROVERBS 22:6 | *Direct your children onto the right path, and when they are older, they will not leave it.*

As a parent, you have the remarkable privilege of living (role modeling) what you want your children to learn, sharing God's truth with them, guiding them in the right way to go, and then watching with joy as your work continues in future generations.

Promise from God ISAIAH 59:21 | *[The Lord said,] "My Spirit will not leave them, and neither will these words I have given you. They will be on your lips and on the lips of your children and your children's children forever."*

CHRISTLIKENESS

What is meant by "Christlikeness"?

LUKE 9:23 | *[Jesus] said to the crowd, "If any of you wants to be my follower, you must turn from your selfish ways, take up your cross daily, and follow me."*

Christ is the ultimate example of how to live a life that is pleasing to God. If you pattern your life after him, you will please God. To be like Christ is your goal. You want to think his thoughts, show his attitudes, and live as he would live here on earth today.

LUKE 6:36 | *You must be compassionate, just as your Father is compassionate.*

A compassionate lifestyle is a sign of Christlikeness.

JOHN 13:14-15 | *Since I, your Lord and Teacher, have washed your feet, you ought to wash each other's feet. I have given you an example to follow. Do as I have done to you.*

1 PETER 2:21, 23 | *God called you to do good, even if it means suffering, just as Christ suffered for you. He is your example, and you must follow in his steps. . . . He did not retaliate when he was insulted, nor threaten revenge when he suffered. He left his case in the hands of God, who always judges fairly.*

A life of humble service is a necessary part of Christlikeness.

How do I become like Christ?

2 CORINTHIANS 3:18 | *All of us who [believe in Christ] can see and reflect the glory of the Lord. And the Lord—who is the Spirit—makes us more and more like him as we are changed into his glorious image.*

EPHESIANS 4:15 | *We will speak the truth in love, growing in every way more and more like Christ, who is the head of his body, the church.*

PHILIPPIANS 1:6 | *God, who began the good work within you, will continue his work until it is finally finished on the day when Christ Jesus returns.*

You become more like Christ by carefully studying how he lived and loved. When you invite him to work his powerful love through you, you will begin to reflect his character.

How will my Christlike character affect my home?

1 CORINTHIANS 7:14 | *The Christian wife brings holiness to her marriage, and the Christian husband brings holiness to his marriage. Otherwise, your children would not be holy, but now they are holy.*

1 PETER 3:1-2 | *Even if some refuse to obey the Good News, your godly lives will speak to them without any words. They will be won over by observing your pure and reverent lives.*

How you model your faith in Christ will have an incredible influence upon those in your household and upon future generations.

Promise from God GALATIANS 5:22-23 | *The Holy Spirit produces this kind of fruit in our lives: love, joy, peace, patience, kindness, goodness, faithfulness, gentleness, and self-control.*

CHURCH

What is the purpose of the church? Why should I attend?

ACTS 2:47 | *Each day the Lord added to [the believers'] fellowship those who were being saved.*

A physical church is a gathering place for those who are saved by faith in Christ. Your attendance encourages other believers and strengthens the body of Christ.

1 CORINTHIANS 3:16-17 | *Don't you realize that all of you together are the temple of God and that the Spirit of God lives in you? God will destroy anyone who destroys this temple. For God's temple is holy, and you are that temple.*

God's church is not a physical building, but the believers who gather inside the building. There, together with other Christians, the Holy Spirit teaches you how to truly change for good and influence others because of your changed lives.

EPHESIANS 4:11-12 | *These are the gifts Christ gave to the church: the apostles, the prophets, the evangelists, and the pastors and teachers. Their responsibility is to equip God's people to do his work and build up the church, the body of Christ.*

The church exists in part to equip God's people to do God's work and to encourage them in their faith.

1 CORINTHIANS 12:12-13 | *The human body has many parts, but the many parts make up one whole body. So it is with the body of Christ. Some of us are Jews, some are Gentiles, some are slaves, and some are free. But we have all been baptized into one body by one Spirit, and we all share the same Spirit.*

All believers together form God's family, but only by meeting together can you bond. The physical church is a place where Christians learn to work together in unity and where the differences between people are reconciled by the Holy Spirit. When you meet together, you can build one another up and help one another.

REVELATION 19:7-8 | *Let us be glad and rejoice, and let us give honor to him. For the time has come for the wedding feast of the Lamb, and his bride has prepared herself. She has been given the finest of pure white linen to wear.*

The church is Christ's bride—a picture of the intimate fellowship that God's people will enjoy with him.

Promise from God MATTHEW 16:18 | *[Jesus said,] "I will build my church, and all the powers of hell will not conquer it."*

COMFORT

How does God comfort me in my times of distress?

PSALM 119:76 | *Let your unfailing love comfort me, just as you promised me, your servant.*

God loves you.

ROMANS 8:26 | *The Holy Spirit helps us in our weakness. For example, we don't know what God wants us to pray for. But the Holy Spirit prays for us with groanings that cannot be expressed in words.*

He prays for you.

PSALM 55:17 | *Morning, noon, and night I cry out in my distress, and the LORD hears my voice.*

He listens to you.

PSALM 94:19 | *When doubts filled my mind, your comfort gave me renewed hope and cheer.*

He gives you hope and joy.

PSALM 119:50, 52 | *Your promise revives me; it comforts me in all my troubles. . . . I meditate on your age-old regulations; O LORD, they comfort me.*

He revives you with his Word.

2 THESSALONIANS 2:16-17 | *May our Lord Jesus Christ himself and God our Father, who loved us and by his grace gave us eternal comfort and a wonderful hope, comfort you and strengthen you in every good thing you do and say.*

He gives you the gift of eternal life.

PSALM 147:3 | *He heals the brokenhearted and bandages their wounds.*

He heals your broken heart.

EXODUS 15:26 | *I am the LORD who heals you.*

He heals your sick body.

How can I comfort others?

JOB 42:11 | *All his brothers, sisters, and former friends came and feasted with him in his home. And they consoled him and*

*comforted him because of all the trials the L*ORD *had brought against him. And each of them brought him a gift of money and a gold ring.*

You can be with them in their time of need. Just being there speaks volumes about how much you care.

JOB 21:2 | *[Job said,] "Listen closely to what I am saying. That's one consolation you can give me."*

You can be a good listener. It is usually more important for you to listen than to talk.

RUTH 2:13 | *"I hope I continue to please you, sir," [Ruth said]. "You have comforted me by speaking so kindly to me, even though I am not one of your workers."*

1 CORINTHIANS 14:3 | *One who prophesies strengthens others, encourages them, and comforts them.*

You can speak kind and encouraging words.

PHILEMON 1:7 | *Your love has given me much joy and comfort, my brother, for your kindness has often refreshed the hearts of God's people.*

You can comfort others with kind actions.

2 CORINTHIANS 1:3-4 | *All praise to God, the Father of our Lord Jesus Christ. God is our merciful Father and the source of all comfort. He comforts us in all our troubles so that we can comfort others. When they are troubled, we will be able to give them the same comfort God has given us.*

Remember the ways God has comforted you, and model that same comfort to others. When you have experienced God's assuring love, his guiding wisdom, and his sustaining power, you are able to comfort others with understanding. The comforted become the comforters.

Promise from God   2 THESSALONIANS 2:16-17 | *May our Lord Jesus Christ himself and God our Father, who loved us and by his grace gave us eternal comfort and a wonderful hope, comfort you and strengthen you in every good thing you do and say.*

COMMUNITY OF BELIEVERS

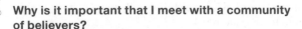

Why is it important that I meet with a community of believers?

MATTHEW 18:20 | *Where two or three gather together as my followers, I am there among them.*

Because Jesus promises to be there with you.

PSALM 55:14 | *What good fellowship we once enjoyed as we walked together to the house of God.*

Because you will enjoy the fellowship of other believers.

1 CORINTHIANS 10:16-17 | *When we bless the cup at the Lord's Table, aren't we sharing in the blood of Christ? And when we break the bread, aren't we sharing in the body of Christ? And though we are many, we all eat from one loaf of bread, showing that we are one body.*

1 CORINTHIANS 11:33 | *Dear brothers and sisters, when you gather for the Lord's Supper, wait for each other.*

Because you can celebrate the Lord with other believers.

ACTS 4:24 | *All the believers lifted their voices together in prayer to God.*

ACTS 12:12 | *[Peter] went to the home of Mary, the mother of John Mark, where many were gathered for prayer.*

Because you can find strength in praying with others.

How can I benefit my community?

ROMANS 12:5-6 | *We are many parts of one body, and we all belong to each other. In his grace, God has given us different gifts for doing certain things well.*

1 CORINTHIANS 14:12 | *Since you are so eager to have the special abilities the Spirit gives, seek those that will strengthen the whole church.*

Since God has given you unique personal gifts, you must find the best way to invest those gifts for him.

Promise from God MATTHEW 18:20 | *Where two or three gather together as my followers, I am there among them.*

COMPASSION

How does God show his compassion to me?

PSALM 103:8 | *The LORD is compassionate and merciful, slow to get angry and filled with unfailing love.*

PSALM 103:13 | *The LORD is like a father to his children, tender and compassionate to those who fear him.*

God shows his compassion to you by giving you blessings you don't deserve and by not giving you what you really do deserve. Instead, he forgives you and restores you to what you were intended to be.

How can I show compassion to others?

2 CORINTHIANS 8:9 | *You know the generous grace of our Lord Jesus Christ. Though he was rich, yet for your sakes he became poor, so that by his poverty he could make you rich.*

In his love and compassion for you, Jesus gave up his most high position to come to earth and die for your sins. Your goal, as a believer in Jesus, is to develop that same depth of love and compassion for others so that you would be willing to even give up your life for their sake.

Promise from God PSALM 145:9 | *The LORD is good to everyone. He showers compassion on all his creation.*

COMPLAINING

What are the dangers of complaining?

JAMES 4:11 | *Don't speak evil against each other, dear brothers and sisters. If you criticize and judge each other, then you are criticizing and judging God's law. But your job is to obey the law, not to judge whether it applies to you.*

JAMES 5:9 | *Don't grumble about each other, brothers and sisters, or you will be judged. For look—the Judge is standing at the door!*

Complaining about others is indirectly complaining about God and his Word.

When I complain, what does it reflect about me?

DEUTERONOMY 1:27-28, 31-32 | *[Moses said,] "You complained in your tents and said, 'The LORD must hate us. . . . Where can we go?' . . . You saw how the LORD your God cared for you all along the way as you traveled through the wilderness, just as a father cares for his child. Now he has brought you to this place. But even after all he did, you refused to trust the LORD your God."*

Complaining demonstrates an ungrateful and selfish heart and shows a lack of gratitude for what God has given you.

It also shows a lack of trust in his care for you. When you complain, you grumble about God!

What effect does my complaining have on others?

PROVERBS 19:13 | *A foolish child is a calamity to a father; a quarrelsome wife is as annoying as constant dripping.*

PROVERBS 21:19 | *It's better to live alone in the desert than with a quarrelsome, complaining wife.*

Those who must listen to constant complaining find it very irritating. No one likes to be around a constant complainer.

What should I do instead of complaining?

PHILIPPIANS 2:14-15 | *Do everything without complaining and arguing, so that no one can criticize you. Live . . . as children of God, shining like bright lights in a world full of crooked and perverse people.*

Instead of complaining about others, say something nice about them. If you can't do that, then don't say anything at all. If you're quiet, you can't be blamed for being negative or critical.

LAMENTATIONS 3:39-40 | *Why should we, mere humans, complain when we are punished for our sins? Instead, let us test and examine our ways. Let us turn back to the LORD.*

Instead of complaining about the sins of others, focus on and repent of your own sins.

LUKE 6:37 | *Do not judge others, and you will not be judged. Do not condemn others, or it will all come back against you. Forgive others, and you will be forgiven.*

Instead of complaining about the weaknesses of others, forgive them as you would like to be forgiven.

Promise from God EPHESIANS 4:29 | *Let everything you say be good and helpful, so that your words will be an encouragement to those who hear them.*

COMPROMISE

When is compromise inappropriate?

ROMANS 6:12 | *Do not let sin control the way you live; do not give in to sinful desires.*

Compromise is inappropriate whenever it involves sin of any kind.

EXODUS 23:2 | *You must not follow the crowd in doing wrong.*

1 SAMUEL 15:24 | *Saul admitted to Samuel, "Yes, I have sinned. I have disobeyed your instructions and the LORD's command, for I was afraid of the people and did what they demanded."*

3 JOHN 1:11 | *Dear friend, don't let this bad example influence you. Follow only what is good.*

When compromise is motivated by people pleasing or following the bad example of others, it is inappropriate.

How do I live in today's culture without compromising my convictions?

DANIEL 1:8, 12-14 | *Daniel was determined not to defile himself by eating the food and wine given to them by the king. He asked the chief of staff for permission not to eat these unacceptable foods. . . . "Please test us for ten days on a diet of vegetables and water," Daniel said. "At the end of the ten days, see how we look compared to the other young men who are eating the king's food. Then make your decision in light of what you see."*

The attendant agreed to Daniel's suggestion and tested them for ten days.

Never be afraid to take a stand for what you know is right and true, but do so in a respectful, humble manner. You will be surprised how often you will be admired for sticking to your beliefs, even if others disagree with them. But even if you meet resistance, you must not compromise by going against God's Word.

EXODUS 34:12 | *Be very careful never to make a treaty with the people who live in the land where you are going. If you do, you will follow their evil ways and be trapped.*

HEBREWS 3:12-13 | *Be careful then, dear brothers and sisters. Make sure that your own hearts are not evil and unbelieving, turning you away from the living God. You must warn each other every day, while it is still "today," so that none of you will be deceived by sin and hardened against God.*

2 JOHN 1:9 | *Anyone who wanders away from [the teaching of Christ] has no relationship with God.*

REVELATION 2:14 | *[God said,] "I have a few complaints against you. You tolerate some among you whose teaching is like that of Balaam, who showed Balak how to trip up the people of Israel. He taught them to sin by eating food offered to idols and by committing sexual sin."*

You must always be on the alert when living or working with those who don't see sin as something wrong. You can easily find yourself compromising and agreeing to commit "little" sins. This will eventually dull your sensitivity to other sins. A "little" sin now and then can lead to a life defined by sin.

JUDGES 16:15-17 | *Delilah pouted, "How can you tell me, 'I love you,' when you don't share your secrets with me? . . . You still haven't told me what makes you so strong!" She tormented him with her nagging day after day until he was sick to death of it. Finally, Samson shared his secret with her.*

You are most likely to compromise in areas where you are spiritually weak. Learn to recognize where you are vulnerable so that you are prepared when the temptation to compromise comes.

Promise from God 1 CHRONICLES 22:13 | *You will be successful if you carefully obey the decrees and regulations that the LORD gave to Israel through Moses. Be strong and courageous; do not be afraid or lose heart!*

CONFESSION

Am I responsible to publicly confess Christ?

MATTHEW 10:32 | *Everyone who acknowledges me publicly here on earth, I will also acknowledge before my Father in heaven.*

ROMANS 10:9 | *If you confess with your mouth that Jesus is Lord and believe in your heart that God raised him from the dead, you will be saved.*

If you want Christ to acknowledge you as his redeemed, you must acknowledge him as your Redeemer. He will claim you on the Day of Judgment as you claim him now.

What is involved in true confession?

PSALM 38:18 | *I confess my sins; I am deeply sorry for what I have done.*

PSALM 51:3-4, 6, 17 | *I recognize my rebellion; it haunts me day and night. Against you, and you alone, have I sinned; I have done what is evil in your sight. . . . You desire honesty from the womb, teaching me wisdom even there. . . . The sacrifice you desire is a broken spirit. You will not reject a broken and repentant heart, O God.*

Expressing sorrow for your sin, displaying humility before God, seeking God and his forgiveness, turning to God in prayer, turning from sin—these are ingredients of true confession to God.

Does God's forgiveness always follow true confession?

PSALM 65:3 | *Though we are overwhelmed by our sins, you forgive them all.*

PSALM 86:5 | *O Lord, you are so good, so ready to forgive, so full of unfailing love for all who ask for your help.*

1 JOHN 1:9 | *If we confess our sins to him, he is faithful and just to forgive us our sins and to cleanse us from all wickedness.*

God's supply of forgiveness far exceeds the number of times you could ever go to him for forgiveness.

In addition to forgiveness, what are other benefits of confession?

PSALM 32:5 | *Finally, I confessed all my sins to you and stopped trying to hide my guilt. I said to myself, "I will confess my rebellion to the LORD." And you forgave me! All my guilt is gone.*

God removes your guilt.

PSALM 51:12 | *Restore to me the joy of your salvation, and make me willing to obey you.*

God restores your joy and helps you want to obey.

JAMES 5:16 | *Confess your sins to each other and pray for each other so that you may be healed. The earnest prayer of a righteous person has great power and produces wonderful results.*

God heals you.

Promise from God   1 JOHN 1:9 | *If we confess our sins to him, he is faithful and just to forgive us our sins and to cleanse us.*

CONFLICT

What causes conflict?

PROVERBS 13:10 | *Pride leads to conflict.*

PROVERBS 28:25 | *Greed causes fighting.*

PROVERBS 30:33 | *As the beating of cream yields butter and striking the nose causes bleeding, so stirring up anger causes quarrels.*

JAMES 4:1 | *What is causing the quarrels and fights among you? Don't they come from the evil desires at war within you?*

Conflict begins when a person, group, or nation isn't getting what it wants and confronts whomever or whatever is in the way. Often pride or greed is involved. You want someone's behavior to be different, you want your way on some issue, you want to win, you want some possession, you want someone's loyalty. The list can go on and on. Unresolved conflict can sometimes lead to open warfare.

ROMANS 7:22-23 | *I love God's law with all my heart. But there is another power within me that is at war with my mind. This power makes me a slave to the sin that is still within me.*

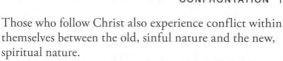

Those who follow Christ also experience conflict within themselves between the old, sinful nature and the new, spiritual nature.

How do I keep conflict with others to a minimum?

PROVERBS 26:17 | *Interfering in someone else's argument is as foolish as yanking a dog's ears.*

It is sometimes tempting to step into an argument in order to "solve it," but doing so often only heats up the issue.

ROMANS 12:18 | *Do all that you can to live in peace with everyone.*

As Christ's ambassadors, you need to work actively to be at peace with others.

EPHESIANS 4:3 | *Make every effort to keep yourselves united in the Spirit, binding yourselves together with peace.*

Spiritual unity and fellowship with God through the Holy Spirit will often help you to bring unity and peace to your relationships.

Promise from God MATTHEW 5:9 | *God blesses those who work for peace, for they will be called the children of God.*

CONFRONTATION

How do I effectively confront others?

MATTHEW 18:15-17 | *If another believer sins against you, go privately and point out the offense. If the other person listens and confesses it, you have won that person back. But if you are unsuccessful, take one or two others with you and go back again, so that everything you say may be confirmed by two or three witnesses. If the person still refuses to listen, take your case to the church. Then if he or she won't accept the church's deci-sion, treat that person as a pagan or a corrupt tax collector.*

Confront them in private. If they do not listen, return later with another concerned friend. If they still refuse to listen, take the matter to the spiritual leaders of your church for guidance and advice.

PROVERBS 27:5 | *An open rebuke is better than hidden love!*

2 TIMOTHY 2:24-25 | *A servant of the Lord must not quarrel but must be kind to everyone, be able to teach, and be patient with difficult people. Gently instruct those who oppose the truth. Perhaps God will change those people's hearts, and they will learn the truth.*

The manner of confrontation is as important as the content. It is essential to consider how you would want others to speak to you. Confront in private, without quarreling and anger. Approach gently, with kindness and patience. Then let God change their hearts!

2 TIMOTHY 1:7 | *God has not given us a spirit of fear and timid-ity, but of power, love, and self-discipline.*

Confront in power and love and with self-discipline!

Under what circumstances should I confront?

EPHESIANS 5:11 | *Take no part in the worthless deeds of evil and darkness; instead, expose them.*

Evil and wickedness must be confronted, or they may consume you.

2 SAMUEL 12:9, 13 | *[Nathan asked,] "Why, then, have you despised the word of the LORD and done this horrible deed?" . . . Then David confessed to Nathan, "I have sinned against*

the Lord." Nathan replied, "Yes, but the Lord has forgiven you, and you won't die for this sin."

LUKE 17:3 | *If another believer sins, rebuke that person; then if there is repentance, forgive.*

Confront others who do wrong, with the purpose of bringing them back into reconciliation with God and others.

How should I respond when others confront me?

PROVERBS 24:26 | *An honest answer is like a kiss of friendship.*

Receive confrontation as an honor, that someone cares enough about you to want what is best for you.

PROVERBS 19:25 | *If you punish a mocker, the simpleminded will learn a lesson; if you correct the wise, they will be all the wiser.*

Confrontation should increase your wisdom. Listen to consider whether you can grow wiser.

Promise from God 2 TIMOTHY 2:25 | *Gently instruct those who oppose the truth. Perhaps God will change those people's hearts, and they will learn the truth.*

CONTENTMENT

How can I find contentment, regardless of life's circumstances?

2 CORINTHIANS 12:10 | *I take pleasure in my weaknesses, and in the insults, hardships, persecutions, and troubles that I suffer for Christ. For when I am weak, then I am strong.*

PHILIPPIANS 4:11-13 | *I have learned how to be content with whatever I have. I know how to live on almost nothing or with everything. I have learned the secret of living in every situation, whether it is with a full stomach or empty, with plenty or little. For I can do everything through Christ, who gives me strength.*

2 PETER 1:3 | *By his divine power, God has given us everything we need for living a godly life. We have received all of this by coming to know him, the one who called us to himself by means of his marvelous glory and excellence.*

When you depend on circumstances for your contentment, you become unhappy when things don't go your way. When you depend on Jesus for your contentment, you are secure because he never fails.

In what or whom should I find contentment?

PSALM 90:14 | *Satisfy us each morning with your unfailing love, so we may sing for joy to the end of our lives.*

PSALM 107:8-9 | *Let them praise the LORD for his great love and for the wonderful things he has done for them. For he satisfies the thirsty and fills the hungry with good things.*

PSALM 119:35 | *Make me walk along the path of your commands, for that is where my happiness is found.*

Looking to God will bring you joy, peace, and contentment because of who he is. He has promised to satisfy all our needs, so as we walk with him we will be at peace.

How can I be a source of contentment in my relationships?

PSALM 106:3 | *There is joy for those who deal justly with others and always do what is right.*

PSALM 119:1 | *Joyful are people of integrity, who follow the instructions of the LORD.*

PSALM 133:1 | *How wonderful and pleasant it is when brothers live together in harmony!*

You can treat people justly, conduct yourself in a godly manner, and try to be pleasant so that your relationships will be harmonious and others will find contentment in them.

Promise from God PSALM 107:9 | *[The Lord] satisfies the thirsty and fills the hungry with good things.*

CRISIS

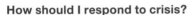

How should I respond to crisis?

PSALM 130:1-2 | *From the depths of despair, O LORD, I call for your help. Hear my cry, O Lord. Pay attention to my prayer.*

JONAH 2:1-2 | *Jonah prayed to the LORD his God from inside the fish. He said, "I cried out to the LORD in my great trouble, and he answered me. I called to you from the land of the dead, and LORD, you heard me!"*

When you reach the end of your rope, call upon the Lord, for your struggle is a time for his strength; your crisis is his opportunity.

PSALM 57:1 | *Have mercy on me, O God, have mercy! I look to you for protection. I will hide beneath the shadow of your wings until the danger passes by.*

When a crisis leaves you vulnerable and exposed, seek the merciful, protective covering of our merciful and all-powerful Lord.

PSALM 28:7 | *The LORD is my strength and shield. I trust him with all my heart. He helps me, and my heart is filled with joy. I burst out in songs of thanksgiving.*

While you are in the midst of a crisis, you may be wonder-ing, "Whom can I trust?" But afterward, you discover that you can always trust the Lord. Praise and thank him for all he has done.

PSALM 119:143 | *As pressure and stress bear down on me, I find joy in your commands.*

When a crisis threatens to overwhelm you, read God's Word for strength and wisdom. It is a firm foundation that will keep you from falling into a bottomless pit.

Where is God in my times of crisis?

PSALM 40:2 | *[The Lord] lifted me out of the pit of despair, out of the mud and the mire. He set my feet on solid ground and steadied me as I walked along.*

PSALM 69:33 | *The LORD hears the cries of the needy; he does not despise his imprisoned people.*

ROMANS 8:35 | *Can anything ever separate us from Christ's love? Does it mean he no longer loves us if we have trouble or calam-ity, or are persecuted, or hungry, or destitute, or in danger, or threatened with death?*

You need not pray for the Lord to be with you in times of crisis—he is already there. Instead, pray that you will recognize his presence and have the humility and discern-ment to accept his help.

JOHN 16:33 | *[Jesus said,] "I have told you all this so that you may have peace in me. Here on earth you will have many trials and sorrows. But take heart, because I have overcome the world."*

God does not say he will always prevent crises in your life— you live in a sinful world where terrible things happen. But God's Son, Jesus, does promise to always be there with you and for you, helping you through your crises. And he promises to help you learn how to have peace and hope in all of them.

How can I help others in their times of crisis?

PROVERBS 27:10 | *Never abandon a friend—either yours or your father's. When disaster strikes, you won't have to ask your brother for assistance. It's better to go to a neighbor than to a brother who lives far away.*

PROVERBS 31:8 | *Speak up for those who cannot speak for themselves; ensure justice for those being crushed.*

1 CORINTHIANS 9:22 | *When I am with those who are weak, I share their weakness, for I want to bring the weak to Christ. Yes, I try to find common ground with everyone, doing everything I can to save some.*

TITUS 3:14 | *Our people must learn to do good by meeting the urgent needs of others; then they will not be unproductive.*

When others face crises, be there with them. The power of your presence may comfort them more than the eloquence of any words.

Promise from God PSALM 46:1 | *God is our refuge and strength, always ready to help in times of trouble.*

CRITICISM

How should I respond to criticism? How do I evaluate whether it is constructive or destructive?

PROVERBS 12:16-18 | *A fool is quick-tempered, but a wise person stays calm when insulted. An honest witness tells the truth;*

a false witness tells lies. Some people make cutting remarks, but the words of the wise bring healing.

If you are criticized, stay calm, and don't lash back. Evaluate whether the criticism is coming from a person with a reputation for telling the truth or telling lies. Ask yourself whether the criticism is meant to heal or to hurt.

ECCLESIASTES 7:5 | *Better to be criticized by a wise person than to be praised by a fool.*

Measure criticism according to the character of the person who is giving it.

1 CORINTHIANS 4:4 | *My conscience is clear, but that doesn't prove I'm right. It is the Lord himself who will examine me and decide.*

Always work to maintain a clear conscience by being honest and trustworthy. This allows you to shrug off criticism that you know is unjustified.

1 PETER 4:14 | *Be happy when you are insulted for being a Christian, for then the glorious Spirit of God rests upon you.*

Consider it a privilege to be criticized for your faith in God. God has special blessings for those who patiently endure this kind of criticism.

Why should I be careful about criticizing others?

ROMANS 14:10 | *Why do you condemn another believer? Why do you look down on another believer? Remember, we will all stand before the judgment seat of God.*

JAMES 4:11 | *If you criticize and judge each other, then you are criticizing and judging God's law.*

Constructive criticism can be a welcome and wholesome gift if given in the spirit of love. But criticism that ridicules,

demeans, or judges someone has at least four harmful consequences: (1) it tears down self-esteem, making a person feel shamed and worthless; (2) it damages your own reputation, making you look mean and merciless; (3) it damages your ability to offer helpful advice because you've made someone become defensive; and (4) it brings greater judgment upon yourself from God, who detests when you hurt others.

How do I offer criticism appropriately?

JOHN 8:7 | *Let the one who has never sinned throw the first stone!*

ROMANS 2:1 | *When you say they are wicked and should be punished, you are condemning yourself, for you who judge others do these very same things.*

Before criticizing another, take an inventory of your own sins and shortcomings so that you can approach the person with clean hands, understanding, and humility.

1 CORINTHIANS 13:5 | *[Love] does not demand its own way. It is not irritable, and it keeps no record of being wronged.*

Constructive criticism is always offered in love, with the motivation to build up. It addresses a specific need in someone else, not a list of his or her shortcomings or character flaws.

Promise from God PROVERBS 12:18 | *Some people make cutting remarks, but the words of the wise bring healing.*

DEBT

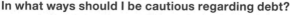

In what ways should I be cautious regarding debt?

PROVERBS 22:7 | *Just as the rich rule the poor, so the borrower is servant to the lender.*

Debt can cause you to be "owned" by those to whom you are indebted.

PSALM 37:21 | *The wicked borrow and never repay, but the godly are generous givers.*

ROMANS 13:7-8 | *Give to everyone what you owe them: Pay your taxes and government fees to those who collect them, and give respect and honor to those who are in authority. Owe nothing to anyone—except for your obligation to love one another.*

Pay your debts in a timely manner, because it is important to honor your commitments. This isn't saying you can never have a home mortgage or car payments, but it does mean that payments should be made in a timely manner. Owing money to someone else is a responsibility not to be taken lightly.

What is the danger of becoming involved in another's debt?

PROVERBS 6:1-3 | *If you have put up security for a friend's debt or agreed to guarantee the debt of a stranger—if you have trapped yourself by your agreement and are caught by what you said— follow my advice and save yourself, for you have placed yourself at your friend's mercy.*

PROVERBS 17:18 | *It's poor judgment to guarantee another person's debt or put up security for a friend.*

PROVERBS 22:26-27 | *Don't agree to guarantee another person's debt or put up security for someone else. If you can't pay it, even your bed will be snatched from under you.*

It's better not to cosign a note for another. If you do cosign a note, be absolutely sure you can repay the entire debt if your friend defaults on the loan. Otherwise, you will be putting yourself and your family at risk.

How did Jesus Christ pay the debt for my sins?

ROMANS 3:25-26 | *God presented Jesus as the sacrifice for sin. . . . This sacrifice shows that God was being fair when he held back and did not punish those who sinned in times past. . . . He declares sinners to be right in his sight when they believe in Jesus.*

ROMANS 5:9, 11 | *Since we have been made right in God's sight by the blood of Christ, he will certainly save us from God's condemnation. . . . So now we can rejoice in our wonderful new relationship with God because our Lord Jesus Christ has made us friends of God.*

Your sins have left you with a debt to God so great that you could never repay it on your own. Jesus Christ paid that debt through his death on the cross. When you trust in Jesus, God mercifully forgives your debt, making you right with God and pure in his sight, and welcomes you to share all the rich blessings he has prepared for you in heaven. He cleared your debt; you owe nothing.

Promise from God HEBREWS 13:5 | *Don't love money; be satisfied with what you have. For God has said, "I will never fail you. I will never abandon you."*

DECISIONS

How can I make good decisions?

ROMANS 2:18 | *You know what [God] wants; you know what is right because you have been taught his law.*

Start by making the basic and obvious decisions to do what the Bible says is right and to avoid what the Bible says is wrong. You won't make big, complicated decisions well if you haven't practiced the fundamental ones.

PSALM 25:4 | *Show me the right path, O LORD; point out the road for me to follow.*

Follow God's direction—his Word shows you which way to go. Stay on the path with God and decide not to do anything that will take you from it.

LUKE 6:12-13 | *One day . . . Jesus went up on a mountain to pray, and he prayed to God all night. At daybreak he called together all of his disciples and chose twelve of them to be apostles.*

Saturate your life with prayer. Talking with God clears your mind, making you more able to hear his counsel.

PSALM 37:30 | *The godly offer good counsel; they teach right from wrong.*

PROVERBS 12:15 | *Fools think their own way is right, but the wise listen to others.*

PROVERBS 18:15 | *Intelligent people are always ready to learn. Their ears are open for knowledge.*

Listen to advice of godly people, and carefully consider it as you make a decision.

PROVERBS 3:5-6 | *Trust in the LORD with all your heart; do not depend on your own understanding. Seek his will in all you do, and he will show you which path to take.*

Don't make a decision without first asking for God's help. Begin all decision making with humility and reverence for God, to whom you are ultimately accountable.

PROVERBS 18:13 | *Spouting off before listening to the facts is both shameful and foolish.*

Make sure you have all the facts before making up your mind.

MATTHEW 16:26 | *What do you benefit if you gain the whole world but lose your own soul? Is anything worth more than your soul?*

Resist the temptation to make choices guided by a desire for personal satisfaction. Such ambition will lead you to make some very bad decisions.

GALATIANS 5:22-23 | *The Holy Spirit produces this kind of fruit in our lives: love, joy, peace, patience, kindness, goodness, faithfulness, gentleness, and self-control.*

Good choices are always in keeping with the character traits produced in us by the Holy Spirit. Bad choices often are a result of neglecting those qualities for selfish ones.

What is the danger of indecision?

ISAIAH 42:20 | *You see and recognize what is right but refuse to act on it. You hear with your ears, but you don't really listen.*

JAMES 1:5-8 | *If you need wisdom, ask our generous God, and he will give it to you. He will not rebuke you for asking. But when you ask him, be sure that your faith is in God alone. Do not waver, for a person with divided loyalty is as unsettled as a wave of the sea that is blown and tossed by the wind. Such people should not expect to receive anything from the Lord. Their loyalty is divided between God and the world, and they are unstable in everything they do.*

Indecision is really a decision not to make a decision. When you procrastinate in making decisions, you forfeit controlling the direction of your life and find yourself at the mercy of the decisions made by others.

Promise from God PROVERBS 3:6 | *Seek his will in all you do, and he will show you which path to take.*

DEPRESSION

What causes depression?

1 SAMUEL 16:14 | *The Spirit of the LORD had left Saul, and the LORD sent a tormenting spirit that filled him with depression and fear.*

When you neglect the Lord, he may honor your decision and leave you alone for a while to "tough out" life's difficult circumstances on your own. Then depression can move easily into the vacant room in your heart. The further you move away from God, the less hope you have of receiving the joy of his presence and his blessings.

JOB 30:16, 27 | *Depression haunts my days. . . . My heart is troubled and restless.*

A broken heart is ripe for depression.

ECCLESIASTES 4:8 | *This is the case of a man who is all alone, without a child or a brother, yet who works hard to gain as much wealth as he can. But then he asks himself, "Who am I working for? Why am I giving up so much pleasure now?" It is all so meaningless and depressing.*

If you spend your life pursuing meaningless things, you may become depressed when you recognize that what you are doing has little lasting value.

JEREMIAH 20:14, 18 | *I curse the day I was born! May no one celebrate the day of my birth. . . . Why was I ever born? My entire life has been filled with trouble, sorrow, and shame.*

The more choices you make that get you into trouble, sorrow, or shame, the deeper your depression will become.

PROVERBS 13:12 | *Hope deferred makes the heart sick, but a dream fulfilled is a tree of life.*

A heart without hope is headed for depression.

How should I handle depression?

PSALM 143:7 | *Come quickly, LORD, and answer me, for my depression deepens. Don't turn away from me, or I will die.*

The Lord's strong presence in your life is the best way to overcome depression. But God often works through other people, so with his guidance, you may also need to seek medical or psychological help and allow him to use it to heal you.

How does God bring healing to those who are depressed?

PSALM 10:17 | *LORD, you know the hopes of the helpless. Surely you will hear their cries and comfort them.*

PSALM 23:4 | *Even when I walk through the darkest valley, I will not be afraid, for you are close beside me. Your rod and your staff protect and comfort me.*

PSALM 34:18 | *The LORD is close to the brokenhearted; he rescues those whose spirits are crushed.*

PSALM 147:3 | *He heals the brokenhearted and bandages their wounds.*

MATTHEW 5:4 | *God blesses those who mourn, for they will be comforted.*

The power of the Lord's presence, coupled with the sensitivity of his listening ear, can bring healing and comfort.

How can I help people who are depressed?

PROVERBS 25:20 | *Singing cheerful songs to a person with a heavy heart is like taking someone's coat in cold weather or pouring vinegar in a wound.*

ROMANS 12:15 | *Be happy with those who are happy, and weep with those who weep.*

2 CORINTHIANS 1:4 | *He comforts us in all our troubles so that we can comfort others. When they are troubled, we will be able to give them the same comfort God has given us.*

The best way to help people who are down is to model the gentle, caring love of Christ. Those dealing with depression need comfort and understanding, not advice and lectures. You can help those who are depressed by your quiet presence, your love, and your encouragement. Telling them to "snap out of it" or minimizing their pain by false cheeriness will just make them feel worse.

Promise from God MATTHEW 11:28 | *Jesus said, "Come to me, all of you who are weary and carry heavy burdens, and I will give you rest."*

DISAPPOINTMENT

What disappoints God?

GENESIS 6:5-6 | *The LORD observed the extent of human wickedness on the earth, and he saw that everything they thought or imagined was consistently and totally evil. So the LORD was sorry he had ever made them and put them on the earth. It broke his heart.*

Wickedness and evil of any kind disappoint God.

HEBREWS 3:17-18 | *Who made God angry for forty years? Wasn't it the people who sinned, whose corpses lay in the wilderness? And to whom was God speaking when he took an oath that they would never enter his rest? Wasn't it the people who disobeyed him?*

Sin and disobedience disappoint God.

MALACHI 1:8, 10 | *"When you give blind animals as sacrifices, isn't that wrong? And isn't it wrong to offer animals that are crippled and diseased? . . . I am not pleased with you," says the LORD of Heaven's Armies, "and I will not accept your offerings."*

Giving God less than your best disappoints him.

2 TIMOTHY 2:4 | *Soldiers don't get tied up in the affairs of civilian life, for then they cannot please the officer who enlisted them.*

Letting other things in your life overshadow the Lord disappoints him.

Is there a way to avoid or minimize disappointment in my life?

HAGGAI 1:6, 9 | *You have planted much but harvest little. . . . Why? Because my house lies in ruins, says the LORD of Heaven's Armies, while all of you are busy building your own fine houses.*

Put God first. Give him the best minutes of your day, the first part of your money, the highest priority in your life. By doing this, you will discover the rewards and satisfaction of a relationship with the God who created you and loves you.

PSALM 22:5 | *They cried out to you and were saved. They trusted in you and were never disgraced.*

PSALM 34:2 | *I will boast only in the LORD; let all who are helpless take heart.*

1 PETER 2:6 | *As the Scriptures say, "I am placing a cornerstone in Jerusalem, chosen for great honor, and anyone who trusts in him will never be disgraced."*

If you live by the principles of Scripture given by God himself, you will face less disappointment because you will have fewer consequences resulting from sinful actions.

GALATIANS 6:4 | *Pay careful attention to your own work, for then you will get the satisfaction of a job well done, and you won't need to compare yourself to anyone else.*

The satisfaction of doing right and performing a job well will minimize disappointment.

How should I respond to disappointment?

GALATIANS 6:9 | *Let's not get tired of doing what is good. At just the right time we will reap a harvest of blessing if we don't give up.*

When others don't seem to notice or appreciate your good deeds or when you don't see them making a difference, you can be disappointed. But anything good you do has immense value, both for you and for others. Don't let disappointment keep you from doing good, if for no other reason than to enjoy the blessings God will reward you with when you meet him face-to-face.

ECCLESIASTES 10:8-9 | *When you dig a well, you might fall in. When you demolish an old wall, you could be bitten by a snake. When you work in a quarry, stones might fall and crush you. When you chop wood, there is danger with each stroke of your ax.*

To live the great adventure of life, you must accept the risks that come with the adventure. See your disappointments as stepping-stones to something greater ahead.

Promise from God PSALM 55:22 | *Give your burdens to the LORD, and he will take care of you.*

DISCIPLINE

What are the benefits of discipline?

PSALM 119:67 | *I used to wander off until you disciplined me; but now I closely follow your word.*

Discipline can keep you following God's Word, saving you much grief and heartache.

PROVERBS 6:20, 23 | *Obey your father's commands, and don't neglect your mother's instruction. . . . For their command is a lamp and their instruction a light; their corrective discipline is the way to life.*

HEBREWS 12:11 | *No discipline is enjoyable while it is happening— it's painful! But afterward there will be a peaceful harvest of right living for those who are trained in this way.*

Discipline promotes right living, bringing a life of joy, satisfaction, and purpose.

How does God discipline you?

HEBREWS 12:7 | *As you endure this divine discipline, remember that God is treating you as his own children. Who ever heard of a child who is never disciplined by its father?*

As a loving father.

DEUTERONOMY 8:5 | *Think about it: Just as a parent disciplines a child, the LORD your God disciplines you for your own good.*

PSALM 119:75 | *I know, O LORD, that your regulations are fair; you disciplined me because I needed it.*

When you need it.

JEREMIAH 31:18 | *You disciplined me severely, like a calf that needs training for the yoke. Turn me again to you and restore me, for you alone are the LORD my God.*

When you deserve it.

How should I discipline my children?

PROVERBS 13:24 | *Those who spare the rod of discipline hate their children. Those who love their children care enough to discipline them.*

With love. Discipline is about relationships, not rules. It is about safety, not retaliation. Your goal is not revenge, but restoration; not to taunt, but to teach.

PROVERBS 19:18 | *Discipline your children while there is hope. Otherwise you will ruin their lives.*

With timeliness. The best discipline is done when they need it—before it is too late.

COLOSSIANS 3:21 | *Fathers, do not aggravate your children, or they will become discouraged.*

Without causing aggravation and discouragement.

HEBREWS 12:10 | *Our earthly fathers disciplined us for a few years, doing the best they knew how. But God's discipline is always good for us, so that we might share in his holiness.*

With wisdom—always doing the best you know how.

Promise from God PSALM 94:12 | *Joyful are those you discipline, LORD, those you teach with your instructions.*

DISTRACTIONS

How do I deal with distractions?

MATTHEW 19:13-15 | *One day some parents brought their children to Jesus so he could lay his hands on them and pray for them. But the disciples scolded the parents for bothering him. But Jesus said, "Let the children come to me. Don't stop them! For the Kingdom of Heaven belongs to those who are like these children." And he placed his hands on their heads and blessed them before he left.*

MARK 10:17 | *As Jesus was starting out on his way to Jerusalem, a man came running up to him, knelt down, and asked, "Good Teacher, what must I do to inherit eternal life?"*

Distractions bombarded Jesus all the time. But he didn't see them as distractions; he saw them as opportunities to save the lost or to help people. When someone needs you, the distraction is a divine opportunity to show him or her the love and care of God. Sometimes God interrupts you for a good reason. Don't miss the chance to focus on the people God brings to you for help.

ACTS 16:29-32 | *The jailer called for lights and ran to the dungeon and fell down trembling before Paul and Silas. Then he brought them out and asked, "Sirs, what must I do to be saved?" They replied, "Believe in the Lord Jesus and you will be saved, along with everyone in your household." And they shared the word of the Lord with him and with all who lived in his household.*

Most people would look at a jail sentence as a definite distraction from their ability to serve God. Not Paul and Silas! Their location didn't stop them from their mission. They were doing a great ministry around the world; now it was confined to a small room with a very small audience. Instead of pushing away the distraction, Paul and Silas embraced it.

Sometimes a distraction seems as restricting as a jail cell. But maybe God wants you to focus for a while on what or who is right in front of you. Your distraction may be a calling from God to minister to new people in a new place.

Does God cause distractions?

EXODUS 3:1-4 | *One day Moses was tending the flock of his father-in-law, Jethro. . . . There the angel of the LORD appeared to him in a blazing fire from the middle of a bush. Moses stared in amazement. Though the bush was engulfed in flames, it didn't burn up. . . . "Why isn't that bush burning up? I must go see it." When the LORD saw Moses coming to take a closer look, God called to him from the middle of the bush, "Moses! Moses!" "Here I am!" Moses replied.*

Moses was just living an ordinary day doing his ordinary job. God used the distraction of a burning bush to get Moses' attention because God had a much bigger job he wanted Moses to begin.

ACTS 9:1, 3-4 | *Saul . . . was eager to kill the Lord's followers. . . . As he was approaching Damascus on this mission, a light from heaven suddenly shone down around him. He fell to the ground and heard a voice saying to him, "Saul! Saul! Why are you persecuting me?"*

God sometimes causes distractions to get you to stop focusing on what *you* think is right and to start focusing on what *he* says is right. Saul (whose name later changed to Paul) sincerely believed that persecuting Christians was the right thing to do—he thought God was pleased with his actions. God had to get his attention with a dramatic distraction that changed the course of his whole life (and the lives of many others!). The more stubborn and passionate you are

about your opinions, the more dramatic God may have to be to get your attention.

Promise from God HEBREWS 12:13 | *Mark out a straight path for your feet so that those who are weak and lame will not fall but become strong.*

DIVORCE

What does the Bible say about divorce?

MALACHI 2:14-16 | *You cry out, "Why doesn't the LORD accept my worship?" I'll tell you why! Because the LORD witnessed the vows you and your wife made when you were young. But you have been unfaithful to her. . . . Didn't the LORD make you one with your wife? In body and spirit you are his. . . . So guard your heart; remain loyal to the wife of your youth. "For I hate divorce!" says the LORD, the God of Israel.*

God sees divorce as wrong because it is breaking a binding commitment you and your spouse made before him. He was a witness at your wedding. It is tearing apart what God bound together into one seamless piece. Divorce occurs when a conscious decision to break this sacred commitment has been made by one or both mates.

MATTHEW 19:3 | *Some Pharisees came and tried to trap him with this question: "Should a man be allowed to divorce his wife for just any reason?"*

Both the Old Testament (Deuteronomy 24:1-4; Malachi 2:14-16) and the New Testament (Matthew 5:31-32; 1 Corinthians 7:10-11) acknowledge the reality of divorce. Even among believers, divorce happens, just like all other

forms of sin, despite the best intentions. Sometimes it is caused by persistent infidelity or abuse by one of the partners, or sometimes a partner simply wants to walk away from the marriage. The fact remains that divorce is wrong, just as any sin is wrong. Another fact is also clear: Any sin can be forgiven. You do not have to forfeit joy and blessing for the rest of your life. God restores you and allows you to move on. So while God clearly lists in the Bible what he considers sin (and divorce is on that list), he also clearly explains how to be forgiven and how to restore your relationship with him, even if your marriage cannot be salvaged.

What are some ways to prevent divorce?

EPHESIANS 5:24-25 | *As the church submits to Christ, so you wives should submit to your husbands in everything. For husbands, this means love your wives, just as Christ loved the church. He gave up his life for her.*

1 THESSALONIANS 5:11 | *Encourage each other and build each other up, just as you are already doing.*

Couples who love each other with the kind of love Christ showed when he died for us, who seek to please each other, who encourage and build up each other are the couples who will likely remain together in a happy marriage. The format is simple, but the fulfillment takes some doing! Don't let anyone convince you that love should be easy. Sin is easy; love is hard work because it requires you to think about your mate more than yourself. But loving and serving others always bring far greater rewards than living just for yourself.

Promise from God MATTHEW 19:6 | *Since they are no longer two but one, let no one split apart what God has joined together.*

EMOTIONS

How can I best handle my emotions?

PROVERBS 4:23 | *Guard your heart above all else, for it determines the course of your life.*

Guard your heart, for it is the source of your emotions. It is the center of the battle between your sinful nature and your new nature as a believer (see Galatians 5:17). This should make you cautious about trusting your emotions, because Satan is trying to get you to think that your sinful feelings are right so it is okay to give in to them.

JOB 7:11 | *I cannot keep from speaking. I must express my anguish. My bitter soul must complain.*

Keep an open dialogue with the Lord and others you trust so that you are not denying your emotions. Share your feelings with a few godly confidants so they can hold you accountable.

EZRA 3:12-13 | *Many of the older priests, Levites, and other leaders who had seen the first Temple wept aloud when they saw the new Temple's foundation. The others, however, were shouting for joy. The joyful shouting and weeping mingled together in a loud noise that could be heard far in the distance.*

A single event can produce multiple emotions. While you celebrate a rainstorm for your garden, others may mourn because it rained on their parade. Try to understand that the feelings of others may be quite different from yours, even over the same event. Don't try to force others to feel the way you do, and don't be obligated to feel the same way others do.

ROMANS 13:14 | *Clothe yourself with the presence of the Lord Jesus Christ. And don't let yourself think about ways to indulge your evil desires.*

EPHESIANS 4:23 | *Let the Spirit renew your thoughts and attitudes.*

When you let the Spirit of Christ control you, he will direct your emotions into healthy behavior.

How can I experience life's most positive emotions?

ROMANS 8:6 | *Letting your sinful nature control your mind leads to death. But letting the Spirit control your mind leads to life and peace.*

GALATIANS 5:22-23 | *The Holy Spirit produces this kind of fruit in our lives: love, joy, peace, patience, kindness, goodness, faithfulness, gentleness, and self-control.*

Life's most positive and healthy emotions come from the fruit of the Spirit of God being lived out in your life.

Promise from God GALATIANS 5:22-23 | *The Holy Spirit produces this kind of fruit in our lives: love, joy, peace, patience, kindness, goodness, faithfulness, gentleness, and self-control.*

ENCOURAGEMENT

When do I most need encouragement?

NUMBERS 13:30-31 | *Caleb tried to quiet the people as they stood before Moses. "Let's go at once to take the land," he said. "We can certainly conquer it!" But the other men who had explored the land with him disagreed. "We can't go up against them! They are stronger than we are!"*

When you stand at life's crossroads and need to move in the right direction. Caleb, in the midst of great opposition, tried to encourage God's people to move in the right direction.

ISAIAH 35:3 | *With this news, strengthen those who have tired hands, and encourage those who have weak knees.*

When you are tired and weak.

ISAIAH 41:10 | *Don't be discouraged, for I am your God. I will strengthen you and help you. I will hold you up with my victorious right hand.*

When you feel that life's challenges are stronger than you are.

TITUS 2:6 | *Encourage the young men to live wisely.*

As you move through life's stages.

DEUTERONOMY 3:28 | *[The Lord said to Moses,] "Commission Joshua and encourage and strengthen him, for he will lead the people across the Jordan. He will give them all the land you now see before you as their possession."*

When you are thrust into a position of leadership.

2 CHRONICLES 35:2 | *Josiah also assigned the priests to their duties and encouraged them in their work at the Temple of the LORD.*

When God has a job for you to do.

How does God encourage me?

1 KINGS 19:4-6 | *[Elijah] went on alone into the wilderness, traveling all day. He sat down under a solitary broom tree and prayed that he might die. "I have had enough, LORD," he said. . . . But as he was sleeping, an angel touched him and told him,*

"Get up and eat!" He looked around and there beside his head was some bread baked on hot stones and a jar of water!

He meets your needs at just the right time.

PSALM 138:3 | *As soon as I pray, you answer me; you encourage me by giving me strength.*

He responds when you talk to him and gives you strength when you are weak.

PSALM 119:25, 28 | *I lie in the dust; revive me by your word. . . . I weep with sorrow; encourage me by your word.*

ROMANS 15:4 | *The Scriptures give us hope and encouragement as we wait patiently for God's promises to be fulfilled.*

He revives you and gives you hope as you spend time in his written Word.

MATTHEW 9:2 | *Some people brought to him a paralyzed man on a mat. Seeing their faith, Jesus said to the paralyzed man, "Be encouraged, my child! Your sins are forgiven."*

MATTHEW 9:22 | *Jesus turned around, and when he saw her he said, "Daughter, be encouraged! Your faith has made you well." And the woman was healed at that moment.*

He heals your wounds, forgives your sins, and renews your faith.

HEBREWS 12:5 | *Have you forgotten the encouraging words God spoke to you as his children? He said, "My child, don't make light of the LORD's discipline, and don't give up when he corrects you."*

He disciplines you to show you how much he cares about you. Be encouraged that God loves you enough to correct you and keep you on the best path for your life.

How can I be an encouragement to others?

1 SAMUEL 23:16 | *Jonathan went to find David and encouraged him to stay strong in his faith in God.*

By inspiring others through your words and actions to stay close to God.

EPHESIANS 4:29 | *Don't use foul or abusive language. Let everything you say be good and helpful, so that your words will be an encouragement to those who hear them.*

By making sure everything you say is kind and uplifting.

2 CHRONICLES 32:8 | *"He may have a great army, but they are merely men. We have the LORD our God to help us and to fight our battles for us!" Hezekiah's words greatly encouraged the people.*

By reminding people what God can do, and wants to do, for and through them.

2 CHRONICLES 30:22 | *Hezekiah encouraged all the Levites regarding the skill they displayed as they served the LORD.*

By complimenting others for a job well done.

TITUS 1:9 | *[An elder] must have a strong belief in the trustworthy message he was taught; then he will be able to encourage others with wholesome teaching and show those who oppose it where they are wrong.*

By sharing God's instruction and correction.

PROVERBS 15:30 | *A cheerful look brings joy to the heart.*

By smiling!

Promise from God 2 THESSALONIANS 2:16-17 | *May our Lord Jesus Christ himself and God our Father, who loved us and by his grace gave us eternal comfort and a wonderful hope, comfort you and strengthen you in every good thing you do and say.*

ENVY

What causes envy?

GENESIS 26:12-14 | *When Isaac planted his crops that year, he harvested a hundred times more grain than he planted, for the LORD blessed him. He became a very rich man, and his wealth continued to grow. He acquired so many flocks of sheep and goats, herds of cattle, and servants that the Philistines became jealous of him.*

JAMES 4:2 | *You want what you don't have, so you scheme and kill to get it. You are jealous of what others have, but you can't get it, so you fight and wage war to take it away from them.*

Envy is desiring what others have and becoming dissatisfied with your situation in life. You are in danger of envying (or longing in an unhealthy way) when you find yourself focused on the success others currently seem to be enjoying.

DANIEL 6:3-4 | *Daniel soon proved himself more capable than all the other administrators and high officers. Because of Daniel's great ability, the king made plans to place him over the entire empire. Then the other administrators and high officers began searching for some fault in the way Daniel was handling government affairs, but they couldn't find anything to criticize or condemn.*

People become jealous when someone has a natural ability to do a better job than they can.

PSALM 73:3 | *I envied the proud when I saw them prosper despite their wickedness.*

It is easy to envy an evil person who prospers more than the righteous.

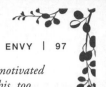

ECCLESIASTES 4:4 | *I observed that most people are motivated to success because they envy their neighbors. But this, too, is meaningless—like chasing the wind.*

Trying to keep up with others is both the cause of envy and the fruit of envy.

What is the result of envy?

JOB 5:2 | *Surely resentment destroys the fool, and jealousy kills the simple.*

PSALM 37:8 | *Stop being angry! Turn from your rage! Do not lose your temper—it only leads to harm.*

PROVERBS 14:30 | *A peaceful heart leads to a healthy body; jealousy is like cancer in the bones.*

PROVERBS 27:4 | *Anger is cruel, and wrath is like a flood, but jealousy is even more dangerous.*

JAMES 3:16 | *Wherever there is jealousy and selfish ambition, there you will find disorder and evil of every kind.*

Envy unchecked can turn to anger, bitterness, and hatred, and it could eventually destroy you.

What can I do about my feelings of envy?

PSALM 37:1, 7 | *Don't worry about the wicked or envy those who do wrong. . . . Be still in the presence of the LORD, and wait patiently for him to act.*

PROVERBS 24:19-20 | *Don't fret because of evildoers; don't envy the wicked. For evil people have no future; the light of the wicked will be snuffed out.*

It is foolish to envy the wicked who prosper, because their prosperity is only temporary. You can let your envy control you and try to get what you don't have, but you will become

frustrated and bitterness will consume you. Or you can learn to be content with what you have and patiently wait for God to act in your life in the way that is best for you. Contentment brings satisfaction and peace of heart and mind.

JOHN 21:20-22 | *Peter turned around and saw behind them the disciple Jesus loved—the one who had leaned over to Jesus during supper and asked, "Lord, who will betray you?" Peter asked Jesus, "What about him, Lord?" Jesus replied, "If I want him to remain alive until I return, what is that to you? As for you, follow me."*

You have a unique role to fulfill. Rather than worrying about others' positions or advantages, trust God to work out his plan for you.

Promise from God PSALM 37:9 | *The wicked will be destroyed, but those who trust in the LORD will possess the land.*

ESCAPE

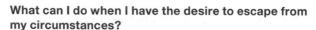

What can I do when I have the desire to escape from my circumstances?

PSALM 139:7 | *I can never escape from your Spirit! I can never get away from your presence!*

JEREMIAH 23:24 | *"Can anyone hide from me in a secret place? Am I not everywhere in all the heavens and earth?" says the LORD.*

Recognize that you cannot escape from God.

PSALM 32:7 | *You are my hiding place; you protect me from trouble. You surround me with songs of victory.*

PSALM 46:1 | *God is our refuge and strength, always ready to help in times of trouble.*

PSALM 57:1 | *Have mercy on me, O God, have mercy! I look to you for protection. I will hide beneath the shadow of your wings until the danger passes by.*

NAHUM 1:7 | *The LORD is good, a strong refuge when trouble comes. He is close to those who trust in him.*

When you have to escape from something, it should be into the arms of your loving God.

How does God provide ways of escape?

GENESIS 7:7 | *[Noah] went on board the boat to escape the flood—he and his wife and his sons and their wives.*

GENESIS 19:17 | *One of the angels ordered, "Run for your lives! And don't look back or stop anywhere in the valley! Escape to the mountains, or you will be swept away!"*

EXODUS 14:21 | *Moses raised his hand over the sea, and the LORD opened up a path through the water with a strong east wind. The wind blew all that night, turning the seabed into dry land.*

Sometimes he provides literal, physical ways to escape.

PROVERBS 14:27 | *Fear of the LORD is a life-giving fountain; it offers escape from the snares of death.*

He offers you escape from sin and spiritual death into a relationship with him.

1 CORINTHIANS 10:13 | *God is faithful. He will not allow the temptation to be more than you can stand. When you are tempted, he will show you a way out so that you can endure.*

He helps you escape from temptation so you can live a life pleasing to God.

Promise from God HEBREWS 6:18 | *God has given both his promise and his oath. These two things are unchangeable because it is impossible for God to lie. Therefore, we who have fled to him for refuge can have great confidence as we hold to the hope that lies before us.*

EXPECTATIONS

What should I expect in life?

PROVERBS 11:23 | *The godly can look forward to a reward, while the wicked can expect only judgment.*

2 CORINTHIANS 3:8, 12 | *Shouldn't we expect far greater glory under the new way, now that the Holy Spirit is giving life? . . . Since this new way gives us such confidence, we can be very bold.*

HEBREWS 10:26-27 | *If we deliberately continue sinning after we have received knowledge of the truth, there is no longer any sacrifice that will cover these sins. There is only the terrible expectation of God's judgment and the raging fire that will consume his enemies.*

If you live for God, you can expect a glorious future, but if you live in rebellion against God, you can expect judgment.

ROMANS 5:3-5 | *We can rejoice, too, when we run into problems and trials, for we know that they help us develop endurance. And endurance develops strength of character, and character strengthens our confident hope of salvation. And this hope will not lead to disappointment. For we know how dearly God loves us, because he has given us the Holy Spirit to fill our hearts with his love.*

If you have trusted in Christ for salvation, you can expect eternal life with God.

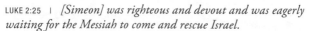

LUKE 2:25 | *[Simeon] was righteous and devout and was eagerly waiting for the Messiah to come and rescue Israel.*

You can live in eager expectation of Christ's coming.

JAMES 1:5-7 | *If you need wisdom, ask our generous God, and he will give it to you. He will not rebuke you for asking. But when you ask him, be sure that your faith is in God alone. Do not waver, for a person with divided loyalty is as unsettled as a wave of the sea that is blown and tossed by the wind. Such people should not expect to receive anything from the Lord.*

When you pray, you should be confident and expect that God will answer you.

Are there expectations I shouldn't have?

PSALM 10:6 | *[The wicked] think, "Nothing bad will ever happen to us! We will be free of trouble forever!"*

ISAIAH 33:1 | *You betray others, but you have never been betrayed. When you are done destroying, you will be destroyed. When you are done betraying, you will be betrayed.*

It is wrong to expect that you can live sinfully and never suffer the consequences.

ECCLESIASTES 10:8-9 | *When you dig a well, you might fall in. When you demolish an old wall, you could be bitten by a snake. When you work in a quarry, stones might fall and crush you. When you chop wood, there is danger with each stroke of your ax.*

You should not expect life to be free from danger and risk.

2 CORINTHIANS 11:7 | *Was I wrong when I humbled myself and honored you by preaching God's Good News to you without expecting anything in return?*

You should not expect to be rewarded by others for serving God and obeying him.

LUKE 13:26-27 | *You will say, "But we ate and drank with you, and you taught in our streets." And he will reply, "I tell you, I don't know you or where you come from. Get away from me, all you who do evil."*

You should not expect to get into heaven by merely knowing about Christ. You must know him personally and trust in him for forgiveness and eternal life.

ISAIAH 55:8 | *"My thoughts are nothing like your thoughts," says the LORD. "And my ways are far beyond anything you could imagine."*

You should not expect God to think or act like you do. He is love, while people struggle to be loving. He is wise, and people are very often foolish. He is all-powerful, and people are weak. He is pure, and people are sinful—the list could go on and on . . .

Promise from God 1 PETER 1:3-4 | *All praise to God, the Father of our Lord Jesus Christ. It is by his great mercy that we have been born again, because God raised Jesus Christ from the dead. Now we live with great expectation, and we have a priceless inheritance—an inheritance that is kept in heaven for you, pure and undefiled, beyond the reach of change and decay.*

FAILURE

How do I keep from failing?

NUMBERS 14:22 | *[The Lord said,] "Not one of these people will ever enter that land. They have all seen my glorious presence*

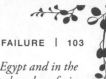

and the miraculous signs I performed both in Egypt and in the wilderness, but again and again they have tested me by refusing to listen to my voice."

JOSHUA 7:7-8, 10-12 | *Joshua cried out, "Oh, Sovereign LORD, why did you bring us across the Jordan River if you are going to let the Amorites kill us? If only we had been content to stay on the other side! Lord, what can I say now that Israel has fled from its enemies?" . . . But the LORD said to Joshua, "Get up! Why are you lying on your face like this? Israel has sinned and broken my covenant! . . . That is why the Israelites are running from their enemies in defeat."*

HEBREWS 4:6 | *God's rest is there for people to enter, but those who first heard this good news failed to enter because they disobeyed God.*

Sin is the cause of many failures. God tells you to live a certain way for a very good reason—to help you make the most of life both now and forever. Sin causes failure because it is contrary to God's plan, which is always best for you. God knows the best way to succeed in life because he created life. You will always fail when you go against God's Word and try to live your own way.

PROVERBS 15:22 | *Plans go wrong for lack of advice; many advisers bring success.*

MATTHEW 7:24-25 | *[Jesus said,] "Anyone who listens to my teaching and follows it is wise, like a person who builds a house on solid rock. Though the rain comes in torrents and the floodwaters rise and the winds beat against that house, it won't collapse because it is built on bedrock."*

Listening to good advice helps prevent failure. A concert of wise counsel makes good music for your success.

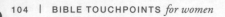

ISAIAH 42:23 | *Who will hear these lessons from the past and see the ruin that awaits you in the future?*

Remember that failure can be helpful: It can teach you important lessons about what to avoid in the future. You need not repeat your own mistakes or copy the mistakes you recognize in others!

When I have failed, how do I get past it and go on?

1 KINGS 8:33-34 | *[Solomon prayed,] "If your people Israel are defeated by their enemies because they have sinned against you, and if they turn to you and acknowledge your name and pray to you here in this Temple, then hear from heaven and forgive the sin of your people Israel."*

Turning to God in repentance and trust is the best response you can have to your failure.

PROVERBS 24:16 | *The godly may trip seven times, but they will get up again. But one disaster is enough to overthrow the wicked.*

MICAH 7:8 | *Though I fall, I will rise again. Though I sit in darkness, the LORD will be my light.*

2 CORINTHIANS 4:9 | *We are hunted down, but never abandoned by God. We get knocked down, but we are not destroyed.*

The best response to failure is to get up again, with the help and hope you receive from God.

Promise from God PSALM 37:23-24 | *The LORD directs the steps of the godly. He delights in every detail of their lives. Though they stumble, they will never fall, for the LORD holds them by the hand.*

FAITH

Why should I have faith in God?

ISAIAH 25:9 | *This is our God! We trusted in him, and he saved us! This is the LORD, in whom we trusted. Let us rejoice in the salvation he brings!*

JOHN 5:24 | *[Jesus said,] "I tell you the truth, those who listen to my message and believe in God who sent me have eternal life."*

According to the Bible (God's own words), faith in God is the only way to heaven, the only doorway to eternal life. And the One who created heaven has told you clearly how to get there.

HEBREWS 11:1 | *Faith is the confidence that what we hope for will actually happen; it gives us assurance about things we cannot see.*

Faith gives you hope. When the world seems to be a crazy, mixed-up place, you can be absolutely confident that Jesus will come and make it right again. Your faith in his promise to do that one day will allow you to keep going today.

How does faith in God affect my life?

GENESIS 15:6 | *Abram believed the LORD, and the LORD counted him as righteous because of his faith.*

ROMANS 3:24-25 | *God, with undeserved kindness, declares that we are righteous. . . . People are made right with God when they believe that Jesus sacrificed his life, shedding his blood.*

Sin breaks your relationship with God because it is rebellion against God. A holy God cannot live with unholy people. But when you accept Jesus as Savior and ask him to forgive your sins, this simple act of faith makes you righteous in God's sight.

ISAIAH 26:3 | *You will keep in perfect peace all who trust in you, all whose thoughts are fixed on you!*

Faith in God frees you from the pressures, priorities, and perspectives of this world. It brings peace of mind and heart because it links you to God's peace and power. Faith that God is sovereign gives you the peaceful assurance that he is still in control, no matter what.

ROMANS 8:5 | *Those who are dominated by the sinful nature think about sinful things, but those who are controlled by the Holy Spirit think about things that please the Spirit.*

GALATIANS 5:22-23 | *The Holy Spirit produces this kind of fruit in our lives: love, joy, peace, patience, kindness, goodness, faithfulness, gentleness, and self-control.*

Faith is inviting God's Holy Spirit to live inside you. It is an act of the mind, but in addition, it taps into the very resources of God so you have the power to live in an entirely new way. If God himself is living in you, your life should change dramatically.

When I'm struggling in my Christian life and have doubts, does it mean I am lacking faith?

GENESIS 15:8 | *Abram replied, "O Sovereign LORD, how can I be sure . . . ?"*

MATTHEW 11:2-3 | *John the Baptist . . . sent his disciples to ask Jesus, "Are you the Messiah we've been expecting, or should we keep looking for someone else?"*

2 PETER 1:4-5 | *Because of [God's] glory and excellence, he has given us great and precious promises. . . . In view of all this, make every effort to respond to God's promises.*

Many people in the Bible whom we consider to be "pillars of faith" had moments of doubt. The key is to bring your doubts to God and allow him to prove himself to you, which he is always gracious to do. Even during moments of doubt, invest the effort and discipline to allow your faith to grow. Doubts are valuable when they bring you closer to God.

Promise from God   1 PETER 1:7 | *When your faith remains strong through many trials, it will bring you much praise and glory and honor on the day when Jesus Christ is revealed to the whole world.*

FAMILY

What is family? How does the Bible define it?

GENESIS 2:24 | *A man leaves his father and mother and is joined to his wife, and the two are united into one.*

EPHESIANS 2:19 | *You are members of God's family.*

JAMES 1:18 | *[God] chose to give birth to us by giving us his true word. And we, out of all creation, became his prized possession.*

The Bible talks about both an earthly family (made up of husband, wife, and children) and the family of God (which includes all believers in Jesus Christ).

GENESIS 4:1 | *Adam had sexual relations with his wife, Eve, and she became pregnant. When she gave birth to Cain, she said, "With the LORD's help, I have produced a man!"*

PSALM 127:3 | *Children are a gift from the LORD; they are a reward from him.*

Children are a wonderful blessing to a family.

1 CHRONICLES 9:1 | *All Israel was listed in the genealogical records in* The Book of the Kings of Israel.

The Bible lists several genealogies, all recorded by family units, showing the family as central and fundamental to the development of people and of nations.

JOSHUA 24:15 | *As for me and my family, we will serve the* LORD.

PROVERBS 6:20, 23 | *My son, obey your father's commands, and don't neglect your mother's instruction. . . . For their command is a lamp and their instruction a light; their corrective discipline is the way to life.*

The family is one of God's greatest resources for communicating truth and effecting change in any community. This change is directly related to the family's spiritual commitment and zeal.

What are my responsibilities to my family, especially my children?

DEUTERONOMY 6:7 | *Repeat [God's commands] again and again to your children. Talk about them when you are at home and when you are on the road, when you are going to bed and when you are getting up.*

PROVERBS 22:6 | *Direct your children onto the right path, and when they are older, they will not leave it.*

Give them spiritual training.

EXODUS 10:2 | *[The Lord said,] "Tell your children and grandchildren about how I made a mockery of the Egyptians and about the signs I displayed among them."*

2 TIMOTHY 1:5 | *I remember your genuine faith, for you share the faith that first filled your grandmother Lois and your mother, Eunice.*

Share spiritual experiences—stories of how God worked in your life—and remind your family of their spiritual heritage.

PROVERBS 29:15 | *To discipline a child produces wisdom, but a mother is disgraced by an undisciplined child.*

EPHESIANS 6:4 | *Bring [your children] up with the discipline and instruction that comes from the Lord.*

Teach your children right from wrong, and discipline them when necessary.

TITUS 2:4-5 | *These older women must train the younger women to love their husbands and their children, to live wisely and be pure, to work in their homes, to do good, and to be submissive to their husbands. Then they will not bring shame on the word of God.*

Teach them proper conduct by being a good role model.

PROVERBS 31:27 | *She carefully watches everything in her household and suffers nothing from laziness.*

Provide for their physical needs.

How can I bring my family closer together?

DEUTERONOMY 12:7 | *You and your families will feast in the presence of the LORD your God, and you will rejoice in all you have accomplished because the LORD your God has blessed you.*

By regularly celebrating God's goodness with your family members.

Promise from God PSALM 102:28 | *The children of your people will live in security. Their children's children will thrive in your presence.*

FAREWELLS

What are some good ways to say good-bye?

RUTH 1:8-9 | *Naomi said to her two daughters-in-law, "Go back to your mothers' homes. And may the LORD reward you for your kindness to your husbands and to me. May the LORD bless you with the security of another marriage."*

Parting with a thankful heart eases the way.

1 SAMUEL 20:42 | *Jonathan said to David, "Go in peace, for we have sworn loyalty to each other in the LORD's name. The LORD is the witness of a bond between us and our children forever." Then David left, and Jonathan returned to the town.*

The heartache of saying good-bye can be softened by entrusting your loved ones into God's care.

GENESIS 24:58-60 | *[Rebekah's brother and mother] called Rebekah. "Are you willing to go with this man?" they asked her. And she replied, "Yes, I will go." So they said good-bye to Rebekah and sent her away with Abraham's servant and his men. The woman who had been Rebekah's childhood nurse went along with her. They gave her this blessing as she parted: "Our sister, may you become the mother of many millions! May your descendants be strong."*

Don't hold on; allow the departure—with a blessing! Let go and trust God to bless the next chapter of your loved one's life, as well as the next chapter of your own.

2 TIMOTHY 1:4 | *I long to see you again, for I remember your tears as we parted. And I will be filled with joy when we are together again.*

Anticipate the next meeting.

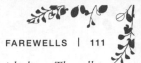

ACTS 20:36-38 | *[Paul] knelt and prayed with them. They all cried as they embraced and kissed him good-bye. They were sad most of all because he had said that they would never see him again.*

Praying together and being open and honest about the pain of parting are important to healthy good-byes.

PHILEMON 1:7 | *Your love has given me much joy and comfort, my brother, for your kindness has often refreshed the hearts of God's people.*

Before parting, thank people for what they have meant to you.

What should be my perspective on farewells caused by death?

ECCLESIASTES 8:8 | *None of us can hold back our spirit from departing.*

Accept that death is inevitable for all.

ISAIAH 25:8 | *He will swallow up death forever! The Sovereign LORD will wipe away all tears. He will remove forever all insults and mockery against his land and people. The LORD has spoken!*

Realize God's ultimate power over death.

MATTHEW 25:46 | *The righteous will go into eternal life.*

REVELATION 7:17 | *The Lamb on the throne will be their Shepherd. He will lead them to springs of life-giving water. And God will wipe every tear from their eyes.*

Remember that there is a wonderful life after death for the Christian.

Promise from God JOHN 14:1-3 | *[Jesus said,] "Don't let your hearts be troubled. Trust in God, and trust also in me.*

There is more than enough room in my Father's home. If this were not so, would I have told you that I am going to prepare a place for you? When everything is ready, I will come and get you, so that you will always be with me where I am."

FASTING

Why should I fast?

2 CHRONICLES 20:3 | *Jehoshaphat was terrified . . . and begged the LORD for guidance. He also ordered everyone in Judah to begin fasting.*

JOEL 1:14 | *Announce a time of fasting; call the people together for a solemn meeting. Bring the leaders and all the people of the land into the Temple of the LORD your God, and cry out to him there.*

Fasting helps you become more focused on the Lord so you can better receive his guidance and mercy.

EZRA 8:21, 23 | *I gave orders for all of us to fast and humble ourselves before our God. We prayed that he would give us a safe journey and protect us, our children, and our goods as we traveled. . . . So we fasted and earnestly prayed that our God would take care of us, and he heard our prayer.*

You can fast to seek God's protection and help.

ESTHER 4:16 | *[Esther said to Mordecai,] "Go and gather together all the Jews of Susa and fast for me. . . . And then, though it is against the law, I will go in to see the king. If I must die, I must die."*

You can fast to seek courage for a specific challenge ahead.

1 CHRONICLES 10:12 | *[The] mighty warriors brought the bodies of Saul and his sons back to Jabesh. Then they buried their bones beneath the great tree at Jabesh, and they fasted for seven days.*

Fasting can help you reinforce your grief in order to show honor to those who have died for your sake and help you focus on the meaning of their sacrifice.

DANIEL 10:2-3 | *I, Daniel, had been in mourning for three whole weeks. All that time I had eaten no rich food. No meat or wine crossed my lips, and I used no fragrant lotions until those three weeks had passed.*

Fasting can be a significant means to keep you from being swallowed up by your culture.

When is it appropriate to fast?

2 SAMUEL 3:35 | *David had refused to eat anything on the day of the funeral.*

In times of mourning.

2 SAMUEL 1:12 | *They mourned and wept and fasted all day for Saul and his son Jonathan, and for the LORD's army and the nation of Israel, because they had died by the sword that day.*

In times of crisis.

DEUTERONOMY 9:18-19 | *[Moses said to the people of Israel,] "I threw myself down before the LORD for forty days and nights. I ate no bread and drank no water because of the great sin you had committed by doing what the LORD hated, provoking him to anger. I feared that the furious anger of the LORD, which turned him against you, would drive him to destroy you. But again he listened to me."*

EZRA 10:6 | *He spent the night there without eating or drinking anything. He was still in mourning because of the unfaithfulness of the returned exiles.*

In times of intercession for others' sins.

ACTS 14:23 | *Paul and Barnabas also appointed elders in every church. With prayer and fasting, they turned the elders over to the care of the Lord, in whom they had put their trust.*

In times of dedication.

2 SAMUEL 12:16 | *David begged God to spare the child. He went without food and lay all night on the bare ground.*

In times of life-threatening illness.

JONAH 3:5 | *The people of Nineveh believed God's message, and from the greatest to the least, they declared a fast and put on burlap to show their sorrow.*

In times of repentance.

What are some guidelines for fasting? How should I fast?

ISAIAH 58:3-5 | *[The Lord says,] "'We have fasted before you!' [my people Israel] say. 'Why aren't you impressed? We have been very hard on ourselves, and you don't even notice it!' 'I will tell you why!' I respond. 'It's because you are fasting to please yourselves. Even while you fast, you keep oppressing your workers. What good is fasting when you keep on fighting and quarreling? . . . Is this what you call fasting? Do you really think this will please the LORD?"'*

The importance of fasting is not your actions or rituals, but your motive. It is not what you do but why you do it. You must truly want to hear from God and be prepared to act on what you hear.

MATTHEW 6:16-18 | *When you fast, don't make it obvious, as the hypocrites do, for they try to look miserable and disheveled so people will admire them for their fasting. I tell you the truth, that is the only reward they will ever get. But when you fast, comb your hair and wash your face. Then no one will notice that you are fasting, except your Father, who knows what you do in private. And your Father, who sees everything, will reward you.*

Fasting, like prayer, is not a public performance but a private relationship with God.

DANIEL 9:3 | *I turned to the Lord God and pleaded with him in prayer and fasting. I also wore rough burlap and sprinkled myself with ashes.*

Fasting and prayer are a spiritual duet. The purpose of fasting is to hear from God.

ACTS 13:2-3 | *One day as these men were worshiping the Lord and fasting, the Holy Spirit said, "Dedicate Barnabas and Saul for the special work to which I have called them." So after more fasting and prayer, the men laid their hands on them and sent them on their way.*

Fasting can also be used in corporate worship when a group of believers needs guidance from the Lord.

Promise from God MATTHEW 6:16, 18 | *When you fast, don't make it obvious. . . . Then no one will notice that you are fasting, except your Father, who knows what you do in private. And your Father, who sees everything, will reward you.*

FORGIVENESS

Do I have to forgive those who hurt me? How many times?

MATTHEW 6:14-15 | *If you forgive those who sin against you, your heavenly Father will forgive you. But if you refuse to forgive others, your Father will not forgive your sins.*

MATTHEW 18:21-22 | *Peter came to [Jesus] and asked, "Lord, how often should I forgive someone who sins against me? Seven times?" "No, not seven times," Jesus replied, "but seventy times seven!"*

MARK 11:25 | *When you are praying, first forgive anyone you are holding a grudge against, so that your Father in heaven will forgive your sins, too.*

Just as God forgives you without limit, you should forgive others without counting how many times.

LUKE 17:3-4 | *If another believer sins, rebuke that person; then if there is repentance, forgive. Even if that person wrongs you seven times a day and each time turns again and asks forgiveness, you must forgive.*

Forgiveness isn't cheap. The hard work of real forgiveness reveals a love that is tough but lasting.

LUKE 23:34 | *Jesus said, "Father, forgive them, for they don't know what they are doing."*

When you find it hard to forgive someone, remember that Jesus forgave those who mocked him and killed him.

COLOSSIANS 3:13 | *Make allowance for each other's faults, and forgive anyone who offends you. Remember, the Lord forgave you, so you must forgive others.*

1 PETER 3:9 | *Don't repay evil for evil. Don't retaliate with insults when people insult you. Instead, pay them back with a blessing. That is what God has called you to do, and he will bless you for it.*

When people say hurtful things about you, God wants you to respond by blessing them.

Is there a limit to how much God will forgive me?

ISAIAH 1:18 | *"Come now, let's settle this," says the LORD. "Though your sins are like scarlet, I will make them as white as snow. Though they are red like crimson, I will make them as white as wool."*

JOEL 2:32 | *Everyone who calls on the name of the LORD will be saved.*

No matter how sinful and disobedient you have been, you can receive God's forgiveness by turning to him in repentance.

PSALM 86:5 | *O Lord, you are so good, so ready to forgive, so full of unfailing love for all who ask for your help.*

PSALM 103:3 | *He forgives all my sins.*

EZEKIEL 18:22 | *All their past sins will be forgotten, and they will live because of the righteous things they have done.*

God is ready to forgive you right now.

MATTHEW 18:23-25, 27 | *The Kingdom of Heaven can be compared to a king who decided to bring his accounts up to date. . . . One of his debtors was brought in who owed him millions of dollars. He couldn't pay. . . . Then his master was filled with pity for him, and he released him and forgave his debt.*

God is merciful toward you even though your debt is great.

LUKE 24:47 | *There is forgiveness of sins for all who repent.*

EPHESIANS 1:7 | *He is so rich in kindness and grace that he purchased our freedom with the blood of his Son and forgave our sins.*

COLOSSIANS 1:13-14 | *He has rescued us from the kingdom of darkness and transferred us into the Kingdom of his dear Son, who purchased our freedom and forgave our sins.*

God will forgive every sin because Christ has already paid the penalty for all sin by his death.

MARK 3:29 | *Anyone who blasphemes the Holy Spirit will never be forgiven. This is a sin with eternal consequences.*

Those who harden themselves against God's Spirit and reject him utterly will never experience his forgiveness because it is the Spirit that works in hearts to bring repentance.

Promise from God 1 JOHN 1:9 | *If we confess our sins to him, he is faithful and just to forgive us our sins and to cleanse us.*

FRIENDSHIP

What is the mark of true friendship?

1 SAMUEL 18:3 | *Jonathan made a solemn pact with David, because he loved him as he loved himself.*

PROVERBS 17:17 | *A friend is always loyal, and a brother is born to help in time of need.*

True friends are bonded together by loyalty and commitment. The friendship remains intact, despite changing external circumstances.

What gets in the way of friendships?

1 SAMUEL 18:9-11 | *Saul kept a jealous eye on David. . . . Saul had a spear in his hand, and he suddenly hurled it at David, intending to pin him to the wall.*

Jealousy is a great dividing force of friendships. Envy over what a friend has will soon turn to anger and bitterness, causing you to separate yourself from the one you truly cared for.

PSALM 41:9 | *Even my best friend, the one I trusted completely . . . has turned against me.*

When trust is seriously damaged, even the closest friendship is at risk.

2 SAMUEL 13:11 | *As she was feeding him, he grabbed her and demanded, "Come to bed with me, my darling sister."*

Friendships are destroyed when boundaries are violated.

What can I do when I'm having trouble making friends?

JOB 19:19 | *My close friends detest me. Those I loved have turned against me.*

JOHN 5:7 | *The sick man said, ". . . I have no one to put me into the pool when the water bubbles up. Someone else always gets there ahead of me."*

Everyone goes through times when he or she feels deserted by friends. Examine your relationships to make sure you are not causing the breach.

MATTHEW 7:12 | *Do to others whatever you would like them to do to you.*

Everyone wants to have good friends, but few are willing to invest the time and effort necessary to build such relationships. You may not make friends quickly and easily, but you can build strong, lasting friendships over time. It might help you to consider the qualities you desire in a good friend— then work to develop those qualities in your own life.

EPHESIANS 4:32 | *Be kind to each other, tenderhearted, forgiving one another, just as God through Christ has forgiven you.*

Keep showing God's love to others, and they will be drawn to you. Acts of kindness and generosity will attract others to you.

JOHN 15:15 | *[Jesus said,] "Now you are my friends, since I have told you everything the Father told me."*

HEBREWS 13:5 | *God has said, "I will never fail you. I will never abandon you."*

Remember that God is your constant friend and will never leave you.

Promise from God MATTHEW 18:20 | *[Jesus said,] "Where two or three gather together as my followers, I am there among them."*

FRUSTRATION

How can I best deal with frustration in my life?

ECCLESIASTES 1:8 | *Everything is wearisome beyond description. No matter how much we see, we are never satisfied. No matter how much we hear, we are not content.*

ECCLESIASTES 2:20 | *I gave up in despair, questioning the value of all my hard work in this world.*

ACTS 17:25 | *Human hands can't serve [God's] needs—for he has no needs. He himself gives life and breath to everything, and he satisfies every need.*

You will become frustrated when you fail to let God be God or when you try to understand the reasons for everything that happens.

PSALM 90:14 | *Satisfy us each morning with your unfailing love, so we may sing for joy to the end of our lives.*

You can choose to be joyful in all circumstances by focusing on God rather than what is going on in your life. When you let go and let God work out what is best for you, you will relieve much of your frustration.

What frustrates God?

PSALM 78:40-42 | *Oh, how often [the people of Israel] rebelled against [God] in the wilderness and grieved his heart in that dry wasteland. Again and again they tested God's patience and provoked the Holy One of Israel. They did not remember his power and how he rescued them from their enemies.*

HOSEA 6:4 | *"O Israel and Judah, what should I do with you?" asks the LORD. "For your love vanishes like the morning mist and disappears like dew in the sunlight."*

It is frustrating to God to give unending love, mercy, and forgiveness to his people, only to see them block these blessings and starve their souls in a spiritual desert.

Promise from God JOSHUA 1:9 | *Be strong and courageous! Do not be afraid or discouraged. For the LORD your God is with you wherever you go.*

GENTLENESS

How is God gentle?

1 KINGS 19:12 | *After the earthquake there was a fire, but the LORD was not in the fire. And after the fire there was the sound of a gentle whisper.*

Although God has the power of the universe at his fingertips, he often speaks most eloquently to us in a gentle whisper.

PSALM 18:35 | *You have given me your shield of victory. Your right hand supports me; your help has made me great.*

PSALM 103:13-14 | *The LORD is like a father to his children, tender and compassionate to those who fear him. For he knows how weak we are; he remembers we are only dust.*

ISAIAH 42:3 | *He will not crush the weakest reed or put out a flickering candle.*

ROMANS 2:4 | *Don't you see how wonderfully kind, tolerant, and patient God is with you? Does this mean nothing to you? Can't you see that his kindness is intended to turn you from your sin?*

God is loving, and he treats you gently because he knows that is what will draw you to him.

How did Jesus demonstrate gentleness?

ISAIAH 40:11 | *He will feed his flock like a shepherd. He will carry the lambs in his arms, holding them close to his heart. He will gently lead the mother sheep with their young.*

MATTHEW 9:36 | *When [Jesus] saw the crowds, he had compassion on them because they were confused and helpless, like sheep without a shepherd.*

MATTHEW 11:28-29 | *Jesus said, "Come to me, all of you who are weary and carry heavy burdens, and I will give you rest. Take my yoke upon you. Let me teach you, because I am humble and gentle at heart, and you will find rest for your souls."*

MARK 6:34 | *Jesus saw the huge crowd as he stepped from the boat, and he had compassion on them because they were like sheep without a shepherd. So he began teaching them many things.*

You can see the heart of Jesus best through images of gentleness: holding his people close, just as a shepherd holds a little lamb; caring for hurting people; lifting heavy burdens; and representing sinful people before almighty God.

How can I be gentler?

GENESIS 33:3-4, 10 | *As [Jacob] approached [Esau], he bowed to the ground seven times before him. Then Esau ran to meet him and embraced him, threw his arms around his neck, and kissed him. And they both wept. . . . [Jacob said,] "If I have found favor with you, please accept this gift from me. And what a relief to see your friendly smile. It is like seeing the face of God!"*

Give a friendly smile in tense times.

1 PETER 3:4 | *You should clothe yourselves instead with the beauty that comes from within, the unfading beauty of a gentle and quiet spirit, which is so precious to God.*

Develop a gentle and quiet spirit, which has lasting beauty.

COLOSSIANS 3:12-13 | *Since God chose you to be the holy people he loves, you must clothe yourselves with tenderhearted mercy, kindness, humility, gentleness, and patience. Make allowance for each other's faults, and forgive anyone who offends you.*

Gentleness is often connected to other spiritual qualities such as mercy, kindness, humility, patience, and forgiveness, demonstrating your desire to live as Jesus did.

JAMES 3:17 | *The wisdom from above is . . . peace loving, gentle at all times.*

Utilize God's wisdom.

GALATIANS 6:1 | *Dear brothers and sisters, if another believer is overcome by some sin, you who are godly should gently and humbly help that person back onto the right path.*

When you need to confront someone, a gentle approach is usually most effective. A gentle response shows you care about the person; a harsh response shows you care only about the behavior.

2 TIMOTHY 2:24-25 | *A servant of the Lord must not quarrel but must be kind to everyone, be able to teach, and be patient with difficult people. Gently instruct those who oppose the truth. Perhaps God will change those people's hearts, and they will learn the truth.*

When teaching others, gentleness and patience are most effective in getting across your message, especially when dealing with difficult people.

PROVERBS 15:1, 4 | *A gentle answer deflects anger, but harsh words make tempers flare. . . . Gentle words are a tree of life; a deceitful tongue crushes the spirit.*

A gentle response to an angry person almost always restrains an argument and keeps it from getting out of control.

Promise from God GALATIANS 5:22-23 | *The Holy Spirit produces this kind of fruit in our lives: love, joy, peace, patience, kindness, goodness, faithfulness, gentleness, and self-control.*

GOSSIP

Why is gossip so bad?

LEVITICUS 19:16 | *Do not spread slanderous gossip among your people.*

Gossip is specifically forbidden by God.

PROVERBS 11:13 | *A gossip goes around telling secrets, but those who are trustworthy can keep a confidence.*

Gossips make poor friends. Gossips are demolition experts who tear others down, while trustworthy people build others up.

ROMANS 1:29 | *Their lives became full of every kind of wickedness, sin, greed, hate, envy, murder, quarreling, deception, malicious behavior, and gossip.*

God catalogs gossip with such sins as greed, hate, envy, and murder.

1 TIMOTHY 5:13 | *If they are on the list [for support], [younger widows] will learn to be lazy and will spend their time gossiping from house to house, meddling in other people's business and talking about things they shouldn't.*

Gossiping often grows out of laziness. When you have nothing better to do than sit around talking about other people, you wind up saying things you might later regret.

MATTHEW 7:1 | *Do not judge others, and you will not be judged.*

When you gossip, you put yourself in the position of judging others—also a sin. In a court of law, rumors and opinions are not allowed because they might unjustly sway the opinion of the jury. So when you turn your living room into a courtroom, you sit as judge and allow rumor and

opinion to color and often damage the reputation of others who can't defend themselves.

PROVERBS 18:8 | *Rumors are dainty morsels that sink deep into one's heart.*

Gossip hurts others. It also destroys your credibility if the gossip proves false.

How do I stop gossip?

PROVERBS 26:20 | *Fire goes out without wood, and quarrels disappear when gossip stops.*

When you hear gossip, decide not to spread it any further. Stop the fires of gossip from spreading beyond you. You could also refuse to listen to the gossip in the first place.

DEUTERONOMY 13:14 | *You must examine the facts carefully.*

If you are concerned about something you've heard, look carefully into the matter instead of assuming what you have been told is true. Go to the source and get the facts straight.

MATTHEW 7:12 | *Do to others whatever you would like them to do to you.*

The Golden Rule can also be applied to your speech—"Talk about others in the same way you would like them to talk about you."

EPHESIANS 4:29 | *Don't use foul or abusive language. Let everything you say be good and helpful, so that your words will be an encouragement to those who hear them.*

When you're tempted to gossip, compliment or encourage someone instead.

COLOSSIANS 3:17 | *Whatever you do or say, do it as a representative of the Lord Jesus.*

If you feel the urge to gossip, ask yourself, *Does the person I'm talking to need to know this? Is it true and accurate, and would it be helpful?*

Promise from God   1 PETER 3:10 | *If you want to enjoy life and see many happy days, keep your tongue from speaking evil and your lips from telling lies.*

GRIEF

What might cause me to grieve?

RUTH 1:9 | *She kissed them good-bye, and they all broke down and wept.*

You grieve when you have to say good-bye to people you love.

NEHEMIAH 2:2-3 | *The king asked me, "Why are you looking so sad?" . . . I replied, "Long live the king! How can I not be sad? For the city where my ancestors are buried is in ruins, and the gates have been destroyed by fire."*

You grieve when you see loved ones hurt or in great need.

JOHN 11:13, 35 | *Lazarus had died. . . . Then Jesus wept.*

You grieve over the death of a loved one.

2 CORINTHIANS 7:10 | *The kind of sorrow God wants us to experience leads us away from sin and results in salvation.*

JAMES 4:9 | *Let there be tears for what you have done. Let there be sorrow and deep grief. Let there be sadness instead of laughter, and gloom instead of joy.*

You grieve over sin. It is right to genuinely grieve for your sins and beg God to forgive them. Until Jesus has cleansed you of those sins, you suffer from them as they lurk within

you. Confession and forgiveness will cleanse sin and wipe away your tears caused by guilt.

LUKE 13:34 | *[Jesus said,] "O Jerusalem, Jerusalem! . . . How often I have wanted to gather your children together as a hen protects her chicks."*

When your heart is in tune with God's, you grieve for those who don't know him.

How do I get over my grief?

GENESIS 50:1 | *Joseph threw himself on his father and wept over him and kissed him.*

2 SAMUEL 18:33 | *The king was overcome with emotion. He went up to the room over the gateway and burst into tears. And as he went, he cried, "O my son Absalom!"*

Recognize that grieving is necessary and important. You need the freedom to grieve. It is an important part of healing because it allows you to release the emotional pressure of your sorrow.

ISAIAH 66:13 | *I will comfort you there in Jerusalem as a mother comforts her child.*

2 CORINTHIANS 1:3 | *All praise to God, the Father of our Lord Jesus Christ. God is our merciful Father and the source of all comfort.*

God knows you grieve, understands your sorrow, and comforts you. He does not promise to protect you from grief, but he does promise to help you through it.

GENESIS 23:2-4 | *Abraham mourned and wept for [Sarah]. Then, leaving her body, he said to the Hittite elders, "Here I am, a stranger and a foreigner among you. Please sell me a piece of land so I can give my wife a proper burial."*

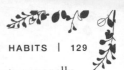

Participate in the process of grief. Take time to personally mourn, but also become involved in the steps necessary to bring closure to your loss.

REVELATION 21:4 | *[God] will wipe every tear from their eyes, and there will be no more death or sorrow or crying or pain.*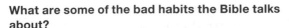

Take hope that there will be no more grief in heaven.

ECCLESIASTES 3:1, 4 | *For everything there is a season. . . . A time to cry and a time to laugh. A time to grieve and a time to dance.*

Grief has its own season, but after you have mourned, God wants you to wipe your tears, move on, and minister to other grieving people.

Promise from God PSALM 147:3 | *[The Lord] heals the brokenhearted and bandages their wounds.*

HABITS

What are some of the bad habits the Bible talks about?

1 JOHN 3:8 | *When people keep on sinning, it shows that they belong to the devil, who has been sinning since the beginning.*

Sinning is a habit you cannot completely stop, but a pattern of sinful living with no change in behavior shows that you are not serious about following God.

EXODUS 8:28, 32 | *"All right, go ahead," Pharaoh replied. "I will let you go." . . . But Pharaoh again became stubborn and refused to let the people go.*

Pharaoh had a hard heart, which led to a bad habit of stubbornness and going back on his word.

NUMBERS 11:1 | *The people began to complain about their hardship.*

The Israelites developed a bad habit of complaining. Chronic complaining quickly turns into bitterness.

1 TIMOTHY 5:13 | *They will learn to be lazy and will spend their time gossiping.*

Having too much time and too little to do can be fertile ground for bad habits to develop. Idleness makes it easy to develop the bad habit of gossiping.

How can I deal with bad habits?

ROMANS 7:15, 25 | *[Paul said,] "I don't really understand myself, for I want to do what is right, but I don't do it. Instead, I do what I hate. . . . The answer is in Jesus Christ."*

One of the best ways to deal with bad habits is to recognize them for what they are and confess them honestly. Paul knew that he could not kick the habit of sin completely. But he did know that, with God's help, he could change. In the same way, you may ask for and receive God's help to rid yourself of your bad habits.

1 JOHN 2:15 | *Do not love this world nor the things it offers you.*

Sinning often appears attractive. In the same way, indulging in bad habits often feels good even though you know they are ultimately bad for you. Breaking a bad habit can be hard because you are losing something you enjoy. Understand that there may be a grieving process, but losing a bad habit ultimately brings a deeper satisfaction from doing what is pleasing to God.

COLOSSIANS 3:2 | *Think about the things of heaven, not the things of earth.*

It will be much easier to break bad habits if you replace them with good habits.

How can I develop good habits?

HEBREWS 10:25 | *Let us not neglect our meeting together, as some people do, but encourage one another.*

Meeting with other believers is a good habit because it provides necessary support and fellowship, it enriches you as you search God's Word together, it keeps you busy when you might otherwise be slipping into bad habits, and it offers accountability.

GENESIS 26:21-22 | *Isaac's men then dug another well, but again there was a dispute over it. . . . Abandoning that one, Isaac moved on and dug another well. This time there was no dispute over it.*

Stay away from the source of your bad habit. Isaac pursued a habit of living in peace. In this case it meant staying away from the source of the conflict, the Philistines, even at great cost.

PSALM 28:7 | *The LORD is my strength and shield. I trust him with all my heart. He helps me, and my heart is filled with joy. I burst out in songs of thanksgiving.*

As a young boy, David developed the habits of talking to God, singing songs about him, and writing psalms. These habits helped him to trust in and follow God all his life.

Promise from God ROMANS 8:5-6 | *Those who are dominated by the sinful nature think about sinful things, but those who are controlled by the Holy Spirit think about things that please the Spirit. So letting your sinful nature control your mind leads to death. But letting the Spirit control your mind leads to life and peace.*

HAND OF GOD

What does the "hand of God" mean?

PSALM 66:5 | *Come and see what our God has done, what awesome miracles he performs for people!*

God works on behalf of his people in miraculous ways—his hand at work, even when you don't see it.

DEUTERONOMY 4:34 | *Has any other god dared to take a nation for himself out of another nation by means of trials, miraculous signs, wonders, war, a strong hand, a powerful arm, and terrifying acts? Yet that is what the LORD your God did for you in Egypt, right before your eyes.*

God works through trials, miraculous signs, wonders, war, awesome power, and even terrifying acts—his hand at work in mighty ways.

DANIEL 6:27 | *He rescues and saves his people; he performs miraculous signs and wonders in the heavens and on earth. He has rescued Daniel from the power of the lions.*

God works to rescue and save his people—his hand at work in personal ways.

JEREMIAH 31:35 | *It is the LORD who provides the sun to light the day and the moon and stars to light the night, and who stirs the sea into roaring waves. His name is the LORD of Heaven's Armies.*

Who but the Creator can control creation? All creation is a testimony to the powerful hand of God. The facts that the sun comes up and warms you, the rain waters the land, and the seasons continue without fail reveal a God who still holds the world in his hand.

What does God's hand provide for me?

JAMES 1:17 | *Whatever is good and perfect comes down to us from God our Father, who created all the lights in the heavens.*

Everything good and perfect comes from God's hand.

JOB 2:10 | *Job [said] . . . "Should we accept only good things from the hand of God and never anything bad?"*

Sometimes God withdraws his hand and allows bad things to happen to good people. Why? Because his long-range eternal plans for your greater good may not fit your short-range view of comfort.

ECCLESIASTES 2:24 | *I decided there is nothing better than to enjoy food and drink and to find satisfaction in work. Then I realized that these pleasures are from the hand of God.*

The pleasure of God's provision transcends the pleasure of the provisions themselves. For example, God's *gift* of bread is far more pleasurable than the taste of bread itself.

Promise from God PSALM 66:5 | *Come and see what our God has done, what awesome miracles he performs for people!*

HEALING

In what ways do I need to be healed?

MARK 1:40 | *A man with leprosy came and knelt in front of Jesus, begging to be healed.*

LUKE 8:42 | *[Jairus's] only daughter, who was about twelve years old, was dying.*

You may need to be healed from sickness and disease.

ISAIAH 61:1 | *[The Lord] has sent me to comfort the brokenhearted.*

Your broken heart may need healing and restoration.

PSALM 30:11 | *You have turned my mourning into joyful dancing.*

You may need healing from grief and sorrow.

PSALM 55:20 | *As for my companion, he betrayed his friends; he broke his promises.*

You may need to be healed from the pain of betrayal.

PSALM 103:3 | *[The Lord] forgives all my sins.*

ROMANS 6:23 | *The wages of sin is death, but the free gift of God is eternal life through Christ Jesus our Lord.*

You need to be healed from sin.

PROVERBS 17:22 | *A cheerful heart is good medicine, but a broken spirit saps a person's strength.*

At times, you may need healing from depression and sadness.

How does God heal?

2 KINGS 20:7 | *Isaiah said, "Make an ointment from figs." So Hezekiah's servants spread the ointment over the boil, and Hezekiah recovered!*

Through physicians and medicine.

PSALM 119:93 | *I will never forget your commandments, for by them you give me life.*

MARK 3:5 | *[Jesus] said to the man, "Hold out your hand." So the man held out his hand, and it was restored!*

Through his words and commands.

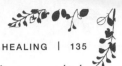

LUKE 5:12-13 | *"Lord," he said, "if you are willing, you can heal me and make me clean." Jesus reached out and touched him. "I am willing," he said. "Be healed!"*

Through miracles.

MARK 2:4-5 | *They couldn't bring him to Jesus because of the crowd, so they dug a hole through the roof above his head. . . . Seeing their faith, Jesus said to the paralyzed man, "My child, your sins are forgiven."*

Through faithful friends.

PSALM 6:2 | *Heal me, LORD, for my bones are in agony.*

JAMES 5:14 | *Are any of you sick? You should call for the elders of the church to come and pray over you, anointing you with oil in the name of the Lord.*

Through prayer.

ISAIAH 38:16 | *Lord, your discipline is good, for it leads to life and health.*

Through discipline.

GENESIS 27:41; 33:4 | *Esau hated Jacob. . . . [Later] Esau ran to meet him and embraced him, threw his arms around his neck, and kissed him. And they both wept.*

Through time.

ISAIAH 53:5 | *He was pierced for our rebellion, crushed for our sins. He was beaten so we could be whole. He was whipped so we could be healed.*

Through Christ's death. His death brought you healing. By accepting your punishment, he set you free.

Promise from God MALACHI 4:2 | *[The Lord said,] "For you who fear my name, the Sun of Righteousness will rise with healing in his wings. And you will go free, leaping with joy like calves let out to pasture."*

HEALTH

How can God use my sickness in a positive way?

ROMANS 5:3-4 | *We can rejoice, too, when we run into problems and trials, for we know that they help us develop endurance. And endurance develops strength of character, and character strengthens our confident hope of salvation.*

2 CORINTHIANS 12:7-9 | *To keep me from becoming proud, I was given a thorn in my flesh. . . . Three different times I begged the Lord to take it away. Each time he said, "My grace is all you need. My power works best in weakness."*

You probably don't welcome sickness, pain, or weakness. But from these challenges you can rejoice in the fruit that often comes—patience, reliance on God's strength, and gratitude to God for what you do have.

How can my attitude affect my health?

PROVERBS 17:22 | *A cheerful heart is good medicine, but a broken spirit saps a person's strength.*

It's both a biblical truth and a fact of life—a positive, cheerful disposition has a positive impact on your health.

How do I keep my soul in good health?

1 TIMOTHY 4:7-8 | *Do not waste time arguing over godless ideas and old wives' tales. Instead, train yourself to be godly. "Physical training is good, but training for godliness is much better, promising benefits in this life and in the life to come."*

Spiritual exercise is as purposeful and strenuous as physical exercise. But the benefits of spiritual fitness last for eternity, while the benefits of physical fitness last only as long as your body lasts.

Promise from God   ISAIAH 58:11 | *The LORD will guide you continually, giving you water when you are dry and restoring your strength. You will be like a well-watered garden, like an ever-flowing spring.*

HEART

What kind of heart does God desire for me?

2 KINGS 23:25 | *Never before had there been a king like Josiah, who turned to the LORD with all his heart and soul and strength, obeying all the laws of Moses.*

God desires that your heart be devoted and obedient.

1 CHRONICLES 29:17 | *I know, my God, that you examine our hearts and rejoice when you find integrity there. You know I have done all this with good motives, and I have watched your people offer their gifts willingly and joyously.*

God desires that your heart be a heart of integrity.

PSALM 51:6, 10, 17 | *You desire honesty from the womb, teaching me wisdom even there. . . . Create in me a clean heart, O God. Renew a loyal spirit within me. . . . The sacrifice you desire is a broken spirit. You will not reject a broken and repentant heart, O God.*

God desires that your heart be honest, clean, and repentant.

PSALM 86:11 | *Teach me your ways, O LORD, that I may live according to your truth! Grant me purity of heart, so that I may honor you.*

MATTHEW 5:8 | *God blesses those whose hearts are pure, for they will see God.*

God desires that your heart be pure.

1 SAMUEL 16:7 | *The LORD doesn't see things the way you see them. People judge by outward appearance, but the LORD looks at the heart.*

God desires to find pure motives in your heart.

How can my heart become the heart God wants?

2 CHRONICLES 12:7 | *When the LORD saw their change of heart, he gave this message to Shemaiah: "Since the people have humbled themselves, I will not completely destroy them and will soon give them some relief."*

Develop an attitude of humility. Then God will begin to work on your behalf.

EZEKIEL 18:31 | *Put all your rebellion behind you, and find yourselves a new heart and a new spirit.*

Get rid of any sinful habit or lifestyle. Practice obeying God's Word, and you will see your heart change for the better.

EZEKIEL 36:26 | *[The Lord says,] "I will give you a new heart, and I will put a new spirit in you. I will take out your stony, stubborn heart and give you a tender, responsive heart."*

Truly desire a change of heart, and then God will do it!

HEBREWS 9:14 | *Just think how much more the blood of Christ will purify our consciences from sinful deeds so that we can worship the living God. For by the power of the eternal Spirit, Christ offered himself to God as a perfect sacrifice for our sins.*

Let Christ's sacrifice purify your heart.

How do I guard and protect my heart?

2 CHRONICLES 19:9 | *You must always act in the fear of the L*ORD*, with faithfulness and an undivided heart.*

PROVERBS 4:23 | *Guard your heart above all else, for it determines the course of your life.*

PROVERBS 23:19 | *My child, listen and be wise: Keep your heart on the right course.*

EPHESIANS 3:17 | *Christ will make his home in your hearts as you trust in him. Your roots will grow down into God's love and keep you strong.*

1 JOHN 5:21 | *Keep away from anything that might take God's place in your hearts.*

Keep God at the center of your heart to prevent anything else from controlling it.

Promise from God PROVERBS 23:19 | *My child, listen and be wise: Keep your heart on the right course.*

HOME

How can I establish my home the way God wants it?

PSALM 127:1 | *Unless the L*ORD *builds a house, the work of the builders is wasted.*

PROVERBS 24:3-4 | *A house is built by wisdom and becomes strong through good sense. Through knowledge its rooms are filled with all sorts of precious riches and valuables.*

Through God's Word you find God's wisdom and his ways for your life and for your home.

How can I experience God's blessing on my home?

PROVERBS 3:33 | *The LORD curses the house of the wicked, but he blesses the home of the upright.*

PROVERBS 12:7 | *The wicked die and disappear, but the family of the godly stands firm.*

PROVERBS 14:11 | *The house of the wicked will be destroyed, but the tent of the godly will flourish.*

PROVERBS 15:6 | *There is treasure in the house of the godly, but the earnings of the wicked bring trouble.*

God promises to bless the homes of those who strive to be righteous.

What are some of my responsibilities in my home?

DEUTERONOMY 11:19-20 | *Teach [God's words] to your children. Talk about them when you are at home and when you are on the road, when you are going to bed and when you are getting up. Write them on the doorposts of your house and on your gates.*

PSALM 101:2 | *I will be careful to live a blameless life—when will you come to help me? I will lead a life of integrity in my own home.*

PROVERBS 31:27 | *[A virtuous and capable woman] carefully watches everything in her household and suffers nothing from laziness.*

As you care for your family members, exhibit godly character and behavior. Serve them with industry, integrity, faithfulness, purity, and an abundance of love.

Promise from God PROVERBS 3:33 | *The LORD curses the house of the wicked, but he blesses the home of the upright.*

HOPE

In what or whom do we hope?

PSALM 39:7 | *Lord, where do I put my hope? My only hope is in you.*

You place your hope in the Lord himself, because he holds you fast today, and he determines your future.

Why should I trust God as my hope?

HEBREWS 6:18-19 | *God has given both his promise and his oath. These two things are unchangeable because it is impossible for God to lie. Therefore, we who have fled to him for refuge can have great confidence as we hold to the hope that lies before us. This hope is a strong and trustworthy anchor for our souls. It leads us through the curtain into God's inner sanctuary.*

HEBREWS 10:23 | *Let us hold tightly without wavering to the hope we affirm, for God can be trusted to keep his promise.*

1 PETER 1:21 | *Through Christ you have come to trust in God. And you have placed your faith and hope in God because he raised Christ from the dead and gave him great glory.*

God cannot lie because he is truth. God, therefore, cannot break his promises. His words stand forever. God must be trusted as your hope because he alone conquered death by raising Christ from the dead.

Where can I go to reinforce my hope?

PSALM 119:43, 74, 81, 114, 147 | *Do not snatch your word of truth from me, for your regulations are my only hope. . . . May all who fear you find in me a cause for joy, for I have put my hope in your word. . . . I am worn out waiting for your rescue, but I have put my hope in your word. . . . You are my refuge and my*

shield; your word is my source of hope. . . . I rise early, before the sun is up; I cry out for help and put my hope in your words.

ROMANS 15:4 | *The Scriptures give us hope and encouragement as we wait patiently for God's promises to be fulfilled.*

Each day I can visit God's Word and have my hope renewed and reinforced. His Word never fails or wavers.

Promise from God PSALM 130:7 | *O Israel, hope in the LORD; for with the LORD there is unfailing love. His redemption overflows.*

HOSPITALITY

How should I show hospitality to others?

GENESIS 19:2 | *"My lords," [Lot] said, "come to my home to wash your feet, and be my guests for the night. You may then get up early in the morning and be on your way again."*

GENESIS 24:32 | *The man went home with Laban, and Laban unloaded the camels, gave him straw for their bedding, fed them, and provided water for the man and the camel drivers to wash their feet.*

1 PETER 4:9 | *Cheerfully share your home with those who need a meal or a place to stay.*

Offering food to eat and providing a place to stay—the basics of good hospitality—are simple acts of kindness that can be offered by almost anyone.

To whom should I be hospitable?

ROMANS 12:13 | *When God's people are in need, be ready to help them. Always be eager to practice hospitality.*

Fellow Christians.

3 JOHN 1:5 | *You are being faithful to God when you care for the traveling teachers who pass through, even though they are strangers to you.*

God's workers—those in ministry.

HEBREWS 13:2 | *Don't forget to show hospitality to strangers, for some who have done this have entertained angels without realizing it!*

Strangers.

ISAIAH 58:7 | *Share your food with the hungry, and give shelter to the homeless. Give clothes to those who need them, and do not hide from relatives who need your help.*

The hungry, poor, needy—including your relatives.

LUKE 14:12-14 | *[Jesus] turned to his host. "When you put on a luncheon or a banquet," he said, "don't invite your friends, brothers, relatives, and rich neighbors. For they will invite you back, and that will be your only reward. Instead, invite the poor, the crippled, the lame, and the blind. Then at the resurrection of the righteous, God will reward you for inviting those who could not repay you."*

Those who cannot repay you.

Promise from God HEBREWS 13:2 | *Don't forget to show hospitality to strangers, for some who have done this have entertained angels without realizing it!*

HUMILITY

What is true humility?

ZEPHANIAH 3:12 | *Those who are left will be the lowly and humble, for it is they who trust in the name of the LORD.*

Humility is not thinking too highly of oneself.

MATTHEW 18:4 | *Anyone who becomes as humble as this little child is the greatest in the Kingdom of Heaven.*

Humility is childlike. It is an attitude of total trust in God.

TITUS 3:2 | *[Believers] must not slander anyone and must avoid quarreling. Instead, they should be gentle and show true humility to everyone.*

Humility is being gentle and amicable to all.

PSALM 51:3-4 | *I recognize my rebellion; it haunts me day and night. Against you, and you alone, have I sinned; I have done what is evil in your sight. You will be proved right in what you say, and your judgment against me is just.*

Humility is being willing to admit and confess sin.

PROVERBS 12:23 | *The wise don't make a show of their knowledge, but fools broadcast their foolishness.*

Humility is refraining from proving what you know, how good you are at something, or that you are always right.

1 PETER 5:5 | *All of you, serve each other in humility, for "God opposes the proud but favors the humble."*

Humility enables you to serve God and others.

PROVERBS 13:10 | *Pride leads to conflict; those who take advice are wise.*

Humility allows you to seek advice.

GENESIS 32:9-10 | *Jacob prayed, "O God . . . you promised me, 'I will treat you kindly.' I am not worthy of all the unfailing love and faithfulness you have shown to me, your servant."*

Humility is recognizing your need for God and how he provides for you!

How was Jesus humble?

ZECHARIAH 9:9 | *Rejoice, O people of Zion! Shout in triumph, O people of Jerusalem! Look, your king is coming to you. He is righteous and victorious, yet he is humble, riding on a donkey—riding on a donkey's colt.*

Jesus was King of kings, yet he rode a lowly donkey on his royal ride into Jerusalem.

PHILIPPIANS 2:5-8 | *You must have the same attitude that Christ Jesus had. Though he was God, he did not think of equality with God as something to cling to. Instead, he gave up his divine privileges; he took the humble position of a slave and was born as a human being. When he appeared in human form, he humbled himself in obedience to God and died a criminal's death on a cross. Therefore, God elevated him to the place of highest honor and gave him the name above all other names, that at the name of Jesus every knee should bow, in heaven and on earth and under the earth, and every tongue confess that Jesus Christ is Lord, to the glory of God the Father.*

Jesus was God, yet he made himself nothing and suffered death on the cross for you.

HEBREWS 2:9 | *What we do see is Jesus, who was given a position "a little lower than the angels"; and because he suffered death for us, he is now "crowned with glory and honor." Yes, by God's grace, Jesus tasted death for everyone.*

Jesus had all glory and honor, but for your sake he died so you could be saved and have eternal life with him.

MATTHEW 11:29 | *Take my yoke upon you. Let me teach you, because I am humble and gentle at heart, and you will find rest for your souls.*

Jesus is the ultimate role model of gentleness and humility.

How does God respond to a humble spirit?

PSALM 69:32 | *The humble will see their God at work and be glad. Let all who seek God's help be encouraged.*

God gives joy to the humble.

PSALM 18:27 | *You rescue the humble, but you humiliate the proud.*

God rescues the humble.

PSALM 138:6 | *Though the LORD is great, he cares for the humble, but he keeps his distance from the proud.*

God takes care of the humble.

PSALM 147:6 | *The LORD supports the humble, but he brings the wicked down into the dust.*

God supports the humble.

ISAIAH 29:19 | *The humble will be filled with fresh joy from the LORD. The poor will rejoice in the Holy One of Israel.*

God refreshes the humble.

MATTHEW 18:4 | *Anyone who becomes as humble as this little child is the greatest in the Kingdom of Heaven.*

God honors and blesses the humble.

Promise from God MATTHEW 23:12 | *Those who exalt themselves will be humbled, and those who humble themselves will be exalted.*

HUSBANDS

What are some ways I can meet my husband's needs?

1 PETER 3:5 | *This is how the holy women of old made themselves beautiful. They trusted God and accepted the authority of their husbands.*

You can accept your husband's authority.

PROVERBS 12:4 | *A worthy wife is a crown for her husband, but a disgraceful woman is like cancer in his bones.*

You can give him joy by acting with grace and dignity.

PROVERBS 31:11 | *Her husband can trust her, and she will greatly enrich his life.*

You can be trustworthy.

1 CORINTHIANS 7:34 | *A married woman has to think about her earthly responsibilities and how to please her husband.*

You can think of ways to please and honor him.

How can I best help my husband if he does not know Jesus Christ as his Savior and Lord?

1 CORINTHIANS 7:13-14, 16 | *If a Christian woman has a husband who is not a believer and he is willing to continue living with her, she must not leave him. For the Christian wife brings holiness to her marriage. . . . Don't you wives realize that your husbands might be saved because of you?*

1 PETER 3:1-2 | *You wives must accept the authority of your husbands. Then, even if some refuse to obey the Good News, your godly lives will speak to them without any words. They will be won over by observing your pure and reverent lives.*

Godly loving is the best way to witness to an unbelieving mate.

Promise from God PROVERBS 12:4 | *A worthy wife is a crown for her husband, but a disgraceful woman is like cancer in his bones.*

INFERTILITY

How can I deal with the tensions infertility causes?

GENESIS 30:1-2 | *When Rachel saw that she wasn't having any children for Jacob, she became jealous of her sister. She pleaded with Jacob, "Give me children, or I'll die!" Then Jacob became furious with Rachel. "Am I God?" he asked. "He's the one who has kept you from having children!"*

PROVERBS 30:15-16 | *There are three things that are never satisfied—no, four that never say, "Enough!": the grave, the barren womb, the thirsty desert, the blazing fire.*

Why does God permit his loved ones to suffer pain, such as the pain of being unable to bear children? Why can't he just give a child to parents who want one so badly? The real answer is that nobody knows. What is known is that you live in a fallen world where life doesn't always go the way you had hoped. For reasons you do not fully understand, God does not always allow you to have what you desire. Maybe it's because he has a different plan. Or maybe it is simply because life is dealing a hard blow. When you get to heaven, you will find out. But for now, trust that God is in control, he loves you, and he is with you in your heartache.

How can I accept God's timing?

GENESIS 16:1-2, 4; 21:2 | *Sarai, Abram's wife, had not been able to bear children for him. But she had an Egyptian servant named Hagar. So Sarai said to Abram, "The LORD has prevented me from having children. Go and sleep with my servant. Perhaps I can have children through her."... So Abram had sexual relations with Hagar, and she became pregnant. But when Hagar knew she was pregnant, she began to treat her mistress, Sarai, with contempt.... [Later, Sarai] became pregnant, and she gave birth to a son for [Abram] in his old age. This happened at just the time God had said it would.*

PSALM 62:1, 5, 8 | *I wait quietly before God, for my victory comes from him.... Let all that I am wait quietly before God, for my hope is in him.... O my people, trust in him at all times. Pour out your heart to him, for God is our refuge.*

ISAIAH 30:18 | *The LORD must wait for you to come to him so he can show you his love and compassion. For the LORD is a faithful God. Blessed are those who wait for his help.*

ISAIAH 64:4 | *Since the world began, no ear has heard and no eye has seen a God like you, who works for those who wait for him!*

LAMENTATIONS 3:25-26 | *The LORD is good to those who depend on him, to those who search for him. So it is good to wait quietly for salvation from the LORD.*

Sometimes God says yes when you pray. Sometimes he says no. Sometimes he wants you to wait. And sometimes you simply have to leave your life in God's control, even when you don't always understand his ways. Rushing ahead may get you what you think you want, but waiting for God's timing will get God's best for you, which is always better.

Is it wrong to continue to plead to God for children?

GENESIS 25:21 | *Isaac pleaded with the LORD on behalf of his wife, because she was unable to have children. The LORD answered Isaac's prayer, and Rebekah became pregnant with twins.*

GENESIS 30:22-24 | *God remembered Rachel's plight and answered her prayers by enabling her to have children. She became pregnant and gave birth to a son. "God has removed my disgrace," she said. And she named him Joseph, for she said, "May the LORD add yet another son to my family."*

PSALM 5:3 | *Listen to my voice in the morning, LORD. Each morning I bring my requests to you and wait expectantly.*

As long as you believe in miracles, pray. As long as you believe in God, pray. Even when you're short on hope, pray. Then let God be God and let him do what he knows is best.

Promise from God PSALM 62:1, 5, 8 | *I wait quietly before God, for my victory comes from him. . . . Let all that I am wait quietly before God, for my hope is in him. . . . O my people, trust in him at all times. Pour out your heart to him, for God is our refuge.*

INTERRUPTIONS

See **DISTRACTIONS.**

INTIMACY

What is the basis for true and lasting intimacy in marriage?

PROVERBS 18:22 | *The man who finds a wife finds a treasure.*

PROVERBS 31:10-11 | *Who can find a virtuous and capable wife? She is more precious than rubies. Her husband can trust her, and she will greatly enrich his life.*

1 CORINTHIANS 7:3, 5 | *The husband should fulfill his wife's sexual needs, and the wife should fulfill her husband's needs. . . . Do not deprive each other of sexual relations, unless you both agree to refrain from sexual intimacy for a limited time so you can give yourselves more completely to prayer.*

EPHESIANS 5:24-26, 28-29 | *As the church submits to Christ, so you wives should submit to your husbands. . . . Husbands . . . love your wives, just as Christ loved the church. He gave up his life for her to make her holy and clean. . . . Husbands ought to love their wives as they love their own bodies. For a man who loves his wife actually shows love for himself. No one hates his own body but feeds and cares for it, just as Christ cares for the church.*

True and lasting intimacy in marriage is based upon the following: (1) faithfulness; (2) rejoicing in one another; (3) satisfying each other in love and sexuality; (4) accepting one's mate as a blessing from the Lord; (5) recognizing the great value of one's mate; (6) recognizing how much one's mate can truly bring delight and satisfaction; (7) living happily with each other; (8) talking together about the Lord and spiritual things; (9) giving thanks to the Lord together; (10) submitting to each other; and (11) loving each other as passionately as Christ loved the church and died for it.

Sexual intimacy is reserved for marriage, and sexual intimacy is a mutual responsibility and pleasure for both partners. One should not deprive the other of this privilege except by mutual agreement.

How can I experience an intimate relationship with God?

GENESIS 5:23-24 | *Enoch lived 365 years, walking in close fellowship with God. Then one day he disappeared, because God took him.*

Walk with God—daily and consistently.

GENESIS 6:9 | *Noah was a righteous man, the only blameless person living on earth at the time, and he walked in close fellowship with God.*

Live the way God wants you to live—daily and consistently.

PSALM 27:8 | *My heart has heard you say, "Come and talk with me." And my heart responds, "LORD, I am coming."*

PSALM 145:18 | *The LORD is close to all who call on him, yes, to all who call on him in truth.*

Talk with God—daily and consistently.

JAMES 4:8 | *Come close to God, and God will come close to you. Wash your hands, you sinners; purify your hearts, for your loyalty is divided between God and the world.*

Stay close to God and purify your heart before him—daily and consistently.

EXODUS 34:14 | *You must worship no other gods, for the LORD, whose very name is Jealous, is a God who is jealous about his relationship with you.*

Worship God only—daily and consistently.

MATTHEW 22:37 | *Jesus [said], "You must love the LORD your God with all your heart, all your soul, and all your mind."*

Love God completely—daily and consistently.

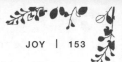

ROMANS 5:11 | *We can rejoice in our wonderful new relationship with God because our Lord Jesus Christ has made us friends of God.*

In light of what Jesus has done for you, put your trust in him—daily and consistently.

Promise from God 1 CHRONICLES 28:9 | *If you seek him, you will find him.*

JOY

Does God promise me joy?

ACTS 5:41 | *The apostles left the high council rejoicing that God had counted them worthy to suffer disgrace for the name of Jesus.*

JAMES 1:2 | *When troubles come your way, consider it an opportunity for great joy.*

God does not promise your life will always be happy; in fact, the Bible assures you problems will come your way. But God does promise lasting joy for you—for all believers—because you have the assurance that the God of the universe loves you, wants to walk with you, promises to comfort and care for you, and has guaranteed your eternal future if you trust him. This kind of joy stays with you despite your problems and helps you get through them without being overwhelmed.

What is the source of true joy?

PSALM 40:16 | *May all who search for you be filled with joy and gladness in you. May those who love your salvation repeatedly shout, "The LORD is great!"*

PSALM 68:3 | *Let the godly rejoice. Let them be glad in God's presence. Let them be filled with joy.*

PSALM 86:4 | *Give me happiness, O Lord, for I give myself to you.*

PSALM 146:5 | *Joyful are those who have the God of Israel as their helper, whose hope is in the LORD their God.*

The Lord himself is the wellspring of true joy. The more you love him, know him, walk with him, and become like him, the greater your joy.

MATTHEW 6:19-21 | *Don't store up treasures here on earth, where moths eat them and rust destroys them, and where thieves break in and steal. Store your treasures in heaven, where moths and rust cannot destroy, and thieves do not break in and steal. Wherever your treasure is, there the desires of your heart will also be.*

True joy comes from the assurance that what is really valuable is waiting for you in heaven. You can hoard material possessions here on earth and have little waiting for you in heaven, or you can send your wealth on ahead for eternal enjoyment by obeying and serving God right now.

How can I be joyful in the midst of difficult circumstances?

1 PETER 4:12-13 | *Don't be surprised at the fiery trials you are going through, as if something strange were happening to you. Instead, be very glad—for these trials make you partners with Christ in his suffering, so that you will have the wonderful joy of seeing his glory when it is revealed to all the world.*

Anticipating God's rewards makes you joyful even in the midst of adversity.

ROMANS 5:2 | *We confidently and joyfully look forward to sharing God's glory.*

HEBREWS 10:34 | *You suffered along with those who were thrown into jail, and when all you owned was taken from you, you accepted it with joy. You knew there were better things waiting for you that will last forever.*

Hope in God's promises of eternal life can make you joyful because you know that what you are presently going through will one day end.

ACTS 5:41 | *The apostles left the high council rejoicing that God had counted them worthy to suffer disgrace for the name of Jesus.*

When you live in such a way that even your suffering brings honor to Jesus, he has a special place of honor for you that will bring you a deep sense of joy.

DANIEL 12:3 | *Those who are wise will shine as bright as the sky, and those who lead many to righteousness will shine like the stars forever.*

You can be joyful because you know this world is not all there is—you know something better is coming. So practice letting God's light shine through you so others can see that no matter what's happening in the world around you, you are joyful in the knowledge of a future in heaven.

How can I bring God joy?

DEUTERONOMY 30:10 | *The LORD your God will delight in you if you obey his voice and keep the commands and decrees written in this Book of Instruction, and if you turn to the LORD your God with all your heart and soul.*

PROVERBS 11:20 | *The LORD . . . delights in those with integrity.*

PROVERBS 15:8 | *The LORD . . . delights in the prayers of the upright.*

PROVERBS 15:26 | *The LORD . . . delights in pure words.*

Can finite, sinful human beings truly bring joy and delight to the Lord, the Creator of the universe? Yes, and it is simple, though not easy—honor him, obey him, respond to his love, seek his forgiveness, and walk daily with him.

How can I bring joy to others?

ROMANS 12:10 | *Love each other with genuine affection, and take delight in honoring each other.*

2 CORINTHIANS 7:13 | *In addition to our own encouragement, we were especially delighted to see how happy Titus was about the way all of you welcomed him and set his mind at ease.*

Treating others with God's love will bring them joy. Just as God is the wellspring of true joy, so you are his conduit of that joy to others.

Promise from God JOHN 15:11 | *[Jesus said,] "I have told you these things so that you will be filled with my joy. Yes, your joy will overflow!"*

KINDNESS

Why should I be kind?

ZECHARIAH 7:9 | *This is what the LORD of Heaven's Armies says: Judge fairly, and show mercy and kindness to one another.*

EPHESIANS 4:32 | *Be kind to each other, tenderhearted, forgiving one another, just as God through Christ has forgiven you.*

Be kind because God has been kind to you and asks you to pass it on to others. It is a way to show others his love.

MATTHEW 7:12 | *Do to others whatever you would like them to do to you.*

If you expect others to be kind to you, you must be kind to them.

RUTH 2:10-11 | *"What have I done to deserve such kindness?" she asked. "I am only a foreigner." "Yes, I know," Boaz replied. "But I also know about everything you have done for your mother-in-law since the death of your husband."*

Kindness is never lost; it keeps on going from person to person until it returns to you.

2 CORINTHIANS 8:9 | *You know the generous grace of our Lord Jesus Christ. Though he was rich, yet for your sakes he became poor, so that by his poverty he could make you rich.*

2 CORINTHIANS 10:1 | *I, Paul, appeal to you with the gentleness and kindness of Christ—though I realize you think I am timid.*

When you are kind, you are following Jesus' example.

MATTHEW 25:34-36 | *The King will say to those on his right, "Come, you who are blessed by my Father, inherit the Kingdom prepared for you from the creation of the world. For I was hungry, and you fed me. I was thirsty, and you gave me a drink. I was a stranger, and you invited me into your home. I was naked, and you gave me clothing. I was sick, and you cared for me. I was in prison, and you visited me."*

PHILIPPIANS 4:17 | *I don't say this because I want a gift from you. Rather, I want you to receive a reward for your kindness.*

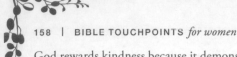

God rewards kindness because it demonstrates unconditional love.

PROVERBS 11:17 | *Your kindness will reward you, but your cruelty will destroy you.*

Kindness to others is like food for your soul.

How can I become kind to others?

GALATIANS 5:22 | *The Holy Spirit produces this kind of fruit in our lives: . . . kindness.*

Kindness is planted in you by the Holy Spirit.

1 CORINTHIANS 13:4 | *Love is patient and kind.*

From the fountains of love flow the rivers of kindness. It is impossible to be truly kind unless you are first truly loving.

LUKE 6:35 | *Love your enemies! Do good to them. Lend to them without expecting to be repaid.*

Kindness is based on the loving heart of the giver, not the actions of the recipient.

How has God shown kindness to me?

TITUS 3:4-5 | *When God our Savior revealed his kindness and love, he saved us, not because of the righteous things we had done, but because of his mercy. He washed away our sins, giving us a new birth and new life through the Holy Spirit.*

God forgives your sins and offers you salvation. If God were not kind, you would get the punishment you deserve. Since he is kind, you get the forgiveness you don't deserve.

PSALM 145:8, 17 | *The LORD is merciful and compassionate, slow to get angry and filled with unfailing love. . . .*

The LORD is righteous in everything he does; he is filled with kindness.

God gives you mercy when you don't deserve it. He is patient with you and doesn't lash out when you do something wrong.

ROMANS 2:4 | *Don't you see how wonderfully kind, tolerant, and patient God is with you? Does this mean nothing to you? Can't you see that his kindness is intended to turn you from your sin?*

God shows his kindness by giving you time to turn from your sin and turn to him.

ACTS 14:17 | *[God] never left [the nations] without evidence of himself and his goodness. For instance, he sends you rain and good crops and gives you food and joyful hearts.*

In kindness, God meets your needs.

JOEL 2:13 | *Return to the LORD your God, for he is merciful and compassionate, slow to get angry and filled with unfailing love. He is eager to relent and not punish.*

Because God is kind, he is slow to anger, eager to withhold punishment, and quick to forgive and show mercy.

How can I show God my gratitude for his kindness to me?

PSALM 92:2 | *It is good to proclaim your unfailing love in the morning, your faithfulness in the evening,*

Remember to thank and praise the Lord daily for his kindness and faithfulness.

Promise from God MATTHEW 10:42 | *If you give even a cup of cold water to one of the least of my followers, you will surely be rewarded.*

LISTENING

Does God really listen when I pray?

PSALM 17:6 | *I am praying to you because I know you will answer, O God. Bend down and listen as I pray.*

PSALM 102:17 | *He will listen to the prayers of the destitute. He will not reject their pleas.*

1 JOHN 5:14-15 | *We are confident that he hears us whenever we ask for anything that pleases him. And since we know he hears us when we make our requests, we also know that he will give us what we ask for.*

God hears every prayer, listens carefully, and answers us. His answer may be "yes," "no," or "wait, not now."

How can I better listen to God?

PSALM 5:3 | *Listen to my voice in the morning, LORD. Each morning I bring my requests to you and wait expectantly.*

Come to God regularly, and wait expectantly. God always answers. Wait patiently!

PSALM 46:10 | *Be still, and know that I am God!*

Find times to be quiet and meditate so you will hear the voice of God when he speaks.

LUKE 8:18 | *[Jesus said,] "Pay attention to how you hear. To those who listen to my teaching, more understanding will be*

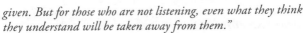

given. But for those who are not listening, even what they think they understand will be taken away from them."

Pay attention to the many ways in which God speaks to you. Don't miss an opportunity for a lesson from the Master Teacher. The more you listen to God, the more you will hear from him.

1 KINGS 19:12 | *After the earthquake there was a fire, but the LORD was not in the fire. And after the fire there was the sound of a gentle whisper.*

Recognize that God's power and greatness are often displayed in quietness and gentleness.

JOHN 10:27 | *My sheep listen to my voice; I know them, and they follow me.*

The more you trust God and follow him, as sheep with their shepherd, the more you will recognize his voice.

In addition to God, to whom should I listen?

PROVERBS 10:20 | *The words of the godly are like sterling silver; the heart of a fool is worthless.*

Listen to godly people.

1 KINGS 10:24 | *People from every nation came to consult [King Solomon] and to hear the wisdom God had given him.*

Listen to those filled with God's wisdom.

1 SAMUEL 3:19 | *As Samuel grew up, the LORD was with him, and everything Samuel said proved to be reliable.*

Listen to those who walk with God.

1 CHRONICLES 13:1 | *David consulted with all his officials, including the generals and captains of his army.*

Listen to wise and skilled leaders.

PROVERBS 5:13 | *Oh, why didn't I listen to my teachers? Why didn't I pay attention to my instructors?*

Listen to people in your life whom God has provided as teachers.

Promise from God PROVERBS 1:23 | *Come and listen to my counsel. I'll share my heart with you and make you wise.*

LONELINESS

Why does God allow me to be lonely?

GENESIS 2:18 | *The LORD God said, "It is not good for the man to be alone. I will make a helper who is just right for him."*

God did not intend for you to be lonely. Quite the contrary, it was God who recognized Adam's need for companionship. He first gave Adam the task of naming the animals so that Adam could recognize his own need for a companion. It was then that God created woman (see Genesis 2:19-22).

ROMANS 8:38-39 | *Nothing can ever separate us from God's love. Neither death nor life, neither angels nor demons, neither our fears for today nor our worries about tomorrow—not even the powers of hell can separate us from God's love. No power in the sky above or in the earth below—indeed, nothing in all creation will ever be able to separate us from the love of God that is revealed in Christ Jesus our Lord.*

God never intended for you to be alone. He promised he will always be there for you. Nothing can separate you from him. When your human relationships fail, take comfort in your friendship with God.

How can I avoid loneliness?

ROMANS 12:5 | *We are many parts of one body, and we all belong to each other.*

HEBREWS 10:25 | *Let us not neglect our meeting together, as some people do, but encourage one another, especially now that the day of his return is drawing near.*

The best way to avoid loneliness is to get together with other believers. Get involved in a local church.

Promise from God PSALM 23:4 | *Even when I walk through the darkest valley, I will not be afraid, for you are close beside me. Your rod and your staff protect and comfort me.*

LOSS

How do I deal with loss in my life?

JOHN 11:13, 35 | *Lazarus had died. . . . Then Jesus wept.*

By not denying your loss. The tears of Jesus at Lazarus's death forever validate your tears of grief.

JOB 1:20-22 | *Job stood up and tore his robe in grief. Then he shaved his head and fell to the ground to worship. He said, "I came naked from my mother's womb, and I will be naked when I leave. The LORD gave me what I had, and the LORD has taken it away. Praise the name of the LORD!" In all of this, Job did not sin by blaming God.*

LAMENTATIONS 3:19-23 | *The thought of my suffering and homelessness is bitter beyond words. I will never forget this awful time, as I grieve over my loss. Yet I still dare to hope when I remember this: The faithful love of the LORD never ends! His*

mercies never cease. Great is his faithfulness; his mercies begin afresh each morning.

By recognizing that pain is not wrong or sinful—loss always brings pain—but is rather a healthy expression of how God created you.

HEBREWS 10:34 | *You suffered along with those who were thrown into jail, and when all you owned was taken from you, you accepted it with joy. You knew there were better things waiting for you that will last forever.*

By allowing yourself to grieve, but there is a time for grieving to end. By serving God and others with all the energy and enthusiasm you can muster, you will begin to find healing. And as a Christian, you have the comfort of knowing that one day you will be with God in heaven, where all grief will be gone forever.

How can God help me survive life's losses?

PSALM 10:17 | *LORD, you know the hopes of the helpless. Surely you will hear their cries and comfort them.*

PSALM 30:11-12 | *You have turned my mourning into joyful dancing. You have taken away my clothes of mourning and clothed me with joy, that I might sing praises to you and not be silent. O LORD my God, I will give you thanks forever!*

PSALM 102:17 | *He will listen to the prayers of the destitute. He will not reject their pleas.*

PSALM 147:3 | *He heals the brokenhearted and bandages their wounds.*

LAMENTATIONS 3:32 | *Though he brings grief, he also shows compassion because of the greatness of his unfailing love.*

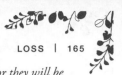

MATTHEW 5:4 | *God blesses those who mourn, for they will be comforted.*

2 CORINTHIANS 1:3 | *All praise to God, the Father of our Lord Jesus Christ. God is our merciful Father and the source of all comfort.*

In times of loss, God comes to you with his presence, comfort, love, peace, and mercy. When you cry out for someone to touch you, God will hold you close.

What can I never lose?

MATTHEW 28:20 | *[Jesus said,] "Be sure of this: I am with you always, even to the end of the age."*

ROMANS 8:35, 38-39 | *Can anything ever separate us from Christ's love? Does it mean he no longer loves us if we have trouble or calamity, or are persecuted, or hungry, or destitute, or in danger, or threatened with death? . . . I am convinced that nothing can ever separate us from God's love. Neither death nor life, neither angels nor demons, neither our fears for today nor our worries about tomorrow—not even the powers of hell can separate us from God's love. No power in the sky above or in the earth below—indeed, nothing in all creation will ever be able to separate us from the love of God that is revealed in Christ Jesus our Lord.*

When you trust in the Lord, you will never lose his love, his presence, or his promise of salvation—the three greatest gifts to see you through life's difficulties and to give you hope.

Promise from God PSALM 34:18 | *The LORD is close to the brokenhearted; he rescues those whose spirits are crushed.*

LOVE

Must I love other people? What if I don't want to?

JOHN 13:34-35 | *[Jesus said,] "I am giving you a new command-ment: Love each other. Just as I have loved you, you should love each other. Your love for one another will prove to the world that you are my disciples."*

1 PETER 4:8 | *Most important of all, continue to show deep love for each other, for love covers a multitude of sins.*

1 JOHN 2:9 | *If anyone claims, "I am living in the light," but hates a Christian brother or sister, that person is still living in darkness.*

1 JOHN 4:12 | *No one has ever seen God. But if we love each other, God lives in us, and his love is brought to full expression in us.*

Being a Christian comes with certain expectations, and one of them is that you will love others—whether you want to or not. Your Christian conduct is proof of whether you love others, and loving others is proof that you belong to Christ.

What are some special things that come from a loving relationship?

PROVERBS 10:12 | *Hatred stirs up quarrels, but love makes up for all offenses.*

1 CORINTHIANS 13:4-7 | *Love is patient and kind. Love is not jealous or boastful or proud or rude. It does not demand its own way. It is not irritable, and it keeps no record of being wronged. It does not rejoice about injustice but rejoices whenever the truth wins out. Love never gives up, never loses faith, is always hopeful, and endures through every circumstance.*

Gifts that come from a loving relationship include forgiveness, patience, kindness, love for truth, justice, acceptance, and loyalty. Love does not allow for jealousy, pride, contempt, selfishness, rudeness, demanding your own way, irritability, or grudges.

Does God really love me? How can I know?

HOSEA 2:19 | *[The Lord says,] "I will make you my wife forever, showing you righteousness and justice, unfailing love and compassion."*

JOHN 3:16 | *God loved the world so much that he gave his one and only Son, so that everyone who believes in him will not perish but have eternal life.*

ROMANS 5:5 | *We know how dearly God loves us, because he has given us the Holy Spirit to fill our hearts with his love.*

ROMANS 8:38 | *Nothing can ever separate us from God's love.*

1 JOHN 4:9-10 | *God showed how much he loved us by sending his one and only Son into the world so that we might have eternal life through him. This is real love.*

God loves you so much that he sent his Son, Jesus, to earth to die for you. Jesus took the punishment you deserve for your sins. His forgiveness is so complete, it is as though you never sinned at all. His love for you can never be changed or broken.

How can I show my love to God?

MATTHEW 10:42 | *[Jesus said,] "If you give even a cup of cold water to one of the least of my followers, you will surely be rewarded."*

Show love to needy people, whom God loves.

JOHN 14:21 | *[Jesus said,] "Those who accept my command-ments and obey them are the ones who love me."*

Love God by obeying him and honoring his commandments.

JOHN 21:15-16 | *[Jesus said to Simon Peter,] "Do you love me more than these? . . . Then take care of my sheep."*

HEBREWS 6:10 | *[God] will not forget how hard you have worked for him and how you have shown your love to him by caring for other believers, as you still do.*

Love God by guiding and helping Jesus' followers and by being an example to others.

PSALM 122:1 | *I was glad when they said to me, "Let us go to the house of the LORD."*

Love God by worshiping him and praising him for his love for you.

Promise from God ROMANS 8:39 | *No power in the sky above or in the earth below—indeed, nothing in all creation will ever be able to separate us from the love of God that is revealed in Christ Jesus our Lord.*

MARRIAGE

What kind of relationship should a marriage be?

GENESIS 2:18 | *The LORD God said, "It is not good for the man to be alone. I will make a helper who is just right for him."*

ECCLESIASTES 4:9-10 | *Two people are better off than one, for they can help each other succeed. If one person falls, the other can reach out and help. But someone who falls alone is in real trouble.*

MATTHEW 19:4-6 | *"Haven't you read the Scriptures?" Jesus replied. "They record that from the beginning 'God made them male and female.' And he said, 'This explains why a man leaves his father and mother and is joined to his wife, and the two are united into one.' Since they are no longer two but one, let no one split apart what God has joined together."*

1 CORINTHIANS 11:3 | *The head of every man is Christ, the head of woman is man, and the head of Christ is God.*

Marriage at its best is a relationship so close and intimate that the two of you work together as one. It involves mutual trust, support, defense, comfort, productivity, vulnerability, and responsibility.

How should a husband treat his wife?

PROVERBS 18:22 | *The man who finds a wife finds a treasure, and he receives favor from the LORD.*

ECCLESIASTES 9:9 | *Live happily with the woman you love through all the meaningless days of life that God has given you under the sun. The wife God gives you is your reward for all your earthly toil.*

EPHESIANS 5:21, 25 | *Submit to one another out of reverence for Christ. . . . For husbands, this means love your wives, just as Christ loved the church. He gave up his life for her.*

1 PETER 3:7 | *You husbands must give honor to your wives. Treat your wife with understanding as you live together. She may be weaker than you are, but she is your equal partner in God's gift of new life. Treat her as you should so your prayers will not be hindered.*

A husband should love his wife sacrificially—with the depth of love that Christ showed when he died for all people.

How should a wife treat her husband?

PROVERBS 31:11-12 | *Her husband can trust her, and she will greatly enrich his life. She brings him good, not harm, all the days of her life.*

EPHESIANS 5:22-24 | *Submit to your husbands as to the Lord. For a husband is the head of his wife as Christ is the head of the church. He is the Savior of his body, the church. As the church submits to Christ, so you wives should submit to your husbands in everything.*

A wife should love her husband sacrificially, helping and supporting him, believing in him, and submitting to him as he submits in Christlike love to her.

What is the importance of loyalty in a marriage?

MALACHI 2:15 | *Didn't the LORD make you one with your wife? In body and spirit you are his. And what does he want? Godly children from your union. So guard your heart; remain loyal to the wife of your youth.*

God doesn't merely suggest that husbands and wives be loyal to one another, he commands it.

PROVERBS 5:15, 18-19 | *Drink water from your own well—share your love only with your wife. . . . Let your wife be a fountain of blessing for you. Rejoice in the wife of your youth. She is a loving deer, a graceful doe. Let her breasts satisfy you always. May you always be captivated by her love.*

1 CORINTHIANS 7:3-4 | *The husband should fulfill his wife's sexual needs, and the wife should fulfill her husband's needs. The wife gives authority over her body to her husband, and the husband gives authority over his body to his wife.*

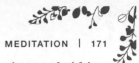

HEBREWS 13:4 | *Give honor to marriage, and remain faithful to one another in marriage. God will surely judge people who are immoral and those who commit adultery.*

Husbands and wives must be faithful to each other, seeking to satisfy and honor each other.

Promise from God EPHESIANS 5:31 | *A man leaves his father and mother and is joined to his wife, and the two are united into one.*

MEDITATION

To whom should my meditation be directed?

PSALM 63:6 | *I lie awake thinking of you, meditating on you through the night.*

Meditation is a time to think about God and communicate with God.

How do I meditate? What is involved in meditation?

PSALM 62:1, 5 | *I wait quietly before God, for my victory comes from him. . . . Let all that I am wait quietly before God, for my hope is in him.*

Meditation involves thinking about God quietly and intently, with confidence that he will hear you and you will hear him.

PSALM 1:2 | *[The godly] delight in the law of the LORD, meditating on it day and night.*

Meditation involves taking the time to read God's Word and consider it. He often speaks to your heart as you read the words he has written for you.

PSALM 16:7 | *I will bless the LORD who guides me; even at night my heart instructs me.*

Meditation is time spent seeking God's guidance and instruction.

PSALM 143:5 | *I remember the days of old. I ponder all your great works and think about what you have done.*

Meditation is time spent reflecting on God's past blessings and thanking him for them.

What should I think about when I meditate?

PSALM 48:9 | *O God, we meditate on your unfailing love as we worship in your Temple.*

Think about God's unfailing love.

PSALM 77:11-12 | *I recall all you have done, O LORD; I remember your wonderful deeds of long ago. They are constantly in my thoughts. I cannot stop thinking about your mighty works.*

Think about all God has done for you.

PSALM 145:5 | *I will meditate on your majestic, glorious splendor and your wonderful miracles.*

Think about God's majestic, glorious splendor, and praise him for it.

ROMANS 8:5 | *Those who are dominated by the sinful nature think about sinful things, but those who are controlled by the Holy Spirit think about things that please the Spirit.*

Think about the Holy Spirit, what pleases him and how you can allow yourself to be used by him.

PHILIPPIANS 4:8 | *Fix your thoughts on what is true, and honorable, and right, and pure, and lovely, and admirable. Think about things that are excellent and worthy of praise.*

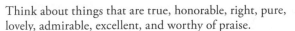

Think about things that are true, honorable, right, pure, lovely, admirable, excellent, and worthy of praise.

PSALM 119:97 | *Oh, how I love your instructions! I think about them all day long.*

Think about God's Word and all the wisdom it holds for your life.

Promise from God 2 TIMOTHY 2:7 | *Think about what I am saying. The Lord will help you understand all these things.*

MEMORIES

What do I do with bad memories?

GENESIS 41:51 | *Joseph named his older son Manasseh, for he said, "God has made me forget all my troubles and everyone in my father's family."*

ISAIAH 54:4 | *Fear not; you will no longer live in shame. Don't be afraid; there is no more disgrace for you. You will no longer remember the shame of your youth and the sorrows of widowhood.*

PHILIPPIANS 3:13-14 | *I focus on this one thing: Forgetting the past and looking forward to what lies ahead, I press on.*

God can help you forget bad memories.

What place does God desire to have in my memory?

EXODUS 31:13 | *[The Lord said,] "Be careful to keep my Sabbath day, for the Sabbath is a sign of the covenant between me and you from generation to generation. It is given so you may know that I am the LORD, who makes you holy."*

DEUTERONOMY 4:9 | *Watch out! Be careful never to forget what you yourself have seen. Do not let these memories escape from your mind as long as you live! And be sure to pass them on to your children and grandchildren.*

PSALM 103:2 | *Let all that I am praise the LORD; may I never forget the good things he does for me.*

PSALM 111:4 | *He causes us to remember his wonderful works. How gracious and merciful is our LORD!*

2 TIMOTHY 2:8 | *[Paul said,] "Always remember that Jesus Christ, a descendant of King David, was raised from the dead. This is the Good News I preach."*

HEBREWS 10:32 | *Think back on those early days when you first learned about Christ. Remember how you remained faithful even though it meant terrible suffering.*

Never forget the Lord and what he has done for you. Keep his commandments fresh in your mind by reading God's Word daily.

What is the danger in forgetting God?

1 SAMUEL 12:9 | *The people soon forgot about the LORD their God, so he handed them over to Sisera, the commander of Hazor's army, and also to the Philistines and to the king of Moab, who fought against them.*

JOB 8:13-14 | *The same happens to all who forget God. The hopes of the godless evaporate. Their confidence hangs by a thread. They are leaning on a spider's web.*

JEREMIAH 3:21 | *Voices are heard high on the windswept mountains, the weeping and pleading of Israel's people. For they have chosen crooked paths and have forgotten the LORD their God.*

EZEKIEL 23:35 | *Because you have forgotten me and turned your back on me, this is what the Sovereign LORD says: You must bear the consequences of all your lewdness and prostitution.*

When you forget God, you have nothing left but sin and self, and what will those do for your eternal future? Forgetting God leaves you vulnerable to temptation, and you will have to cope with the consequences of your sin without the benefits of God's gracious mercy.

Promise from God PSALM 119:16, 93 | *I will delight in your decrees and not forget your word. . . . I will never forget your commandments, for by them you give me life.*

MERCY

What is mercy?

PSALM 103:8-10 | *The LORD is compassionate and merciful, slow to get angry and filled with unfailing love. He will not constantly accuse us, nor remain angry forever. He does not punish us for all our sins; he does not deal harshly with us, as we deserve.*

ISAIAH 63:9 | *In all their suffering he also suffered, and he personally rescued them. In his love and mercy he redeemed them. He lifted them up and carried them through all the years.*

LAMENTATIONS 3:22 | *The faithful love of the LORD never ends! His mercies never cease.*

MICAH 7:18 | *Where is another God like you, who pardons the guilt of the remnant, overlooking the sins of his special people? You will not stay angry with your people forever, because you delight in showing unfailing love.*

1 PETER 1:3 | *All praise to God, the Father of our Lord Jesus Christ. It is by his great mercy that we have been born again, because God raised Jesus Christ from the dead.*

Mercy is more than exemption from the punishment you deserve for your sins: It is receiving the undeserved gift of salvation as well. Mercy is experiencing favor with almighty God through his forgiveness.

Who receives mercy?

PSALM 119:132 | *Come and show me your mercy, as you do for all who love your name.*

MATTHEW 5:7 | *God blesses those who are merciful, for they will be shown mercy.*

LUKE 1:50 | *He shows mercy from generation to generation to all who fear him.*

God promises his mercy to those who love him, fear (revere) him, and show mercy to others.

ROMANS 9:15-16 | *God said to Moses, "I will show mercy to anyone I choose, and I will show compassion to anyone I choose." So it is God who decides to show mercy. We can neither choose it nor work for it.*

Ultimately, God chooses who will receive his mercy. We cannot earn it. We are, literally, at his mercy.

How can I show mercy?

COLOSSIANS 3:12-13 | *Since God chose you to be the holy people he loves, you must clothe yourselves with tenderhearted mercy, kindness, humility, gentleness, and patience. Make allowance for each other's faults, and forgive anyone who offends you. Remember, the Lord forgave you, so you must forgive others.*

Forgive others as God has forgiven you.

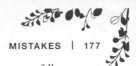

MATTHEW 18:33 | *Shouldn't you have mercy on your fellow servant, just as I had mercy on you?*

Be merciful to others even when they don't deserve it.

MICAH 6:8 | *The LORD has told you what is good, and this is what he requires of you: to do what is right, to love mercy, and to walk humbly with your God.*

Show mercy as an act of obedience to God.

ZECHARIAH 7:9 | *This is what the LORD of Heaven's Armies says: Judge fairly, and show mercy and kindness to one another.*

You can show mercy by judging fairly and honestly and by showing kindness to others.

JAMES 3:17 | *The wisdom from above is first of all pure. It is also peace loving, gentle at all times, and willing to yield to others. It is full of mercy and good deeds. It shows no favoritism and is always sincere.*

Being merciful is the result of wisdom from God. Ask God for his wisdom so you can know how to share his mercy with others.

Promise from God PSALM 103:8 | *The LORD is compassionate and merciful, slow to get angry and filled with unfailing love.*

MISTAKES

How can I learn from my mistakes?

GENESIS 3:11-13 | *[God asked,] "Have you eaten from the tree whose fruit I commanded you not to eat?" The man replied, "It was the woman you gave me who gave me the fruit, and I ate it." Then the LORD God asked the woman, "What have you done?" "The serpent deceived me," she replied. "That's why I ate it."*

Both Adam and Eve responded to their mistakes by trying to shift the blame. When you've made a mistake, it's essential to admit it.

EXODUS 2:12 | *After looking in all directions to make sure no one was watching, Moses killed the Egyptian and hid the body in the sand.*

Everyone, even the most godly people, makes mistakes. Moses, whom God handpicked to lead the Israelites out of slavery, made several immature and terrible mistakes. When you make a mistake, confess it to God and others and ask for forgiveness and help.

GENESIS 4:6-7 | *"Why are you so angry?" the LORD asked Cain. "Why do you look so dejected? You will be accepted if you do what is right. But if you refuse to do what is right, then watch out! Sin is crouching at the door, eager to control you. But you must subdue it and be its master."*

PROVERBS 29:1 | *Whoever stubbornly refuses to accept criticism will suddenly be destroyed beyond recovery.*

When you are told you have made a mistake, respond with humility. Consider the source and the substance of the criticism, then listen and learn for the future.

JUDGES 16:17, 21, 28 | *Finally, Samson shared his secret with her. . . . So the Philistines captured him and gouged out his eyes. . . . Then Samson prayed to the LORD, "Sovereign LORD, remember me again."*

God can still use you despite your mistakes. Samson's life, although filled with foolish mistakes, was still mightily used by God.

1 SAMUEL 13:11-13 | *Samuel said, "What is this you have done?" Saul replied, "I saw my men scattering from me, and you didn't arrive when you said you would, and the Philistines are at Micmash ready for battle. . . . So I felt compelled to offer the burnt offering myself before you came." "How foolish!" Samuel exclaimed. "You have not kept the command the LORD your God gave you."*

Mistakes are often created by the impatient pursuit of your own agenda. Learning patience can help you avoid making mistakes in the future.

JAMES 3:2 | *Indeed, we all make many mistakes. For if we could control our tongues, we would be perfect and could also control ourselves in every other way.*

One of the most common mistakes is saying something you later regret. Practice thinking about the consequences of your words before you open your mouth.

JONAH 1:3 | *But Jonah . . . went in the opposite direction to get away from the LORD.*

One of the worst mistakes you can make is to run from God. It is always better to run to him, not away from him.

MATTHEW 26:74 | *Peter swore, "A curse on me if I'm lying—I don't know the man!"*

Following Jesus means allowing him to forgive your mistakes. Jesus restored Peter to fellowship—and leadership—even after his most painful mistake (see John 21:15-17).

Promise from God PHILIPPIANS 3:13-14 | *I focus on this one thing: Forgetting the past and looking forward to what lies ahead, I press on to reach the end of the race and receive the heavenly prize for which God, through Christ Jesus, is calling us.*

MODESTY

What is the importance of modesty?

1 TIMOTHY 2:15 | *Women will be saved through childbearing, assuming they continue to live in faith, love, holiness, and modesty.*

Modesty is maintaining a standard of appropriateness that cannot be criticized and keeps you from being a stumbling block to others. It is keeping your appearance in harmony with your faith, love, and holiness. Modesty frees you from focusing excessive time and attention on yourself and worrying about how you appear to others.

How can I be modest in my appearance?

1 CORINTHIANS 6:19-20 | *Don't you realize that your body is the temple of the Holy Spirit, who lives in you and was given to you by God? You do not belong to yourself, for God bought you with a high price. So you must honor God with your body.*

1 TIMOTHY 2:9 | *[Paul said,] "I want women to be modest in their appearance. They should wear decent and appropriate clothing and not draw attention to themselves by the way they fix their hair or by wearing gold or pearls or expensive clothes."*

1 PETER 3:3-4 | *Don't be concerned about the outward beauty of fancy hairstyles, expensive jewelry, or beautiful clothes. You should clothe yourselves instead with the beauty that comes from within, the unfading beauty of a gentle and quiet spirit, which is so precious to God.*

Modesty focuses on inward beauty, the kind of beauty that remains strong and youthful long after your body turns old and frail.

How should I show modesty in my behavior?

ROMANS 13:13 | *Because we belong to the day, we must live decent lives for all to see. Don't participate in the darkness of wild parties and drunkenness, or in sexual promiscuity and immoral living, or in quarreling and jealousy.*

EPHESIANS 5:8 | *Once you were full of darkness, but now you have light from the Lord. So live as people of light!*

TITUS 2:12 | *We are instructed to turn from godless living and sinful pleasures. We should live in this evil world with wisdom, righteousness, and devotion to God.*

If you have committed yourself to following Jesus, your behavior should reflect his as much as possible. You can show modesty by avoiding wrong and indecent behavior and by serving others with grace and kindness.

Promise from God PROVERBS 31:30 | *Charm is deceptive, and beauty does not last; but a woman who fears the LORD will be greatly praised.*

MONEY

What is a proper attitude toward money?

MATTHEW 6:21 | *Wherever your treasure is, there the desires of your heart will also be.*

MATTHEW 6:24 | *No one can serve two masters. . . . You cannot serve both God and money.*

The Bible mentions many wealthy people who loved God, while saying nothing negative about the amount of wealth they owned (Abraham, David, Joseph of Arimathea, Lydia). Scripture doesn't focus on how much money you can or cannot have, but rather on what you do with it. Jesus made one thing clear: Wherever you put your money, your heart will follow after it. So work hard and succeed without guilt, but work just as hard at finding ways to please God with your money.

PSALM 119:36 | *Give me an eagerness for your laws rather than a love for money!*

ECCLESIASTES 5:10 | *Those who love money will never have enough. How meaningless to think that wealth brings true happiness!*

1 TIMOTHY 6:10 | *The love of money is the root of all kinds of evil. And some people, craving money, have wandered from the true faith and pierced themselves with many sorrows.*

HEBREWS 13:5 | *Don't love money; be satisfied with what you have. For God has said, "I will never fail you. I will never abandon you."*

It's not having money that's wrong, but the love of money that can get your priorities out of line. Loving money can cultivate a dangerous craving—the more you have, the more you want. It is a vicious cycle that never has a satisfactory conclusion. Keep reminding yourself that God must be first in your life and that money cannot satisfy your deepest needs.

PROVERBS 11:28 | *Trust in your money and down you go!*

ISAIAH 55:2 | *Why spend your money on food that does not give you strength? . . . Listen to me, and you will eat what is good. You will enjoy the finest food.*

Do you ever buy things to try to fill a void or satisfy an emotional need in your life? The Bible points to the way to acquire a deep and lasting happiness that always satisfies.

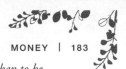

PROVERBS 19:1 | *Better to be poor and honest than to be dishonest and a fool.*

No amount of money is worth deception or dishonesty. Taking advantage of others to make money is stealing. Those who do this lose far more than they gain.

PSALM 23:1 | *The LORD is my shepherd; I have all that I need.*

PHILIPPIANS 4:11-12 | *I have learned how to be content with whatever I have. . . . I have learned the secret of living in every situation, whether it is with a full stomach or empty, with plenty or little.*

PHILIPPIANS 4:19 | *This same God who takes care of me will supply all your needs from his glorious riches, which have been given to us in Christ Jesus.*

The Bible promises that God will supply all your needs. The problem comes when your definition of "need" is different from God's. When you study God's Word, you will discover what you truly need for a fulfilling life.

How can I best handle my money?

MARK 12:43 | *Jesus called his disciples to him and said, "I tell you the truth, this poor widow has given more than all the others who are making contributions."*

1 JOHN 3:17 | *If someone has enough money to live well and sees a brother or sister in need but shows no compassion—how can God's love be in that person?*

Consistent and generous giving is one of the most effective ways to keep you from being greedy with your money. When your giving meets needs in the lives of others, you will find much deeper satisfaction than if you had spent the money on yourself—or hoarded it.

PROVERBS 3:9-10 | *Honor the LORD with your wealth and with the best part of everything you produce. Then he will fill your barns with grain, and your vats will overflow with good wine.*

MALACHI 3:10 | *"Bring all the tithes into the storehouse. . . . If you do," says the LORD of Heaven's Armies, "I will open the windows of heaven for you. I will pour out a blessing so great you won't have enough room to take it in! Try it! Put me to the test!"*

Instead of viewing money as yours, to use as you wish, see it as God's, to use as he wishes. Giving back to God the first part of everything you receive will help you maintain this perspective.

PROVERBS 21:20 | *The wise have wealth and luxury, but fools spend whatever they get.*

PROVERBS 28:19 | *A hard worker has plenty of food, but a person who chases fantasies ends up in poverty.*

MATTHEW 25:14 | *He called together his servants and entrusted his money to them while he was gone.*

LUKE 6:38 | *Give, and you will receive.*

1 CORINTHIANS 4:12 | *We work wearily with our own hands to earn our living.*

2 CORINTHIANS 9:6 | *A farmer who plants only a few seeds will get a small crop. But the one who plants generously will get a generous crop.*

1 THESSALONIANS 4:12 | *People who are not Christians will respect the way you live, and you will not need to depend on others.*

Properly handling money requires good stewardship in earning, giving, spending, and saving your money. God understands the importance of providing for the needs of your family and the future. But he also expects you to use your money generously to help others.

Why don't I ever seem to have enough money?

ECCLESIASTES 10:19 | *A party gives laughter, wine gives happiness, and money gives everything!*

It's human nature to believe that if you just had more money, you could be happier and fix almost any problem. But when you get more, you will want even more, and you will never seem to have enough.

ISAIAH 55:2 | *Why spend your money on food that does not give you strength?*

Review your finances. You might be surprised at how much you are spending on frivolous things you don't really need.

HAGGAI 1:4, 6 | *[The Lord said,] "Why are you living in luxurious houses while my house lies in ruins? . . . You eat but are not satisfied. . . . Your wages disappear as though you were putting them in pockets filled with holes!"*

When you're not managing your money by God's priorities, you will feel as though you never have enough. God's priorities would have you ask "How can I help?" not "What can I get?"

MARK 8:36 | *And what do you benefit if you gain the whole world but lose your own soul?*

LUKE 12:15 | *Guard against every kind of greed. Life is not measured by how much you own.*

You may be depending on your money to bring security. But this is false thinking. Your money is never secure on earth and can disappear suddenly. Only in heaven are your treasures completely secure.

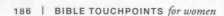

MARK 10:21-22 | *[Jesus said,] "Go and sell all your possessions and give the money to the poor, and you will have treasure in heaven. Then come, follow me." At this the man's face fell, and he went away sad, for he had many possessions.*

We accumulate money because we believe that money and wealth can make us happier. But how much happier and more productive we could be if we set our minds to accumulating treasure in heaven!

Promise from God MATTHEW 6:31-33 | *Don't worry about these things, saying, "What will we eat? What will we drink? What will we wear?" These things dominate the thoughts of unbelievers, but your heavenly Father already knows all your needs. Seek the Kingdom of God above all else, and live righteously, and he will give you everything you need.*

MOTHERS

What qualities should a mother possess?

1 KINGS 3:26-27 | *The woman who was the real mother of the living child, and who loved him very much, cried out, "Oh no, my lord! Give her the child—please do not kill him!" But the other woman said, "All right, he will be neither yours nor mine; divide him between us!" Then the king said, "Do not kill the child, but give him to the woman who wants him to live, for she is his mother!"*

A good mother should love her children unselfishly, wanting what is best for the child more than what is best for herself.

1 THESSALONIANS 2:7 | *As apostles of Christ . . . we were like a mother feeding and caring for her own children.*

A caring mother is gentle with her children.

HEBREWS 11:23 | *It was by faith that Moses' parents hid him for three months when he was born. They saw that God had given them an unusual child, and they were not afraid to disobey the king's command.*

A godly mother exercises great faith on behalf of her children.

PROVERBS 14:1 | *A wise woman builds her home, but a foolish woman tears it down with her own hands.*

A wise mother builds her family up rather than tearing it down with hurtful words.

What are some of the responsibilities of a mother?

PROVERBS 4:3 | *I, too, was once my father's son, tenderly loved as my mother's only child.*

A mother should love her children tenderly.

LUKE 18:15 | *One day some parents brought their little children to Jesus so he could touch and bless them. But when the disciples saw this, they scolded the parents for bothering him.*

A mother should lead her children to Jesus.

2 TIMOTHY 1:5 | *I remember your genuine faith, for you share the faith that first filled your grandmother Lois and your mother, Eunice. And I know that same faith continues strong in you.*

A mother should be a woman with strong faith in God, which can become a great heritage for her family.

DEUTERONOMY 8:5 | *Just as a parent disciplines a child, the LORD your God disciplines you for your own good.*

A mother should discipline her children with the same loving hand the Lord shows to her.

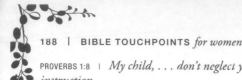

PROVERBS 1:8 | *My child, . . . don't neglect your mother's instruction.*

A mother should teach her children God's ways.

ISAIAH 66:12-13 | *This is what the LORD says: "I will give Jerusalem a river of peace and prosperity. The wealth of the nations will flow to her. Her children will be nursed at her breasts, carried in her arms, and held on her lap. I will comfort you there in Jerusalem as a mother comforts her child."*

A mother should comfort her children.

MARK 10:7 | *A man leaves his father and mother and is joined to his wife.*

A mother should raise her children to become mature and independent young people.

Promise from God EXODUS 20:12 | *Honor your father and mother. Then you will live a long, full life in the land the LORD your God is giving you.*

MOTIVES

How can I have purer motives?

PSALM 19:14 | *May the words of my mouth and the meditation of my heart be pleasing to you, O LORD, my rock and my redeemer.*

Start by asking God to change the way you think by changing your heart.

PSALM 26:2 | *Put me on trial, LORD, and cross-examine me. Test my motives and my heart.*

PROVERBS 17:3 | *Fire tests the purity of silver and gold, but the LORD tests the heart.*

1 CORINTHIANS 4:4 | *My conscience is clear, but that doesn't prove I'm right. It is the Lord himself who will examine me and decide.*

Remember that God alone knows your heart. Ask him to reveal to you any area in which your motives are less than pure. Welcome it when God tests your motives. This gives you an opportunity to grow.

What are some wrong motives?

JAMES 3:15 | *Jealousy and selfishness are not God's kind of wisdom. Such things are earthly, unspiritual, and demonic.*

1 JOHN 3:12 | *We must not be like Cain, who belonged to the evil one and killed his brother. And why did he kill him? Because Cain had been doing what was evil, and his brother had been doing what was righteous.*

If you let jealousy motivate you, your actions will be selfish and will hurt others.

1 SAMUEL 18:17 | *Saul thought, "I'll send him out against the Philistines and let them kill him rather than doing it myself."*

PROVERBS 10:11 | *The words of the godly are a life-giving fountain; the words of the wicked conceal violent intentions.*

If you intend to harm someone, you are being motivated by hatred.

EZEKIEL 33:31 | *[The Lord said to Ezekiel the prophet,] "My people come pretending to be sincere and sit before you. They listen to your words, but they have no intention of doing what you say. Their mouths are full of lustful words, and their hearts seek only after money."*

Pretending to be close to God is displeasing to him because your motives are insincere—you are just trying to make yourself look good.

MATTHEW 6:1 | *Watch out! Don't do your good deeds publicly, to be admired by others, for you will lose the reward from your Father in heaven.*

You shouldn't do good in order to be admired by people— out of vanity—you should do it simply to please God.

MATTHEW 22:16-18 | *"Teacher," they said, "we know how honest you are. You teach the way of God truthfully. You are impartial and don't play favorites. Now tell us what you think about this: Is it right to pay taxes to Caesar or not?" But Jesus knew their evil motives. "You hypocrites!" he said. "Why are you trying to trap me?"*

Appearing sincere while being motivated only by a desire to trap others into looking bad is hypocritical.

What kinds of motives are right motives?

EXODUS 25:2 | *Tell the people of Israel to bring me their sacred offerings. Accept the contributions from all whose hearts are moved to offer them.*

ISAIAH 11:3 | *He will delight in obeying the LORD.*

To desire to serve God simply because you want to please him is right and good.

2 KINGS 2:9 | *Elijah said to Elisha, "Tell me what I can do for you before I am taken away." And Elisha replied, "Please let me inherit a double share of your spirit and become your successor."*

Wanting to follow in the footsteps of a godly person so you can become more godly is a noble motive.

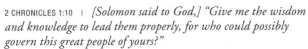

2 CHRONICLES 1:10 | *[Solomon said to God,] "Give me the wisdom and knowledge to lead them properly, for who could possibly govern this great people of yours?"*

Solomon's motive, to grow in wisdom and knowledge in order to be a better king to God's people, was pleasing to God.

JOHN 21:17 | *[Jesus] asked him, "Simon son of John, do you love me?" Peter . . . said, "Lord, you know everything. You know that I love you." Jesus said, "Then feed my sheep."*

God wants you to help others out of love for Jesus, not out of a desire for personal praise or as a way to impress.

Promise from God PROVERBS 14:22 | *If you plan to do evil, you will be lost; if you plan to do good, you will receive unfailing love and faithfulness.*

MOURNING

See **GRIEF.**

MOVING

How can I best handle a move?

JOSHUA 1:9 | *This is my command—be strong and courageous! Do not be afraid or discouraged. For the LORD your God is with you wherever you go.*

PSALM 139:3, 5, 7, 9-10 | *You see me when I travel and when I rest at home. You know everything I do. . . . You go before me and follow me. You place your hand of blessing on my head. . . . I can never escape from your Spirit! I can never get away from your presence! . . . If I ride the wings of the morning, if I dwell by the farthest oceans, even there your hand will guide me, and your strength will support me.*

When you move to a new place, recognize that God is already there, preparing that place for you and you for that place.

NUMBERS 10:13 | *The people set out for the first time, following the instructions the LORD had given through Moses.*

PROVERBS 19:2 | *Enthusiasm without knowledge is no good; haste makes mistakes.*

Before any move, seek the Lord's direction. Pray specifically and think carefully.

NUMBERS 9:21 | *Sometimes the cloud stayed only overnight and lifted the next morning. But day or night, when the cloud lifted, the people broke camp and moved on.*

When you move to a new place, pray that you will recognize the signs of God's presence and that you will walk through the doors of opportunity he opens for you.

GENESIS 13:18 | *Abram moved his camp to Hebron and settled near the oak grove belonging to Mamre. There he built another altar to the LORD.*

Throughout any move continue to worship the Lord consistently, for he is the guardian of your move. It is easy to let the myriad of details distract you from prayer, Bible study, and worship.

How can God help me in my move?

EXODUS 33:14-15 | *The LORD [said], "I will personally go with you, Moses, and I will give you rest—everything will be fine for you." Then Moses said, "If you don't personally go with us, don't make us leave this place."*

2 SAMUEL 2:1 | *David asked the LORD, "Should I move back to one of the towns of Judah?" "Yes," the LORD replied. Then David asked, "Which town should I go to?" "To Hebron," the LORD answered.*

EZRA 8:21 | *I gave orders for all of us to fast and humble ourselves before our God. We prayed that he would give us a safe journey and protect us, our children, and our goods as we traveled.*

ISAIAH 41:13 | *I hold you by your right hand—I, the LORD your God. And I say to you, "Don't be afraid. I am here to help you."*

If you ask him, God will guide you, give you wisdom and courage, and be with you wherever your move takes you.

Promise from God JOSHUA 1:9 | *The LORD your God is with you wherever you go.*

NEEDS

What—and whom—do I really need?

MATTHEW 5:3 | *God blesses those who are poor and realize their need for him, for the Kingdom of Heaven is theirs.*

HEBREWS 7:26 | *[Jesus] is the kind of high priest we need because he is holy and blameless, unstained by sin. He has been set apart from sinners and has been given the highest place of honor in heaven.*

You need God—his love, his mercy, his presence, his salvation, his forgiveness, and his promise of eternal life.

LUKE 17:5 | *The apostles said to the Lord, "Show us how to increase our faith."*

EPHESIANS 6:16 | *In addition to all of these, hold up the shield of faith to stop the fiery arrows of the devil.*

You need faith to stand firm in the face of temptation.

PSALM 119:19 | *I am only a foreigner in the land. Don't hide your commands from me!*

You need God's guidance so that you know where to go in life's journey.

JAMES 1:5 | *If you need wisdom, ask our generous God, and he will give it to you. He will not rebuke you for asking.*

You need God's wisdom so that you will do what is right, what is appropriate, and what is pleasing to him.

COLOSSIANS 1:11 | *We also pray that you will be strengthened with all his glorious power so you will have all the endurance and patience you need.*

HEBREWS 10:36 | *Patient endurance is what you need now, so that you will continue to do God's will. Then you will receive all that he has promised.*

You need patient endurance to continue to do God's will.

2 CORINTHIANS 12:9 | *[God] said, "My grace is all you need. My power works best in weakness." So now I am glad to boast about my weaknesses, so that the power of Christ can work through me.*

HEBREWS 4:16 | *Let us come boldly to the throne of our gracious God. There we will receive his mercy, and we will find grace to help us when we need it most.*

You need God's power, mercy, and grace in times of weakness or when you fail him.

PSALM 119:75 | *I know, O LORD, that your regulations are fair; you disciplined me because I needed it.*

You need the Lord's discipline to keep you following his ways.

ROMANS 12:4-5 | *Just as our bodies have many parts and each part has a special function, so it is with Christ's body. We are many parts of one body, and we all belong to each other.*

You need other Christians, encouraging you and serving with you.

PSALM 145:15 | *The eyes of all look to you in hope; you give them their food as they need it.*

You need food and other provisions of life.

What do I need to do?

ACTS 13:24 | *Before [Jesus] came, John the Baptist preached that all the people of Israel needed to repent of their sins and turn to God and be baptized.*

You need to repent of your sins and turn to God.

PSALM 138:3 | *As soon as I pray, you answer me; you encourage me by giving me strength.*

LUKE 18:1 | *Jesus told his disciples a story to show that they should always pray and never give up.*

You need to pray, to keep you in constant communication with God.

PHILIPPIANS 4:13 | *I can do everything through Christ, who gives me strength.*

You need to depend on God's strength to do what you can't do on your own.

Does God really care about my daily needs?

ISAIAH 46:4 | *I will be your God throughout your lifetime— until your hair is white with age. I made you, and I will care for you. I will carry you along and save you.*

2 CORINTHIANS 9:8-9 | *God will generously provide all you need. Then you will always have everything you need and plenty left over to share with others. As the Scriptures say, "They share freely and give generously to the poor. Their good deeds will be remembered forever."*

PHILIPPIANS 4:19 | *This same God who takes care of me will supply all your needs from his glorious riches, which have been given to us in Christ Jesus.*

When you learn to distinguish between your wants and your needs, you will begin to understand how God provides and you will realize how much he truly cares for you. God doesn't promise to give you a lot of possessions, but he does promise to help you possess the character traits that reflect his nature so that you can accomplish his plan for you. He doesn't promise to preserve your physical life, but he does promise to keep your soul for all eternity if you've pledged your allegiance to him.

Promise from God PHILIPPIANS 4:19 | *This same God who takes care of me will supply all your needs from his glorious riches, which have been given to us in Christ Jesus.*

NEIGHBORS

Who is my neighbor?

LUKE 10:29-34, 36-37 | *The man . . . asked Jesus, "And who is my neighbor?" Jesus replied with a story: "A Jewish man was travel- ing from Jerusalem down to Jericho, and he was attacked by bandits. They stripped him of his clothes, beat him up, and left him half dead beside the road. By chance a priest came along . . . and passed him by. A Temple assistant walked over . . . but he also passed by on the other side. Then a despised Samaritan came along, and when he saw the man, he felt compassion for him. . . . He took care of him. . . . Now which of these three would you say was a neighbor to the man who was attacked by bandits?" Jesus asked. The man replied, "The one who showed him mercy." Then Jesus said, "Yes, now go and do the same."*

Your neighbor is anyone around you who needs help, mercy, forgiveness, compassion, or friendship.

What are my responsibilities to my neighbor?

DEUTERONOMY 22:1, 3-4 | *If you see your neighbor's ox or sheep or goat wandering away, don't ignore your responsibility. Take it back to its owner. . . . Do the same if you find your neighbor's donkey, clothing, or anything else your neighbor loses. Don't ignore your responsibility. If you see that your neighbor's donkey or ox has collapsed on the road, do not look the other way. Go and help your neighbor get it back on its feet!*

PROVERBS 3:28 | *If you can help your neighbor now, don't say, "Come back tomorrow, and then I'll help you."*

Help your neighbor in times of need.

ROMANS 13:9-10 | *The commandments say, "You must not commit adultery. You must not murder. You must not steal. You must not covet." These—and other such commandments— are summed up in this one commandment: "Love your neighbor as yourself." Love does no wrong to others, so love fulfills the requirements of God's law.*

JAMES 2:8 | *Yes indeed, it is good when you obey the royal law as found in the Scriptures: "Love your neighbor as yourself."*

Love your neighbor, regardless of your differences.

LEVITICUS 19:18 | *[The Lord said,] "Do not seek revenge or bear a grudge against a fellow Israelite, but love your neighbor as yourself. I am the LORD."*

Never try to get back at your neighbor for some wrong committed against you. Let the Lord deal with him or her.

LEVITICUS 19:15-17 | *Always judge people fairly. Do not spread slanderous gossip among your people. . . . Confront people directly so you will not be held guilty for their sin.*

EPHESIANS 4:25 | *Stop telling lies. Let us tell our neighbors the truth, for we are all parts of the same body.*

Be honest with your neighbor and always tell the truth, even when it is painful.

EXODUS 20:16 | *You must not testify falsely against your neighbor.*

Don't tell lies or gossip about your neighbor.

PROVERBS 3:29 | *Don't plot harm against your neighbor, for those who live nearby trust you.*

Don't break your neighbors' trust by plotting against them.

PROVERBS 11:12 | *It is foolish to belittle one's neighbor; a sensible person keeps quiet.*

Don't make fun of your neighbor.

DEUTERONOMY 5:21 | *You must not covet your neighbor's wife. You must not covet your neighbor's house or land, male or female servant, ox or donkey, or anything else that belongs to your neighbor.*

Don't envy what your neighbor has.

PROVERBS 25:17 | *Don't visit your neighbors too often, or you will wear out your welcome.*

PROVERBS 27:14 | *A loud and cheerful greeting early in the morning will be taken as a curse!*

Respect your neighbor's time and privacy.

How should I live among my non-Christian neighbors?

GALATIANS 5:14 | *The whole law can be summed up in this one command: "Love your neighbor as yourself."*

COLOSSIANS 4:5-6 | *Live wisely among those who are not believers, and make the most of every opportunity. Let your conversation be gracious and attractive so that you will have the right response for everyone.*

JAMES 4:12 | *God alone, who gave the law, is the Judge. He alone has the power to save or to destroy. So what right do you have to judge your neighbor?*

1 PETER 2:12 | *Be careful to live properly among your unbelieving neighbors. Then even if they accuse you of doing wrong, they will see your honorable behavior, and they will give honor to God when he judges the world.*

Treat your non-Christian neighbors with love and respect, live honorably and graciously before them, be an example of godliness, and refuse to condemn them. If they don't know God, why should you expect them to live as though they do? Instead of judging them, win them over with friendship.

Promise from God JAMES 2:8 | *Yes indeed, it is good when you obey the royal law as found in the Scriptures: "Love your neighbor as yourself."*

OBEDIENCE

Is obedience to God really necessary, since I am saved by faith?

DEUTERONOMY 10:12-13 | *What does the LORD your God require of you? He requires only that you fear the LORD your God, and live in a way that pleases him, and love him and serve him with all your heart and soul. And you must always obey the LORD's commands and decrees . . . for your own good.*

PHILIPPIANS 2:12 | *[Paul said,] "Dear friends, you always followed my instructions when I was with you. And now that I am away, it is even more important. Work hard to show the results of your salvation, obeying God with deep reverence and fear."*

God's call for your obedience is based on his own commitment to your well-being. Since God is the Creator of life, he knows how life is supposed to work. Obedience demonstrates your willingness to accept that what he says is best and your trust that God's way is best for you.

JEREMIAH 7:23 | *Obey me, and I will be your God, and you will be my people.*

Obedience to God is an intrinsic element of a covenant relationship with him.

HEBREWS 11:8 | *It was by faith that Abraham obeyed.*

Obedience is an act of faith. It shows you trust God enough to follow his commands for your life.

TITUS 1:16 | *Such people claim they know God, but they deny him by the way they live. They are detestable and disobedient, worthless for doing anything good.*

If you are consistently disobedient to God, your claim to knowing him is meaningless.

LEVITICUS 9:6 | *Moses said, "This is what the LORD has commanded you to do so that the glory of the LORD may appear to you."*

Obedience to God brings you into fellowship with him, synchronizing you with his will.

ACTS 5:32 | *We are witnesses of these things and so is the Holy Spirit, who is given by God to those who obey him.*

God's presence in your life is evidence that you obey him.

In what ways does God want me to obey him?

GENESIS 6:22 | *Noah did everything exactly as God had commanded him.*

DEUTERONOMY 5:32 | *You must be careful to obey all the commands of the LORD your God, following his instructions in every detail.*

God wants you to do everything he asks of you. Obedience is not about "generally" following God's commands, or following any of his instructions that suit you. True obedience is about following every detail of all his commands to the best of your ability.

1 SAMUEL 15:22 | *What is more pleasing to the LORD: your burnt offerings and sacrifices or your obedience to his voice? Listen! Obedience is better than sacrifice, and submission is better than offering the fat of rams.*

Obedience to God involves listening to and doing what he says.

EXODUS 1:17 | *Because the midwives feared God, they refused to obey the king's orders. They allowed the boys to live.*

EXODUS 12:28 | *The people of Israel did just as the LORD had commanded through Moses and Aaron.*

ACTS 4:19-20 | *Peter and John [said], "Do you think God wants us to obey you rather than him? We cannot stop telling about everything we have seen and heard."*

ACTS 5:29 | *Peter and the apostles [said], "We must obey God rather than any human authority."*

ROMANS 13:1 | *Everyone must submit to governing authorities. For all authority comes from God, and those in positions of authority have been placed there by God.*

HEBREWS 13:7 | *Remember your leaders who taught you the word of God. Think of all the good that has come from their lives, and follow the example of their faith.*

God also commands you to obey your leaders, unless what they ask contradicts God's Word.

Promise from God EXODUS 19:5 | *[The Lord said,] "If you will obey me and keep my covenant, you will be my own special treasure from among all the peoples on earth; for all the earth belongs to me."*

PAIN

See **SUFFERING.**

PARENTING

What does the Bible say about the role of parents?

2 TIMOTHY 3:15 | *You have been taught the holy Scriptures from childhood.*

Parents are to take responsibility for teaching their children to love the Word of God.

PROVERBS 3:12 | *The LORD corrects those he loves, just as a father corrects a child in whom he delights.*

HEBREWS 12:11 | *No discipline is enjoyable while it is happening—it's painful! But afterward there will be a peaceful harvest of right living for those who are trained in this way.*

Parents are to discipline their children with consistency, wisdom, and love. Parents do their children a favor when they sincerely seek what God wants for their children, not necessarily what their children want. Indulgent parents do not help their children develop character.

GENESIS 25:28 | *Isaac loved Esau . . . but Rebekah loved Jacob.*

Parents are not to show favoritism between children.

LUKE 15:20 | *Filled with love and compassion, he ran to his son, embraced him, and kissed him.*

A mark of a loving parent is the willingness to forgive.

How are children to relate to parents?

EXODUS 20:12 | *Honor your father and mother. Then you will live a long, full life in the land the LORD your God is giving you.*

EPHESIANS 6:1 | *Children, obey your parents because you belong to the Lord, for this is the right thing to do.*

Children have a responsibility to obey, honor, and show respect to their parents.

What if I am a single parent or grew up in a single-parent home?

PSALM 68:5 | *Father to the fatherless, defender of widows— this is God, whose dwelling is holy.*

God has a special place in his heart for those who are lonely or abandoned. Turn to him for comfort and help.

Promise from God PROVERBS 22:6 | *Direct your children onto the right path, and when they are older, they will not leave it.*

PAST

How do I deal with regrets?

PSALM 51:7, 9-10 | *Purify me from my sins, and I will be clean; wash me, and I will be whiter than snow. . . . Don't keep looking at my sins. Remove the stain of my guilt. Create in me a clean heart, O God. Renew a loyal spirit within me.*

ISAIAH 1:18 | *"Come now, let's settle this," says the LORD. "Though your sins are like scarlet, I will make them as white as snow. Though they are red like crimson, I will make them as white as wool."*

ROMANS 4:6-8 | *David . . . described the happiness of those who are declared righteous without working for it: "Oh, what joy for those whose disobedience is forgiven, whose sins are put out of sight. Yes, what joy for those whose record the LORD has cleared of sin."*

PHILIPPIANS 3:13-14 | *I have not achieved [perfection], but I focus on this one thing: Forgetting the past and looking forward to what lies ahead, I press on.*

Regrets are like a dirty window that keeps you from seeing clearly what is in front of you. But God is in the cleaning business. He washes away the sins of the past as well as the guilt over those sins. If he can forget them completely, so can you. You can choose to move forward joyfully, without carrying the burden of regret.

How can I recover from a hurtful past?

GENESIS 27:41; 33:4 | *Esau hated Jacob . . . and Esau began to scheme: "I will . . . kill my brother, Jacob." . . . [Later] Esau ran to meet [Jacob] and embraced him, threw his arms around his neck, and kissed him. And they both wept.*

GENESIS 50:19-20 | *Joseph [said], "Don't be afraid of me. Am I God, that I can punish you? You intended to harm me, but God intended it all for good."*

MATTHEW 18:21-22 | *Peter came to [Jesus] and asked, "Lord, how often should I forgive someone who sins against me? Seven times?" "No, not seven times," Jesus replied, "but seventy times seven!"*

LUKE 23:33, 34 | *[The soldiers] nailed [Jesus] to the cross. . . . Jesus said, "Father, forgive them, for they don't know what they are doing."*

Forgiving is essential to the healing process. As you release those hurts, you are free to be healed and to grow beyond the pain.

How can I benefit from the past?

DEUTERONOMY 32:7 | *Remember the days of long ago; think about the generations past. Ask your father, and he will inform you. Inquire of your elders, and they will tell you.*

PSALM 78:4 | *We will not hide these truths from our children; we will tell the next generation about the glorious deeds of the LORD, about his power and his mighty wonders.*

ISAIAH 42:23 | *Who will hear these lessons from the past and see the ruin that awaits you in the future?*

1 CORINTHIANS 10:1, 5, 11 | *I don't want you to forget, dear brothers and sisters, about our ancestors in the wilderness long ago. . . . God was not pleased with most of them, and their bodies were scattered in the wilderness. . . . These things happened to them as examples for us. They were written down to warn us who live at the end of the age.*

From the past you learn wise lessons of God at work. You also learn from others—what worked well and what didn't. You learn not to repeat failures and to how to build on successes.

Promise from God HEBREWS 8:12 | *[God said,] "I will forgive their wickedness, and I will never again remember their sins."*

PATIENCE

How can I develop more patience?

EXODUS 5:22; 6:2 | *Moses went back to the LORD and protested, . . . "Why did you send me?" . . . And God said to Moses, "I am Yahweh—'the LORD.'"*

Focusing less on your agenda and more on God's agenda for you will provide a "big picture" perspective and help you be less impatient.

PSALM 40:1 | *I waited patiently for the LORD to help me, and he turned to me and heard my cry.*

Prayer is a necessary tool in developing patience and giving you God's perspective on your situation.

HABAKKUK 2:3 | *If it seems slow in coming, wait patiently, for it will surely take place. It will not be delayed.*

If God is going to do what is best for you, then his plan for you will be accomplished on his schedule, not yours. Keeping that in mind, you can actually become excited about waiting for him to act, anticipating the good things he will work in your life.

GALATIANS 5:22 | *The Holy Spirit produces this kind of fruit in our lives: love, joy, peace, patience.*

The more you let the Holy Spirit fill and inspire you, the more patient you will become. All fruit takes time to grow and mature, including the fruit of the Holy Spirit.

ROMANS 8:25 | *If we look forward to something we don't yet have, we must wait patiently and confidently.*

ROMANS 12:12 | *Rejoice in our confident hope. Be patient in trouble, and keep on praying.*

God uses life's circumstances to develop your patience. You can't always choose the circumstances that come your way, but you can choose to learn and grow from them.

Promise from God ISAIAH 30:18 | *The LORD is a faithful God. Blessed are those who wait for his help.*

POVERTY

Doesn't God care that I'm poor? I feel so lonely when I realize that so many others seem to have all they need, and I'm struggling.

ISAIAH 25:4 | *You are a tower of refuge to the poor, O LORD, a tower of refuge to the needy in distress. You are a refuge from the storm and a shelter from the heat.*

ROMANS 8:35, 37 | *Does it mean he no longer loves us if we have trouble or calamity, or are persecuted, or hungry, or destitute, or in danger, or threatened with death? . . . No, despite all these things, overwhelming victory is ours through Christ, who loved us.*

HEBREWS 13:5 | *Don't love money; be satisfied with what you have. For God has said, "I will never fail you. I will never abandon you."*

If you are poor, suffering from a crippling disease, grieving over the loss of a loved one, lonely or abandoned, or living in constant danger, your greatest hope as a believer is that this condition is temporary. God promises that you will be free from all trouble when you live with him in heaven. While you may not understand why some people seem to get all the breaks on earth, you can be assured that those who love God will get all the breaks in eternity.

Does God really care about the poor?

PSALM 35:10 | *LORD, who can compare with you? Who else rescues the helpless from the strong? Who else protects the help-less and poor from those who rob them?*

PSALM 40:17 | *Since I am poor and needy, let the Lord keep me in his thoughts.*

PSALM 72:12 | *He will rescue the poor when they cry to him;*
he will help the oppressed, who have no one to defend them.

PSALM 102:17 | *He will listen to the prayers of the destitute.*
He will not reject their pleas.

PSALM 113:6-8 | *He stoops to look down on heaven and on earth.*
He lifts the poor from the dust and the needy from the garbage
dump. He sets them among princes, even the princes of his own
people!

God cares deeply for the poor. And he commands all
believers to care for them too.

What is my responsibility to the poor?

LEVITICUS 25:39 | *If one of your fellow Israelites falls into poverty*
and is forced to sell himself to you, do not treat him as a slave.

PROVERBS 19:17 | *If you help the poor, you are lending to the*
LORD—and he will repay you!

PROVERBS 22:9 | *Blessed are those who are generous, because they*
feed the poor.

ISAIAH 58:10 | *Feed the hungry, and help those in trouble. Then*
your light will shine out from the darkness, and the darkness
around you will be as bright as noon.

MATTHEW 7:12 | *Do to others whatever you would like them to*
do to you.

JAMES 2:9 | *If you favor some people over others, you are*
committing a sin.

God has compassion for the poor, so if you want to please
God, you must also have compassion for them. If it does
not reach into your checkbook or onto your "to do" list, it
is not godly compassion. Helping the poor is not merely an

obligation; it is also a privilege that brings not only great joy from helping others but a reward from God himself.

Promise from God PSALM 41:1 | *Oh, the joys of those who are kind to the poor! The LORD rescues them when they are in trouble.*

PRAISE

Why is it so important to praise God?

1 CHRONICLES 16:25-26 | *Great is the LORD! He is most worthy of praise! He is to be feared above all gods. The gods of other nations are mere idols, but the LORD made the heavens!*

PSALM 89:5 | *All heaven will praise your great wonders, LORD; myriads of angels will praise you for your faithfulness.*

PSALM 92:1 | *It is good to give thanks to the LORD, to sing praises to the Most High.*

PSALM 106:2 | *Who can list the glorious miracles of the LORD? Who can ever praise him enough?*

LUKE 19:36-37 | *As [Jesus] rode along, the crowds spread out their garments on the road ahead of him. When he reached the place where the road started down the Mount of Olives, all of his followers began to shout and sing as they walked along, praising God for all the wonderful miracles they had seen.*

ACTS 16:23, 25 | *[Paul and Silas] were severely beaten, and then they were thrown into prison. . . . Around midnight Paul and Silas were praying and singing hymns to God, and the other prisoners were listening.*

Consider how great God is—the awesome Creator of the universe! Next, consider how sinful and mortal you are.

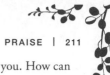

Finally, consider how great God's love is for you. How can you help but praise him? He is powerful enough to sustain the universe and loving enough to redeem it.

How can I express praise to God?

PSALM 35:10 | *With every bone in my body I will praise him.*

PSALM 86:12 | *With all my heart I will praise you, O Lord my God. I will give glory to your name forever.*

Express your praise to God wholeheartedly.

1 CHRONICLES 23:30 | *Each morning and evening they stood before the LORD to sing songs of thanks and praise to him.*

PSALM 104:33 | *I will sing to the LORD as long as I live. I will praise my God to my last breath!*

Praise the Lord as you begin your day and at night as you recall his acts of goodness in your life. Praise him with a grateful heart until the day you die!

ROMANS 15:6 | *All of you can join together with one voice, giving praise and glory to God, the Father of our Lord Jesus Christ.*

Express your praise to God through worship and fellowship with other believers.

2 CHRONICLES 20:19 | *The Levites from the clans of Kohath and Korah stood to praise the LORD, the God of Israel, with a very loud shout.*

PSALM 34:1 | *I will praise the LORD at all times. I will constantly speak his praises.*

Express your praise out loud.

1 CHRONICLES 16:42 | *They used their trumpets, cymbals, and other instruments to accompany their songs of praise to God.*

PSALM 33:3 | *Sing a new song of praise to him; play skillfully on the harp, and sing with joy.*

PSALM 47:6-7 | *Sing praises to God, sing praises; sing praises to our King, sing praises! For God is the King over all the earth. Praise him with a psalm!*

PSALM 149:1 | *Praise the LORD! Sing to the LORD a new song. Sing his praises in the assembly of the faithful.*

PSALM 150:3-5 | *Praise him with a blast of the ram's horn; praise him with the lyre and harp! Praise him with the tambourine and dancing; praise him with strings and flutes! Praise him with a clash of cymbals; praise him with loud clanging cymbals.*

God is the creator of music, and he is pleased when you use it to express your heartfelt praise for him.

PSALM 54:6 | *I will sacrifice a voluntary offering to you; I will praise your name, O LORD, for it is good.*

Express your praise with offerings to support God's work.

What is the importance of praising others?

PROVERBS 27:2 | *Let someone else praise you, not your own mouth—a stranger, not your own lips.*

PROVERBS 31:28 | *Her children stand and bless her. Her husband praises her.*

PROVERBS 31:31 | *Reward her for all she has done. Let her deeds publicly declare her praise.*

MATTHEW 3:16-17 | *After his baptism, as Jesus came up out of the water, the heavens were opened and he saw the Spirit of God descending like a dove and settling on him. And a voice from heaven said, "This is my dearly loved Son, who brings me great joy."*

MATTHEW 25:21 | *The master was full of praise. "Well done, my good and faithful servant. You have been faithful in handling this small amount, so now I will give you many more responsibilities. Let's celebrate together!"*

There is a difference between praising God, which is worship, and praising others, which is supporting and encouraging them through affirmation.

Promise from God PSALM 31:21 | *Praise the LORD, for he has shown me the wonders of his unfailing love.*

PRAYER

What is prayer?

PSALM 145:18 | *The LORD is close to all who call on him, yes, to all who call on him in truth.*

Prayer is conversation with God. It is simply talking with God and listening to him, honestly telling him your thoughts and feelings, praising him, thanking him, confessing sin, and asking for his help and advice. The essence of prayer is humbly entering the very presence of almighty God.

PSALM 38:18 | *I confess my sins; I am deeply sorry for what I have done.*

1 JOHN 1:9 | *If we confess our sins to him, he is faithful and just to forgive us our sins and to cleanse us from all wickedness.*

Prayer includes confession of sin, which demonstrates the humility necessary for open lines of communication with the almighty, holy God.

1 SAMUEL 14:36 | *The priest said, "Let's ask God first."*

2 SAMUEL 5:19 | *David asked the LORD, "Should I go out to fight the Philistines?"*

Prayer is asking God for guidance and waiting for his direction and leading.

MARK 1:35 | *Before daybreak the next morning, Jesus got up and went out to an isolated place to pray.*

Prayer is an expression of an intimate relationship with your heavenly Father, who makes his own love and resources available to you.

PSALM 9:1-2 | *I will praise you, LORD, with all my heart. . . . I will sing praises to your name, O Most High.*

Through prayer, you praise your mighty God.

Does the Bible teach a "right" way to pray?

1 SAMUEL 23:2 | *David asked the LORD, "Should I go . . . ?"*

NEHEMIAH 1:4 | *For days I mourned, fasted, and prayed to the God of heaven.*

PSALM 18:1 | *I love you, LORD; you are my strength.*

PSALM 32:5 | *Finally, I confessed all my sins to you and stopped trying to hide my guilt. I said to myself, "I will confess my rebellion to the LORD." And you forgave me! All my guilt is gone.*

EPHESIANS 6:18 | *Pray in the Spirit at all times and on every occasion. Stay alert and be persistent in your prayers for all believers everywhere.*

Throughout the Bible, effective prayer includes elements of adoration, fasting, confession, petition, and persistence.

MATTHEW 6:9-13 | *[Jesus said,] "Pray like this: Our Father in heaven, may your name be kept holy. May your Kingdom come soon. May your will be done on earth, as it is in heaven. Give*

us today the food we need, and forgive us our sins, as we have
forgiven those who sin against us. And don't let us yield to
temptation, but rescue us from the evil one."

Jesus taught his disciples that prayer is an intimate conversation with the Father that includes a dependency for daily needs, a commitment to obedience, and confession of sin.

LUKE 18.1 | *Jesus told his disciples a story to show that they*
should always pray and never give up.

Prayer is to be consistent and persistent.

NEHEMIAH 2:4-5 | *The king asked, "Well, how can I help you?"*
With a prayer to the God of heaven, I replied.

Prayer can be spontaneous.

Does God always answer prayer?

GENESIS 30:17 | *God answered Leah's prayers. She became*
pregnant again and gave birth to a fifth son for Jacob.

PSALM 116:1-2 | *I love the LORD because he hears my voice and*
my prayer for mercy. Because he bends down to listen, I will
pray as long as I have breath!

1 PETER 3:12 | *The eyes of the Lord watch over those who do*
right, and his ears are open to their prayers. But the Lord turns
his face against those who do evil.

God listens carefully to every prayer request and answers it. His answer may be yes, no, or wait. At different times, any loving parent gives all three of these responses to a child. God's answering yes to every request would spoil you and be dangerous to your well-being. Answering no to every request would be damaging to your spirit. Answering wait to every prayer would be frustrating.

But sometimes God just wants to talk to you because it is through conversation that you learn and grow your relationship. Many of the best times with a parent are spent just talking. The same is true with God.

JAMES 5:16 | *Confess your sins to each other and pray for each other so that you may be healed. The earnest prayer of a righteous person has great power and produces wonderful results.*

1 JOHN 5:14-15 | *He hears us whenever we ask for anything that pleases him. And . . . he will give us what we ask for.*

As you maintain a close relationship with Jesus and consistently study his Word, your prayers will be more aligned with his will. When that happens, God is delighted to grant your requests.

2 CORINTHIANS 12:8-9 | *Three different times [Paul] begged the Lord to take [the thorn in his flesh] away. Each time he said, "My grace is all you need. My power works best in weakness."*

Sometimes, like Paul, you will find that God answers prayer by giving you something better than you asked for.

EXODUS 14:15 | *The LORD said to Moses, "Why are you crying out to me? Tell the people to get moving!"*

Effective prayer is accompanied by a willingness to obey. When God opens a door, walk through it!

Promise from God 2 CHRONICLES 7:14 | *[The Lord said,] "If my people who are called by my name will humble themselves and pray and seek my face and turn from their wicked ways, I will hear from heaven and will forgive their sins."*

PRIORITIES

What should be my highest priority?

MARK 12:29-30 | *Jesus [said], "The most important commandment is this: 'Listen, O Israel! The LORD our God is the one and only LORD. And you must love the LORD your God with all your heart, all your soul, all your mind, and all your strength.'"*

Jesus clearly stated the greatest priority for every person: Love God, and do it with all you've got. When you sincerely love God, you will also then love others.

How can I tell if God is really my first priority?

EXODUS 20:3 | *You must not have any other god but me.*

DEUTERONOMY 10:12-13 | *What does the LORD your God require of you? He requires only that you fear the LORD your God, and live in a way that pleases him, and love him and serve him with all your heart and soul. And you must always obey the LORD's commands and decrees that I am giving you today for your own good.*

JOSHUA 24:15 | *If you refuse to serve the LORD, then choose today whom you will serve. . . . But as for me and my family, we will serve the LORD.*

LUKE 12:34 | *Wherever your treasure is, there the desires of your heart will also be.*

If you honestly search your heart, you will know if God is your first priority or you have set up some other "gods" in your life. Loving God first does not come naturally, but the Holy Spirit is anxious to help you straighten out your priorities.

What are some benefits of living with right priorities and the dangers of living with wrong priorities?

PSALM 127:1-2 | *Unless the L*ORD *builds a house, the work of the builders is wasted. Unless the L*ORD *protects a city, guarding it with sentries will do no good. It is useless for you to work so hard from early morning until late at night, anxiously working for food to eat; for God gives rest to his loved ones.*

PSALM 128:1-4 | *How joyful are those who fear the L*ORD—*all who follow his ways! You will enjoy the fruit of your labor. How joyful and prosperous you will be! Your wife will be like a fruitful grapevine, flourishing within your home. Your children will be like vigorous young olive trees as they sit around your table. That is the L*ORD's *blessing for those who fear him.*

PROVERBS 14:26 | *Those who fear the L*ORD *are secure; he will be a refuge for their children.*

The proper priorities bring lasting joy, regardless of life's circumstances, and a deep sense of satisfaction that you are doing the right thing, making a lasting impact, and pleasing God. Living with wrong priorities, however, often produces feelings of anxiety, hopelessness, and uselessness.

Promise from God PROVERBS 3:6 | *Seek his will in all you do, and he will show you which path to take.*

PURITY

Why is purity so important?

PSALM 18:20-21 | *The L*ORD *rewarded me for doing right; he restored me because of my innocence. For I have kept the ways of the L*ORD; *I have not turned from my God to follow evil.*

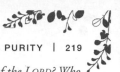

PSALM 24:3-6 | *Who may climb the mountain of the LORD? Who may stand in his holy place? Only those whose hands and hearts are pure, who do not worship idols and never tell lies. They will receive the LORD's blessing and have a right relationship with God their savior. Such people may seek you and worship in your presence, O God of Jacob.*

MATTHEW 5:8 | *God blesses those whose hearts are pure, for they will see God.*

2 TIMOTHY 2:21 | *If you keep yourself pure, you will be a special utensil for honorable use. Your life will be clean, and you will be ready for the Master to use you for every good work.*

For a Christian, purity is the desire to be like Jesus in thought, words, and actions. While you can never be fully free of sin in this life, you can strive for that—and keep clean and pure by asking for forgiveness whenever you do sin. God honors those who strive for pure hearts because it demonstrates a sincere commitment to be like Jesus.

How can I possibly be pure when I mess up so often?

PSALM 51:6, 10 | *You desire honesty from the womb, teaching me wisdom even there. . . . Create in me a clean heart, O God. Renew a loyal spirit within me.*

PSALM 86:11 | *Teach me your ways, O LORD, that I may live according to your truth! Grant me purity of heart, so that I may honor you.*

PHILIPPIANS 4:8 | *Fix your thoughts on what is true, and honorable, and right, and pure, and lovely, and admirable. Think about things that are excellent and worthy of praise.*

1 TIMOTHY 1:5 | *[Paul said,] "The purpose of my instruction is that all believers would be filled with love that comes from a pure heart, a clear conscience, and genuine faith."*

JAMES 3:17 | *The wisdom from above is first of all pure.*

1 PETER 1:22 | *You were cleansed from your sins when you obeyed the truth, so now you must show sincere love to each other as brothers and sisters. Love each other deeply with all your heart.*

God knows you will mess up sometimes. What he desires is your sincerity to be pure.

What if I have not been living a pure life?

PSALM 51:2, 7 | *Wash me clean from my guilt. . . . Purify me from my sins, and I will be clean; wash me, and I will be whiter than snow.*

1 CORINTHIANS 1:30 | *God has united you with Christ Jesus. For our benefit God made him to be wisdom itself. Christ made us right with God; he made us pure and holy, and he freed us from sin.*

HEBREWS 9:14 | *Just think how much more the blood of Christ will purify our consciences from sinful deeds so that we can worship the living God.*

HEBREWS 10:22 | *Let us go right into the presence of God with sincere hearts fully trusting him. For our guilty consciences have been sprinkled with Christ's blood to make us clean, and our bodies have been washed with pure water.*

1 JOHN 1:9 | *If we confess our sins to him, he is faithful and just to forgive us our sins and to cleanse us from all wickedness.*

Christ saves you from any and all sin. Seek his cleansing by being truly sorry for your sin and asking him to forgive you. You will experience the freedom of a clear conscience and a forgiven heart.

Promise from God   PSALM 51:7 | *Purify me from my sins, and I will be clean; wash me, and I will be whiter than snow.*

RAPE

Where is God when rape happens? Doesn't he care enough to prevent it?

PSALM 10:17 | *LORD, you know the hopes of the helpless. Surely you will hear their cries and comfort them.*

PSALM 55:17 | *Morning, noon, and night I cry out in my distress, and the LORD hears my voice.*

PSALM 118:5 | *In my distress I prayed to the LORD, and the LORD answered me and set me free.*

PSALM 119:76 | *Let your unfailing love comfort me, just as you promised me, your servant.*

It is hard to know why God allows this kind of tragedy to enter a woman's life, especially when she's been faithful to him. But you can know that God hurts deeply with a rape victim and loves her more than she'll ever know. God didn't create sin and evil, nor does he condone it. As long as people live on this earth, their sinful nature will cause them to do sinful and evil acts. God has chosen to allow sin to run its course for now, but that will not be the case forever. He promises a future place—heaven—where sin and evil will never, ever exist again. In the meantime, he will comfort her and give her the strength to work through her pain.

GENESIS 37:28 | *When the Ishmaelites, who were Midianite traders, came by, Joseph's brothers pulled him out of the cistern and sold him to them for twenty pieces of silver.*

Sometimes the things that happen are results of the sins of others.

JOHN 9:2-3 | *"Rabbi," his disciples asked him, "why was this man born blind? Was it because of his own sins or his parents' sins?" "It was not because of his sins or his parents' sins," Jesus answered.*

Sometimes the suffering that comes is not the victim's fault, as is the case with rape.

What is the Lord's response to rape?

PSALM 11:5 | *The LORD examines both the righteous and the wicked. He hates those who love violence.*

PSALM 12:5 | *The LORD [said], "I have seen violence done to the helpless, and I have heard the groans of the poor. Now I will rise up to rescue them, as they have longed for me to do."*

God hates all violence, and he hates it when his loved ones suffer at the hands of evil people. God sees all that happens, and he will remember those who have acted violently toward others and will judge them accordingly.

PSALM 118:5 | *In my distress I prayed to the LORD, and the LORD answered me and set me free.*

God has a special place in his heart for those who are abused, oppressed, or victims of violence, and he gives them an extra measure of comfort and healing.

Does the victim of a rape share the blame for the crime?

DEUTERONOMY 22:25-26 | *If the man meets the engaged woman out in the country, and he rapes her, then only the man must die. Do nothing to the young woman; she has committed no crime worthy of death. She is as innocent as a murder victim.*

PROVERBS 16:29 | *Violent people mislead their companions, leading them down a harmful path.*

PROVERBS 24:2 | *[Evil people's] hearts plot violence, and their words always stir up trouble.*

Rape is a violent act against an innocent victim. There is no excuse for such a terrible crime. A rape victim does not share the blame and does not have to feel guilty.

How can a rape victim let go of feelings of anger and hatred?

2 SAMUEL 13:11-12, 14-15, 22, 29 | *As she was feeding him, he grabbed her and demanded, "Come to bed with me, my darling sister." "No, my brother!" she cried. "Don't be foolish! Don't do this to me! Such wicked things aren't done in Israel." . . . But Amnon wouldn't listen to her, and since he was stronger than she was, he raped her. Then suddenly Amnon's love turned to hate. . . . [Absalom] hated Amnon deeply because of what he had done to his sister. . . . So at Absalom's signal they murdered Amnon.*

PSALM 37:8 | *Stop being angry! Turn from your rage! Do not lose your temper—it only leads to harm.*

EPHESIANS 4:31-32 | *Get rid of all bitterness, rage, anger, harsh words, and slander, as well as all types of evil behavior. Instead, be kind to each other, tenderhearted, forgiving one another, just as God through Christ has forgiven you.*

If a rape victim fills her heart and mind with God and his good things, she will empty her heart and mind of anger, hatred, and thoughts of revenge, which only continue the cycle of hatred and violence.

How can the answer to anger possibly be forgiveness?

MATTHEW 5:44 | *Love your enemies! Pray for those who persecute you!*

MATTHEW 18:21-22 | *Peter came to [Jesus] and asked, "Lord, how often should I forgive someone who sins against me? Seven times?" "No, not seven times," Jesus replied, "but seventy times seven!"*

MARK 11:25 | *When you are praying, first forgive anyone you are holding a grudge against, so that your Father in heaven will forgive your sins, too.*

ROMANS 12:21 | *Don't let evil conquer you, but conquer evil by doing good.*

Christ forgave those who crucified him. There is nothing harder—or more healing—than forgiving someone who has greatly wronged another. The rapist should still have to face the consequences and punishment for his actions, but the act of forgiveness frees the victim to move on with her life.

Promise from God REVELATION 21:4 | *[God] will wipe every tear from their eyes, and there will be no more death or sorrow or crying or pain. All these things are gone forever.*

RECONCILIATION

What does the Bible say about reconciliation between people?

MATTHEW 5:23-24 | *If you are presenting a sacrifice at the altar in the Temple and you suddenly remember that someone has something against you, leave your sacrifice there at the altar.*

Go and be reconciled to that person. Then come and offer your sacrifice to God.

Being reconciled with other people is important to God because it demonstrates a humble and forgiving spirit.

MATTHEW 5:25-26 | *When you are on the way to court with your adversary, settle your differences quickly. Otherwise, your accuser may hand you over to the judge, who will hand you over to an officer, and you will be thrown into prison. And if that happens, you surely won't be free again until you have paid the last penny.*

Working toward reconciliation with others is important to your health and peace of mind.

MATTHEW 18:15 | *If another believer sins against you, go privately and point out the offense. If the other person listens and confesses it, you have won that person back.*

God wants you to resolve your differences with others because doing so promotes unity.

EPHESIANS 2:14 | *Christ himself has brought peace to us. He united Jews and Gentiles into one people when, in his own body on the cross, he broke down the wall of hostility that separated us.*

God, through Christ, has made a way for groups at enmity with one another to make peace and be fully reconciled.

What does it mean to be reconciled to God?

ISAIAH 53:5 | *He was pierced for our rebellion, crushed for our sins. He was beaten so we could be whole. He was whipped so we could be healed.*

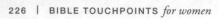

ROMANS 5:10 | *Since our friendship with God was restored by the death of his Son while we were still his enemies, we will certainly be saved through the life of his Son.*

EPHESIANS 2:13 | *You have been united with Christ Jesus. Once you were far away from God, but now you have been brought near to him through the blood of Christ.*

COLOSSIANS 1:20-21 | *Through [Christ] God reconciled everything to himself. He made peace with everything in heaven and on earth by means of Christ's blood on the cross. This includes you who were once far away from God.*

COLOSSIANS 2:14 | *[God] canceled the record of the charges against us and took it away by nailing it to the cross.*

One of the most fundamental truths taught in the Bible is that you, along with all people, were born with a sinful nature, and sin separates you from God. If you want a personal relationship with him, you must be reconciled to him, and that begins with the recognition that without the work of Jesus Christ on the cross, you cannot approach God. He chose to have his Son, Jesus, take your punishment so you could approach God. Accept God's gift of bridging the gap so you can be reconciled to him and have a relationship with him. This is the greatest gift ever offered—and the only way to be reconciled to God.

ROMANS 5:1 | *We have been made right in God's sight by faith.*

2 CORINTHIANS 5:19-21 | *God was in Christ, reconciling the world to himself, no longer counting people's sins against them. And he gave us this wonderful message of reconciliation. So we are Christ's ambassadors; God is making his appeal through us. We speak for Christ when we plead, "Come back to God!" For God made Christ, who never sinned, to be the offering for our sin, so that we could be made right with God through Christ.*

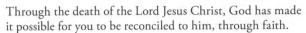

Through the death of the Lord Jesus Christ, God has made it possible for you to be reconciled to him, through faith.

Promise from God   JEREMIAH 3:22 | *"My wayward children," says the LORD, "come back to me, and I will heal your wayward hearts."*

REGRETS

How can I deal with the regrets in my life?

2 CORINTHIANS 5:17 | *Anyone who belongs to Christ has become a new person. The old life is gone; a new life has begun!*

When you come to faith in Jesus, he forgives your sins—all of them. Your past is forgotten to him, and he gives you a fresh start. You may still have to live with the consequences of your sins, but because God has forgiven you completely, you can move forward without any of the tremendous guilt that can accompany regret.

PSALM 51:1, 12 | *Have mercy on me, O God, because of your unfailing love. Because of your great compassion, blot out the stain of my sins. . . . Restore to me the joy of your salvation, and make me willing to obey you.*

Because God no longer holds your sins against you, you no longer have to hold them against yourself. Now you can be free from self-condemnation.

EZEKIEL 6:9-10 | *At last they will hate themselves for all their detestable sins. They will know that I alone am the LORD.*

Ask yourself what God may be communicating through your regrets. God sometimes uses brokenness and remorse

to bring spiritual insight and growth. Regrets that drive you to God are redemptive.

PHILIPPIANS 3:13 | *I focus on this one thing: Forgetting the past and looking forward to what lies ahead.*

Focus on God, who controls the future, not on regrets of the past. The past is over, so don't live a "what if" life of regret, feeling angry at yourself for what you did and bitter toward God for allowing you to do it. God doesn't cause regrets; he washes them away when you ask him to walk with you into the future.

In the future, how can I avoid regrets?

MATTHEW 7:12 | *Do to others whatever you would like them to do to you. This is the essence of all that is taught in the law and the prophets.*

When you treat others the way you like to be treated, you will have no regrets.

1 TIMOTHY 1:19 | *Cling to your faith in Christ, and keep your conscience clear. For some people have deliberately violated their consciences; as a result, their faith has been shipwrecked.*

HEBREWS 13:18 | *Pray for us, for our conscience is clear and we want to live honorably in everything we do.*

Follow your conscience and always do what is right. This will keep you from getting into situations you will later regret.

Promise from God 2 CORINTHIANS 7:10 | *The kind of sorrow God wants us to experience leads us away from sin and results in salvation. There's no regret for that kind of sorrow. But worldly sorrow, which lacks repentance, results in spiritual death.*

RELATIONSHIPS

See **FRIENDSHIP**.

REMEMBERING

How can remembering God help me in my spiritual walk?

NEHEMIAH 4:14 | *As I looked over the situation, I called together the nobles and the rest of the people and said to them, "Don't be afraid of the enemy! Remember the Lord, who is great and glorious, and fight for your brothers, your sons, your daughters, your wives, and your homes!"*

Remember God as the One who helps you fight and win life's battles. Remembering that he is working through you to accomplish his purposes and defeat sin's grip will help you confidently fight your battles without fear.

JONAH 2:7 | *As my life was slipping away, I remembered the LORD. And my earnest prayer went out to you in your holy Temple.*

When you're ready to give up, remembering God as the source of hope will keep you from quitting.

DEUTERONOMY 8:11, 14 | *Beware that in your plenty you do not forget the LORD your God and disobey his commands, regulations, and decrees that I am giving you today. . . . Do not become proud at that time and forget the LORD your God, who rescued you from slavery in the land of Egypt.*

Remembering God when you have plenty will keep you humble, because he blessed you with it. Remembering

God's goodness can help you wait patiently when times are hard.

What are some specific times I can remember God?

EXODUS 31:13 | *[The Lord said,] "Be careful to keep my Sabbath day, for the Sabbath is a sign of the covenant between me and you from generation to generation. It is given so you may know that I am the Lord, who makes you holy."*

As you rest on the Lord's Day, remember him. Thank him for understanding your need to rest and play, and appreciate his blessings.

PSALM 63:6 | *I lie awake thinking of you, meditating on you through the night.*

Remember God day and night. Meditate on him and his great love for you.

GENESIS 9:16 | *[God said,] "When I see the rainbow in the clouds, I will remember the eternal covenant between God and every living creature on earth."*

When you see a rainbow, remember God's promises. Reflecting on how God has kept his promises in the past can help you trust him to fulfill his promises in the future.

LUKE 22:19 | *[Jesus] took some bread and gave thanks to God for it. Then he broke it in pieces and gave it to the disciples, saying, "This is my body, which is given for you. Do this to remember me."*

When you participate in Communion, remember Jesus' sacrifice for you. Meditating on what Jesus gave up for you will help you live with a grateful heart.

2 PETER 1:12-13 | *[Peter said,] "I will always remind you about these things—even though you already know them and are standing firm in the truth you have been taught. And it is only right that I should keep on reminding you as long as I live."*

When you talk about God with others, you remember his blessings together.

2 PETER 3:1-2 | *[Peter said,] "I have tried to stimulate your wholesome thinking and refresh your memory. I want you to remember what the holy prophets said long ago and what our Lord and Savior commanded through your apostles."*

Reading God's Word helps you remember who he is and what he has done for his faithful followers throughout history.

ESTHER 9:28 | *These days would be remembered and kept from generation to generation and celebrated by every family throughout the provinces and cities of the empire. This Festival of Purim would never cease to be celebrated among the Jews, nor would the memory of what happened ever die out among their descendants.*

Celebrating special days and special objects associated with God's blessings will remind you of God's past blessings and help you anticipate his blessings in the future, too.

Promise from God PSALM 78:4 | *We will not hide these truths from our children; we will tell the next generation about the glorious deeds of the LORD, about his power and his mighty wonders.*

RENEWAL

My life is a mess, and I feel like I need to start over again. How can I experience renewal?

JEREMIAH 31:18 | *You disciplined me severely, like a calf that needs training for the yoke. Turn me again to you and restore me, for you alone are the LORD my God.*

If you truly want to change, your heart is ready for the renewal that only God's Spirit can bring.

ACTS 3:19 | *Repent of your sins and turn to God, so that your sins may be wiped away.*

EPHESIANS 4:22-24 | *Throw off your old sinful nature and your former way of life, which is corrupted by lust and deception. Instead, let the Spirit renew your thoughts and attitudes. Put on your new nature, created to be like God—truly righteous and holy.*

Sometimes you are weary because you are clinging to sin and disobedience. If this is the case, confess your sins, and let God cleanse your heart and life. He promises to give you a fresh, new start.

PSALM 51:10 | *Create in me a clean heart, O God. Renew a loyal spirit within me.*

EZEKIEL 36:26-27 | *[The sovereign Lord said,] "I will give you a new heart, and I will put a new spirit in you. I will take out your stony, stubborn heart and give you a tender, responsive heart. And I will put my Spirit in you so that you will follow my decrees and be careful to obey my regulations."*

COLOSSIANS 3:10 | *Put on your new nature, and be renewed as you learn to know your Creator and become like him.*

Renewal comes with the gift of a new heart from the Holy Spirit. God will change everything about you if you let him.

In what ways does God renew me?

PSALM 19:7 | *The instructions of the LORD are perfect, reviving the soul. The decrees of the LORD are trustworthy, making wise the simple.*

God revives your soul by the safety of the boundaries he gives you.

PSALM 119:25 | *I lie in the dust; revive me by your word.*

God revives you by the inspiration, comfort, and encouragement of his Word.

PSALM 23:3 | *He renews my strength. He guides me along right paths, bringing honor to his name.*

God renews your strength and guides you on safe pathways.

PSALM 94:19 | *When doubts filled my mind, your comfort gave me renewed hope and cheer.*

God renews your hope with his comfort.

PSALM 119:40, 93 | *I long to obey your commandments! Renew my life with your goodness. . . . I will never forget your commandments, for by them you give me life.*

God restores your joy and health with his goodness as you obey him.

2 CORINTHIANS 4:16 | *We never give up. Though our bodies are dying, our spirits are being renewed every day.*

God renews your spirit in spite of your physical troubles.

Promise from God PSALM 23:3 | *[The Lord] renews my strength. He guides me along right paths, bringing honor to his name.*

REPENTANCE

Why is repentance necessary?

LEVITICUS 26:40 | *[The Lord said,] "At last my people will confess their sins and the sins of their ancestors for betraying me and being hostile toward me."*

You need to repent because you have sinned and are hostile toward God.

2 CHRONICLES 30:9 | *The LORD your God is gracious and merciful. If you return to him, he will not continue to turn his face from you.*

Repentance is necessary for an ongoing relationship with God. Turn away from anything that is preventing you from worshiping and obeying God wholeheartedly.

PROVERBS 28:13 | *People who conceal their sins will not prosper, but if they confess and turn from them, they will receive mercy.*

ISAIAH 55:7 | *Let the wicked change their ways and banish the very thought of doing wrong. Let them turn to the LORD that he may have mercy on them. Yes, turn to our God, for he will forgive generously.*

JEREMIAH 3:12 | *The LORD says: "O Israel, my faithless people, come home to me again, for I am merciful. I will not be angry with you forever."*

Repentance is your only hope of receiving God's mercy. Those who refuse to see and admit their sins can't be forgiven for them and have placed themselves outside God's mercy and blessing.

EZEKIEL 18:30-32 | *I will judge each of you, O people of Israel, according to your actions, says the Sovereign LORD. Repent, and turn from your sins. Don't let them destroy you! Put all your rebellion behind you, and find yourselves a new heart and a new spirit. For why should you die, O people of Israel? I don't want you to die, says the Sovereign LORD. Turn back and live!*

EZEKIEL 33:11 | *As surely as I live, says the Sovereign LORD, I take no pleasure in the death of wicked people. I only want them to turn from their wicked ways so they can live. Turn! Turn from your wickedness, O people of Israel! Why should you die?*

Repentance allows you to receive a new life from God— literally, a life where the very Spirit of God lives within you.

MATTHEW 3:2 | *Repent of your sins and turn to God, for the Kingdom of Heaven is near.*

LUKE 24:47 | *There is forgiveness of sins for all who repent.*

ACTS 2:37-38 | *Peter's words pierced [the people's] hearts, and they said to him and to the other apostles, "Brothers, what should we do?" Peter replied, "Each of you must repent of your sins and turn to God, and be baptized in the name of Jesus Christ for the forgiveness of your sins. Then you will receive the gift of the Holy Spirit."*

Repentance allows you to receive forgiveness for your sin. If you are sincere when you come to God and ask him humbly, he will forgive your sin.

MATTHEW 11:20, 23 | *Then Jesus began to denounce the towns where he had done so many of his miracles, because they hadn't repented of their sins and turned to God. . . . "And you people of Capernaum, will you be honored in heaven? No, you will go down to the place of the dead."*

Refusing to turn away from your sins will bring God's judgment.

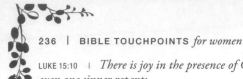

LUKE 15:10 | *There is joy in the presence of God's angels when even one sinner repents.*

All heaven rejoices when you repent.

Promise from God 2 CHRONICLES 7:14 | *[The Lord said,] "If my people who are called by my name will humble themselves and pray and seek my face and turn from their wicked ways, I will hear from heaven and will forgive their sins and restore their land."*

RESENTMENT

What causes feelings of resentment?

2 SAMUEL 6:16 | *As the Ark of the LORD entered the City of David, Michal, the daughter of Saul, looked down from her window. When she saw King David leaping and dancing before the LORD, she was filled with contempt for him.*

The inability to respect someone's actions or behaviors (even when they are good) can cause resentment.

GENESIS 27:36 | *Esau exclaimed, "No wonder his name is Jacob, for now he has cheated me twice. First he took my rights as the firstborn, and now he has stolen my blessing. Oh, haven't you saved even one blessing for me?"*

Being deceived can cause resentment.

GENESIS 4:3-5, 8 | *When it was time for the harvest, Cain presented some of his crops as a gift to the LORD. Abel also brought a gift—the best of the firstborn lambs from his flock. The LORD accepted Abel and his gift, but he did not accept Cain and his gift. This made Cain very angry, and he looked*

dejected. . . . While they were in the field, Cain attacked his brother, Abel, and killed him.

Jealousy can cause resentment.

LUKE 15:27-30 | *"Your brother is back," he was told, "and your father has killed the fattened calf. We are celebrating because of his safe return." The older brother was angry and wouldn't go in. His father came out and begged him, but he replied, "All these years I've slaved for you and never once refused to do a single thing you told me to. And in all that time you never gave me even one young goat for a feast with my friends. Yet when this son of yours comes back after squandering your money on prostitutes, you celebrate by killing the fattened calf!"*

Feeling left out or unappreciated can cause resentment.

GENESIS 37:2-4 | *This is the account of Jacob and his family. When Joseph was seventeen years old, he often tended his father's flocks. He worked for his half brothers, the sons of his father's wives Bilhah and Zilpah. But Joseph reported to his father some of the bad things his brothers were doing. Jacob loved Joseph more than any of his other children because Joseph had been born to him in his old age. So one day Jacob had a special gift made for Joseph—a beautiful robe. But his brothers hated Joseph because their father loved him more than the rest of them. They couldn't say a kind word to him.*

Favoritism can cause resentment.

How do I handle my feelings of resentment?

PROVERBS 10:12 | *Hatred stirs up quarrels, but love makes up for all offenses.*

MARK 11:25 | *When you are praying, first forgive anyone you are holding a grudge against, so that your Father in heaven will forgive your sins, too.*

EPHESIANS 4:26-27, 31-32 | *"Don't sin by letting anger control you." Don't let the sun go down while you are still angry, for anger gives a foothold to the devil. . . . Get rid of all bitterness, rage, anger, harsh words, and slander, as well as all types of evil behavior. Instead, be kind to each other, tenderhearted, forgiving one another, just as God through Christ has forgiven you.*

1 THESSALONIANS 5:15 | *See that no one pays back evil for evil, but always try to do good to each other and to all people.*

JAMES 5:9 | *Don't grumble about each other, brothers and sisters, or you will be judged. For look—the Judge is standing at the door!*

Only love and forgiveness are strong enough to overcome feelings of resentment. Pray for God's strength to love and forgive until it forces the resentment from your heart. This is an area where you can demonstrate to the world that God's power can make a difference.

Promise from God MARK 11:25 | *When you are praying, first forgive anyone you are holding a grudge against, so that your Father in heaven will forgive your sins, too.*

RESPECT

How can I show respect to God?

LEVITICUS 19:30 | *Keep my Sabbath days of rest, and show reverence toward my sanctuary. I am the LORD.*

DEUTERONOMY 10:12 | *What does the LORD your God require of you? He requires only that you fear the LORD your God, and live in a way that pleases him, and love him and serve him with all your heart and soul.*

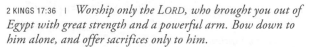

2 KINGS 17:36 | *Worship only the LORD, who brought you out of Egypt with great strength and a powerful arm. Bow down to him alone, and offer sacrifices only to him.*

PSALM 96:7-9 | *O nations of the world, recognize the LORD; recognize that the LORD is glorious and strong. Give to the LORD the glory he deserves! Bring your offering and come into his courts. Worship the LORD in all his holy splendor. Let all the earth tremble before him.*

HEBREWS 12:28-29 | *Since we are receiving a Kingdom that is unshakable, let us be thankful and please God by worshiping him with holy fear and awe. For our God is a devouring fire.*

We should show our respect for God by serving and worshiping him with reverence.

PSALM 22:23 | *Praise the LORD, all you who fear him! Honor him, all you descendants of Jacob! Show him reverence, all you descendants of Israel!*

ISAIAH 33:13 | *[The Lord said,] "You that are near, acknowledge my might!"*

REVELATION 19:5 | *Praise our God, all his servants, all who fear him, from the least to the greatest.*

Praising God for who he is and what he has done shows respect for him.

ECCLESIASTES 5:1 | *As you enter the house of God, keep your ears open and your mouth shut.*

HABAKKUK 2:20 | *The LORD is in his holy Temple. Let all the earth be silent before him.*

ZEPHANIAH 1:7 | *Stand in silence in the presence of the Sovereign LORD.*

Keeping silent in God's presence shows respect for him.

EXODUS 20:20 | *"Don't be afraid," Moses [said], "for God has come in this way to test you, and so that your fear of him will keep you from sinning!"*

Your reverence for God should keep you from sinning.

LEVITICUS 22:32 | *Do not bring shame on my holy name, for I will display my holiness among the people of Israel. I am the LORD who makes you holy.*

Respect for God means you show reverence for his name.

PSALM 115:11 | *All you who fear the LORD, trust the LORD! He is your helper and your shield.*

When we trust in God, we show that we truly respect him.

ECCLESIASTES 12:13 | *Fear God and obey his commands, for this is everyone's duty.*

Obedience to God is a way to respect him.

2 CHRONICLES 19:6 | *Always think carefully before pronouncing judgment. Remember that you do not judge to please people but to please the LORD.*

NEHEMIAH 5:15 | *[Nehemiah said,] "The former governors, in contrast, had laid heavy burdens on the people, demanding a daily ration of food and wine, besides forty pieces of silver. Even their assistants took advantage of the people. But because I feared God, I did not act that way."*

When you truly respect God, you treat other people with fairness and justice.

ACTS 10:2 | *He was a devout, God-fearing man, as was everyone in his household. He gave generously to the poor and prayed regularly to God.*

Generous giving is a way to show your reverence for God.

Promise from God PSALM 33:18 | *The LORD watches over those who fear him, those who rely on his unfailing love.*

RIGHTEOUSNESS

What is righteousness?

GENESIS 6:9 | *Noah was a righteous man, the only blameless person living on earth at the time, and he walked in close fellowship with God.*

JOB 1:1 | *There once was a man named Job who lived in the land of Uz. He was blameless—a man of complete integrity. He feared God and stayed away from evil.*

ROMANS 4:3 | *The Scriptures tell us, "Abraham believed God, and God counted him as righteous because of his faith."*

Righteousness is consistently following God's Word and will, being forgiven of sin, walking with God daily, having an unwavering faith in God and his promises, loving him deeply, demonstrating persistent integrity, and avoiding evil. When you sincerely work at this kind of life, God calls you "blameless." Because he has forgiven your sins, he sees you as though you have no sin in you.

How can I be considered righteous?

ROMANS 1:17 | *This Good News tells us how God makes us right in his sight. This is accomplished from start to finish by faith. As the Scriptures say, "It is through faith that a righteous person has life."*

ROMANS 3:22 | *We are made right with God by placing our faith in Jesus Christ. And this is true for everyone who believes, no matter who we are.*

ROMANS 5:1-2 | *Since we have been made right in God's sight by faith, we have peace with God because of what Jesus Christ our Lord has done for us. Because of our faith, Christ has brought us into this place of undeserved privilege where we now stand, and we confidently and joyfully look forward to sharing God's glory.*

ROMANS 10:10 | *It is by believing in your heart that you are made right with God, and it is by confessing with your mouth that you are saved.*

2 CORINTHIANS 5:21 | *God made Christ, who never sinned, to be the offering for our sin, so that we could be made right with God through Christ.*

PHILIPPIANS 3:9 | *I no longer count on my own righteousness through obeying the law; rather, I become righteous through faith in Christ. For God's way of making us right with himself depends on faith.*

You are considered righteous before God when you trust in Jesus Christ to save you from the punishment you deserve for your sins.

How can I pursue and practice righteousness?

PROVERBS 21:21 | *Whoever pursues righteousness and unfailing love will find life, righteousness, and honor.*

MATTHEW 25:37-40 | *Then these righteous ones will reply, "Lord, when did we ever see you hungry and feed you? Or thirsty and give you something to drink? Or a stranger and show you hospitality? Or naked and give you clothing? When did we ever see you sick or in prison and visit you?" And the King will say, "I tell you the truth, when you did it to one of the least of these my brothers and sisters, you were doing it to me!"*

1 TIMOTHY 6:11 | *You, Timothy, are a man of God; so run from all these evil things. Pursue righteousness and a godly life, along with faith, love, perseverance, and gentleness.*

1 JOHN 3:7 | *When people do what is right, it shows that they are righteous, even as Christ is righteous.*

Do your best to follow Jesus' example of living. This means pursuing that which Jesus saw as important.

Promise from God ROMANS 3:22 | *We are made right with God by placing our faith in Jesus Christ. And this is true for everyone who believes, no matter who we are.*

ROUTINE

See **BOREDOM.**

SALVATION

What does it mean to be saved?

PSALM 103:12 | *He has removed our sins as far from us as the east is from the west.*

ROMANS 3:24 | *God, with undeserved kindness, declares that we are righteous.*

ROMANS 4:7-8 | *Oh, what joy for those whose disobedience is forgiven, whose sins are put out of sight. Yes, what joy for those whose record the LORD has cleared of sin.*

Being saved means your sins have been completely forgiven by God. They no longer count against you, and you are spared from an eternal death sentence. Instead, you are

given the free gift of eternal life. Being saved does not spare you from earthly troubles, but it does save you from eternal punishment.

PSALM 51:9-10 | *Remove the stain of my guilt. Create in me a clean heart, O God.*

Being saved means the stain of guilt has been washed away. Guilt not only *appears* to be gone, it *is* gone! You are given a clean slate!

1 PETER 2:10 | *Once you received no mercy; now you have received God's mercy.*

Being saved means you have received mercy from God.

JOHN 10:27-29 | *[Jesus said,] "My sheep listen to my voice; I know them, and they follow me. I give them eternal life, and they will never perish. No one can snatch them away from me, for my Father has given them to me, and he is more powerful than anyone else. No one can snatch them from the Father's hand."*

Being saved means you are assured of living forever in heaven. You will live on a new earth where there will no longer be sin, pain, or suffering (see Revelation 21:4).

How can I be saved?

ROMANS 10:13 | *Everyone who calls on the name of the LORD will be saved.*

God's Word promises salvation to those who ask Jesus to forgive their sins. Call out to him and tell him you need him to save you. He promises he will.

JOHN 3:16 | *God loved the world so much that he gave his one and only Son, so that everyone who believes in him will not perish but have eternal life.*

JOHN 5:24 | *[Jesus said,] "I tell you the truth, those who listen to my message and believe in God who sent me have eternal life."*

Jesus himself promised that if you believe in him, you will be saved.

Is salvation available to anyone?

JOHN 3:16 | *[Jesus said,] "God loved the world so much that he gave his one and only Son, so that everyone who believes in him will not perish but have eternal life."*

Jesus promised that those who believe in him will be saved. All you have to do is accept what Jesus did for you.

HEBREWS 9:27 | *Each person is destined to die once and after that comes judgment.*

Salvation is available to all, but a time will come when it will be too late to receive it.

How can I be sure of my salvation?

JOHN 1:12 | *To all who believed him and accepted him, he gave the right to become children of God.*

Just as a child cannot be "un-born," God's children— those who have believed in Jesus Christ—cannot be "un-born-again."

ROMANS 8:14 | *All who are led by the Spirit of God are children of God.*

The Holy Spirit takes up residence in your heart only when you are God's child.

How does salvation affect my daily life?

2 CORINTHIANS 5:17 | *Anyone who belongs to Christ has become a new person. The old life is gone; a new life has begun!*

Salvation gives you hope not only for eternity but also for today. You have been given a new life and new power for living.

ROMANS 6:6-8 | *We know that our old sinful selves were crucified with Christ so that sin might lose its power in our lives. We are no longer slaves to sin. For when we died with Christ we were set free from the power of sin. And since we died with Christ, we know we will also live with him.*

Salvation brings you freedom from the power of sin and freedom to live a new life.

ROMANS 5:1 | *Since we have been made right in God's sight by faith, we have peace with God because of what Jesus Christ our Lord has done for us.*

Salvation brings you peace with God.

EPHESIANS 2:10 | *[God] has created us anew in Christ Jesus, so we can do the good things he planned for us long ago.*

God created you for a purpose. Salvation enables you to fulfill that purpose by the power of God at work within you.

Promise from God ROMANS 10:9 | *If you confess with your mouth that Jesus is Lord and believe in your heart that God raised him from the dead, you will be saved.*

SATISFACTION

See **CONTENTMENT.**

SECURITY

With so much change and instability in the world, how can my faith help me feel secure?

PSALM 40:1-2 | *I waited patiently for the LORD to help me, and he turned to me and heard my cry. He lifted me out of the pit of despair, out of the mud and the mire. He set my feet on solid ground and steadied me as I walked along.*

PSALM 125:1 | *Those who trust in the LORD are as secure as Mount Zion; they will not be defeated but will endure forever.*

PROVERBS 1:33 | *All who listen to [wisdom] will live in peace, untroubled by fear of harm.*

MATTHEW 7:24-25 | *[Jesus said,] "Anyone who listens to my teaching and follows it is wise, like a person who builds a house on solid rock. Though the rain comes in torrents and the floodwaters rise and the winds beat against that house, it won't collapse because it is built on bedrock."*

When you build your faith day by day upon the truths of God's Word, you build a solid foundation that will not crack under the world's pressure. Upon that foundation you begin building your place in the world. When life's battles come your way, some may be strong enough to knock down some walls, but your foundation remains strong, steady, and not easily moved because God's truths are eternal. A secure foundation gives you greater courage to face whatever troubles come your way.

How does God provide security?

PSALM 3:3 | *You, O LORD, are a shield around me; you are my glory, the one who holds my head high.*

PSALM 9:9-10 | *The LORD is a shelter for the oppressed, a refuge in times of trouble. Those who know your name trust in you, for you, O LORD, do not abandon those who search for you.*

PSALM 46:1-3 | *God is our refuge and strength, always ready to help in times of trouble. So we will not fear when earthquakes come and the mountains crumble into the sea. Let the oceans roar and foam. Let the mountains tremble as the waters surge!*

PSALM 57:1 | *Have mercy on me, O God, have mercy! I look to you for protection. I will hide beneath the shadow of your wings until the danger passes by.*

PSALM 63:8 | *I cling to you; your strong right hand holds me securely.*

PROVERBS 14:26 | *Those who fear the LORD are secure; he will be a refuge for their children.*

PROVERBS 18:10 | *The name of the LORD is a strong fortress; the godly run to him and are safe.*

No matter how much the battles and storms of life batter you, you are secure for eternity when you put your faith in God. Nothing can ever separate you from his eternal presence and security.

How can I feel secure about the future?

ROMANS 8:38-39 | *Nothing can ever separate us from God's love. Neither death nor life, neither angels nor demons, neither our fears for today nor our worries about tomorrow—not even the powers of hell can separate us from God's love. No power in the sky above or in the earth below—indeed, nothing in all creation will ever be able to separate us from the love of God that is revealed in Christ Jesus our Lord.*

2 CORINTHIANS 1:22 | *[God] has identified us as his own by placing the Holy Spirit in our hearts as the first installment that guarantees everything he has promised us.*

TITUS 3:7 | *Because of [God's] grace he declared us righteous and gave us confidence that we will inherit eternal life.*

1 PETER 1:4-5 | *We have a priceless inheritance—an inheritance that is kept in heaven for you, pure and undefiled, beyond the reach of change and decay. And through your faith, God is protecting you by his power until you receive this salvation, which is ready to be revealed on the last day for all to see.*

1 JOHN 5:18 | *We know that God's children do not make a practice of sinning, for God's Son holds them securely, and the evil one cannot touch them.*

REVELATION 3:5 | *All who are victorious will be clothed in white. I will never erase their names from the Book of Life, but I will announce before my Father and his angels that they are mine.*

The most powerful security in the world is knowing that nothing can separate you from God's love.

Promise from God PROVERBS 14:26 | *Those who fear the LORD are secure; he will be a refuge for their children.*

SELF-ESTEEM

See **WORTH/WORTHINESS.**

SERVICE

What are some requirements for serving God?

PSALM 2:11 | *Serve the LORD with reverent fear, and rejoice with trembling.*

A joyful heart and reverent awe of God.

PSALM 101:6 | *I will search for faithful people to be my companions. Only those who are above reproach will be allowed to serve me.*

A desire to please God and walk in his ways.

MATTHEW 6:24 | *No one can serve two masters. For you will hate one and love the other; you will be devoted to one and despise the other.*

Loyalty to God above all else.

ROMANS 7:6 | *Now we have been released from the law, for we died to it and are no longer captive to its power. Now we can serve God, not in the old way of obeying the letter of the law, but in the new way of living in the Spirit.*

A desire to be led by the Holy Spirit.

ACTS 20:19 | *I have done the Lord's work humbly and with many tears.*

Humility.

GALATIANS 5:13 | *You have been called to live in freedom, my brothers and sisters. But don't use your freedom to satisfy your sinful nature. Instead, use your freedom to serve one another in love.*

Love for others.

How can I serve God today?

JOSHUA 22:5 | *Love the LORD your God, walk in all his ways, obey his commands, hold firmly to him, and serve him with all your heart and all your soul.*

Obey and love God.

JOSHUA 24:15 | *Choose today whom you will serve. . . . As for me and my family, we will serve the LORD.*

Honor God by making your relationship with him your first priority.

1 CORINTHIANS 12:4-5, 7 | *There are different kinds of spiritual gifts, but the same Spirit is the source of them all. There are different kinds of service, but we serve the same Lord. . . . A spiritual gift is given to each of us so we can help each other.*

Exercise your spiritual gifts (see Romans 12:6-8; 1 Corinthians 12:4-11; 1 Peter 4:10-11).

MATTHEW 25:40 | *The King will say, "I tell you the truth, when you did it to one of the least of these my brothers and sisters, you were doing it to me!"*

Demonstrate love and kindness to all people, especially those in need.

ROMANS 12:11 | *Never be lazy, but work hard and serve the Lord enthusiastically.*

Serve with enthusiasm.

How did Jesus serve?

MATTHEW 20:26, 28 | *Whoever wants to be a leader among you must be your servant. . . . For even the Son of Man came not to be served but to serve others and to give his life as a ransom for many.*

Jesus served to the point of sacrificing his very life
for you.

PHILIPPIANS 2:7 | *[Christ Jesus] gave up his divine privileges;
he took the humble position of a slave and was born as a
human being.*

He humbled himself, becoming human so that he could
understand human life, its struggles and temptations.

MATTHEW 20:32 | *When Jesus heard [the blind men shouting],
he stopped and called, "What do you want me to do for you?"*

He made himself available to serve people who needed him.

JOHN 13:5, 14-15 | *[Jesus] began to wash the disciples' feet, drying
them with the towel he had around him. . . . "Since I, your
Lord and Teacher, have washed your feet, you ought to wash
each other's feet. I have given you an example to follow. Do as
I have done to you."*

He washed his disciples' feet. Jesus' greatness and leadership
were shown through this profound and deeply humble act
of service. It was the attitude of his heart that made him a
true servant.

What is meant by having a servant's heart?
How can I have a servant's heart?

PHILIPPIANS 2:5-8 | *You must have the same attitude that Christ
Jesus had. Though he was God, he did not think of equal-
ity with God as something to cling to. Instead, he gave up his
divine privileges; he took the humble position of a slave and was
born as a human being. When he appeared in human form,
he humbled himself in obedience to God and died a criminal's
death on a cross.*

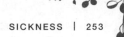

A servant's heart comes through humbling yourself as Jesus did and obediently doing what God wants. The more you obey, the more your heart becomes like Jesus'.

ROMANS 6:13 | *Use your whole body as an instrument to do what is right for the glory of God.*

By submitting yourself to obey Jesus' commands and live by his words, you put your heart in a position ready for heart-felt action.

GENESIS 24:18-20 | *"Yes, my lord," she answered, "have a drink." And she quickly lowered her jug from her shoulder and gave him a drink. When she had given him a drink, she said, "I'll draw water for your camels, too, until they have had enough to drink." So she quickly emptied her jug into the watering trough and ran back to the well to draw water for all his camels.*

Look for opportunities to help those who need you.

LUKE 1:38 | *Mary responded, "I am the Lord's servant. May everything you have said about me come true." And then the angel left her.*

Be willing to be used by God.

Promise from God GALATIANS 5:13 | *You have been called to live in freedom, my brothers and sisters. But don't use your freedom to satisfy your sinful nature. Instead, use your freedom to serve one another in love.*

SICKNESS

See **HEALING; HEALTH.**

SIGNIFICANCE

Do I have to be important for God to use me?

1 CORINTHIANS 1:26-29 | *Few of you were wise in the world's eyes or powerful or wealthy when God called you. Instead, God chose things the world considers foolish in order to shame those who think they are wise. And he chose things that are power-less to shame those who are powerful. God chose things despised by the world, things counted as nothing at all, and used them to bring to nothing what the world considers important. As a result, no one can ever boast in the presence of God.*

Significance in the eyes of the world may be insignificant in God's eyes. Insignificance in the world's eyes may be signifi-cant in God's eyes. God takes joy in using people the world considers "insignificant" to accomplish marvelous things for his Kingdom.

What are some of the most significant things in life?

1 CORINTHIANS 13:2-3 | *If I had the gift of prophecy, and if I understood all of God's secret plans and possessed all knowledge, and if I had such faith that I could move mountains, but didn't love others, I would be nothing. If I gave everything I have to the poor and even sacrificed my body, I could boast about it; but if I didn't love others, I would have gained nothing.*

Loving God and others.

ACTS 20:24 | *My life is worth nothing to me unless I use it for finishing the work assigned me by the Lord Jesus—the work of telling others the Good News about the wonderful grace of God.*

Serving the Lord.

PHILIPPIANS 3:8 | *Everything else is worthless when compared with the infinite value of knowing Christ Jesus my Lord. For his sake I have discarded everything else, counting it all as garbage, so that I could gain Christ.*

Knowing Christ personally.

How can I cope with feelings of insignificance?

PSALM 8:4-5 | *What are mere mortals that you should think about them, human beings that you should care for them? Yet you made them only a little lower than God and crowned them with glory and honor.*

Remember that the Creator of the universe considers you significant.

MATTHEW 10:29-31 | *What is the price of two sparrows—one copper coin? But not a single sparrow can fall to the ground without your Father knowing it. And the very hairs on your head are all numbered. So don't be afraid; you are more valuable to God than a whole flock of sparrows.*

You matter to God. God thinks every event and detail of your life are important.

PSALM 119:37 | *Turn my eyes from worthless things, and give me life through your word.*

Although you may feel insignificant at times, remember that God himself gives you life.

Promise from God PSALM 8:4-5 | *What are mere mortals that you should think about them, human beings that you should care for them? Yet you made them only a little lower than God and crowned them with glory and honor.*

SPIRITUAL WARFARE

What does the Bible say about spiritual warfare?

EPHESIANS 6:11-12 | *Put on all of God's armor so that you will be able to stand firm against all strategies of the devil. For we are not fighting against flesh-and-blood enemies, but against evil rulers and authorities of the unseen world, against mighty powers in this dark world, and against evil spirits in the heavenly places.*

Spiritual warfare is the unseen battle that is being waged for your soul and your Christian testimony. Winning this battle requires preparation—through prayer, unwavering faith, and knowledge of biblical truth—to defeat your spiritual enemy.

1 PETER 5:8 | *Stay alert! Watch out for your great enemy, the devil. He prowls around like a roaring lion, looking for someone to devour.*

You must be alert at all times for the sneak attacks of the devil.

PHILIPPIANS 2:10 | *At the name of Jesus every knee should bow, in heaven and on earth and under the earth.*

JAMES 4:7 | *Resist the devil, and he will flee from you.*

When you resist the devil in the name and power of Jesus, the devil will flee from you. At the name of Jesus, Satan has no power.

MATTHEW 4:1, 3-4 | *Jesus was led by the Spirit into the wilderness to be tempted there by the devil. . . . During that time the devil came and said to him, "If you are the Son of God, tell these stones to become loaves of bread." But Jesus told him, "No! The Scriptures say . . ."*

When under attack by Satan, Jesus relied on the Word of God to combat the lies of his adversary.

Promise from God   EPHESIANS 6:11 | *Put on all of God's armor so that you will be able to stand firm against all strategies of the devil.*

STRESS

What causes stress?

GENESIS 3:6, 23 | *[Eve] took some of the fruit and ate it. Then she gave some to her husband . . . and he ate it, too. . . . So the LORD God banished them from the Garden of Eden.*

2 SAMUEL 11:4; 12:13-14 | *David sent messengers to get [Bathsheba, the wife of Uriah]; and when she came to the palace, he slept with her. . . . David confessed to Nathan, "I have sinned against the LORD." Nathan replied, "Yes, but the LORD has forgiven you, and you won't die for this sin. Nevertheless, because you have shown utter contempt for the LORD by doing this, your child will die."*

LUKE 22:56-57, 61-62 | *[A servant girl] said, "This man was one of Jesus' followers!" But Peter denied it. "Woman," he said, "I don't even know him!" . . . The Lord turned and looked at Peter. . . . And Peter left the courtyard, weeping bitterly.*

Often stress is the result of your own actions. Sin brings the stress of painful consequences.

EXODUS 16:2-3 | *The whole community of Israel complained about Moses and Aaron. "If only the LORD had killed us back in Egypt," they moaned.*

Stress comes when you fail to trust God for help.

JAMES 1:2-4 | *When troubles come your way, consider it an opportunity for great joy. For you know that when your faith is*

tested, your endurance has a chance to grow. So let it grow, for when your endurance is fully developed, you will be perfect and complete, needing nothing.

Adversity and the normal problems of life cause stress.

How can I deal with stress?

PSALM 55:22 | *Give your burdens to the LORD, and he will take care of you. He will not permit the godly to slip and fall.*

JOHN 14:1 | *[Jesus said,] "Don't let your hearts be troubled. Trust in God, and trust also in me."*

The first step in dealing with stress is to bring your burdens to the Lord. Only he can bring true peace of heart and mind. God's availability and promises are effective stress reducers.

2 CORINTHIANS 4:9 | *We are hunted down, but never abandoned by God. We get knocked down, but we are not destroyed.*

GALATIANS 6:9 | *Let's not get tired of doing what is good. At just the right time we will reap a harvest of blessing if we don't give up.*

Keep going! Knowing that God is by your side during times of trouble and stress can help you to not give up.

2 SAMUEL 22:7 | *In my distress I cried out to the LORD; yes, I cried to my God for help. He heard me from his sanctuary; my cry reached his ears.*

PSALM 86:7 | *I will call to you whenever I'm in trouble, and you will answer me.*

Be persistent in prayer.

MATTHEW 11:28-29 | *Jesus said, "Come to me, all of you who are weary and carry heavy burdens, and I will give you rest. Take my yoke upon you. Let me teach you, because I am humble and gentle at heart, and you will find rest for your souls."*

When you allow Jesus to carry your burdens and teach you from his humble and gentle Spirit, you will find your stress melting away, and you will experience peacefulness in your soul instead. Jesus' humility and gentleness counteract the pride and irritability that fuel so much of the conflict and stress in life.

Promise from God ISAIAH 41:10 | *Don't be afraid, for I am with you. Don't be discouraged, for I am your God. I will strengthen you and help you. I will hold you up with my victorious right hand.*

SUBMISSION

What is submission to God?

GENESIS 12:1, 4 | *The LORD had said to Abram, "Leave your native country, your relatives, and your father's family, and go to the land that I will show you." . . . So Abram departed as the LORD had instructed.*

EXODUS 7:6 | *Moses and Aaron did just as the LORD had commanded them.*

MATTHEW 26:42 | *Jesus . . . prayed, "My Father! If this cup cannot be taken away unless I drink it, your will be done."*

JOHN 18:11 | *Jesus said to Peter, "Put your sword back into its sheath. Shall I not drink from the cup of suffering the Father has given me?"*

HEBREWS 5:7-9 | *While Jesus was here on earth, he offered prayers and pleadings, with a loud cry and tears, to the one who could rescue him from death. And God heard his prayers because of his deep reverence for God. Even though Jesus was God's Son, he learned obedience from the things he suffered. In this way, God qualified him as a perfect High Priest, and he became the source of eternal salvation for all those who obey him.*

Submission to God is obedience to him; it is learning to find joy in doing what he commands. Submission involves seeking God's will and following it wholeheartedly out of a genuine love and deep respect for him.

Why is submission important? What are the benefits of submission?

PROVERBS 29:18 | *When people do not accept divine guidance, they run wild. But whoever obeys the law is joyful.*

Submitting yourself to God, your Protector, keeps you from submitting to the destructive forces of evil.

MATTHEW 20:27 | *Whoever wants to be first among you must become your slave.*

HEBREWS 2:9 | *What we do see is Jesus, who was given a position "a little lower than the angels"; and because he suffered death for us, he is now "crowned with glory and honor." Yes, by God's grace, Jesus tasted death for everyone.*

Submission is the way to greatness in God's eyes—the first shall be last and the last first.

To whom should I submit?

ROMANS 6:13 | *Do not let any part of your body become an instrument of evil to serve sin. Instead, give yourselves completely to God,*

for you were dead, but now you have new life. So use your whole body as an instrument to do what is right for the glory of God.

Submit your body to God so he can help you become all he created you to be.

MATTHEW 26:39 | *[Jesus] went on a little farther and bowed with his face to the ground, praying, "My Father! If it is possible, let this cup of suffering be taken away from me. Yet I want your will to be done, not mine."*

Submit yourself to God's will so that you can be connected to God's great plan for you.

HEBREWS 12:9 | *Since we respected our earthly fathers who disciplined us, shouldn't we submit even more to the discipline of the Father of our spirits, and live forever?*

Submit to authority and discipline so that you will be spared from foolish behavior.

EPHESIANS 5:21-22 | *Submit to one another out of reverence for Christ. For wives, this means submit to your husbands as to the Lord.*

Submit to your spouse so that you will build him up and encourage him, which will strengthen your marriage.

HEBREWS 13:17 | *Obey your spiritual leaders, and do what they say. Their work is to watch over your souls, and they are accountable to God. Give them reason to do this with joy.*

Submit to spiritual leaders so they can guide you.

ROMANS 13:1 | *Everyone must submit to governing authorities. For all authority comes from God, and those in positions of authority have been placed there by God.*

TITUS 3:1 | *Remind the believers to submit to the government and its officers. They should be obedient, always ready to do what is good.*

Submit to government, for God gave leaders their authority.

TITUS 2:9-10 | *Slaves must always obey their masters and do their best to please them. They must not talk back or steal, but must show themselves to be entirely trustworthy and good. Then they will make the teaching about God our Savior attractive in every way.*

Submit to your superiors at work, and pray for wisdom for them.

What are some ways to show submission?

ROMANS 12:10 | *Love each other with genuine affection, and take delight in honoring each other.*

Show love and respect to others.

PHILIPPIANS 2:3-4 | *Don't be selfish; don't try to impress others. Be humble, thinking of others as better than yourselves. Don't look out only for your own interests, but take an interest in others, too.*

Be humble toward others, and honor them as you honor yourself.

JAMES 3:17 | *The wisdom from above is first of all pure. It is also peace loving, gentle at all times, and willing to yield to others. It is full of mercy and good deeds. It shows no favoritism and is always sincere.*

Be peace loving and gentle, merciful and full of good deeds.

Promise from God PROVERBS 29:18 | *When people do not accept divine guidance, they run wild. But whoever obeys the law is joyful.*

SUFFERING

Why am I suffering? Doesn't God care about me?

GENESIS 37:28 | *When the Ishmaelites, who were Midianite traders, came by, Joseph's brothers pulled him out of the cistern and sold him to them for twenty pieces of silver.*

JEREMIAH 32:18 | *You show unfailing love to thousands, but you also bring the consequences of one generation's sin upon the next.*

Sometimes you suffer because of the sins of others, not your own sins.

JOHN 9:2-3 | *"Rabbi," his disciples asked him, "why was this man born blind? Was it because of his own sins or his parents' sins?" "It was not because of his sins or his parents' sins," Jesus answered. "This happened so the power of God could be seen in him."*

Sometimes the suffering that comes to you just happens, for no reason you can see. It is how you react to the suffering that matters.

GENESIS 3:6, 23 | *[The woman] saw that the tree was beautiful and its fruit looked delicious. . . . So she took some of the fruit and ate it. . . . So the LORD God banished them from the Garden of Eden.*

LEVITICUS 26:43 | *At last the people will pay for their sins, for they have continually rejected my regulations and despised my decrees.*

PROVERBS 3:11-12 | *My child, don't reject the LORD's discipline, and don't be upset when he corrects you. For the LORD corrects those he loves, just as a father corrects a child in whom he delights.*

Sometimes God sends suffering as punishment for sin. He disciplines you because he loves you and wants to correct you and restore you to him. Thank God for this kind of suffering because his actions to get your attention could save you from even greater consequences later.

DEUTERONOMY 8:2 | *Remember how the LORD your God led you through the wilderness for these forty years, humbling you and testing you to prove your character, and to find out whether or not you would obey his commands.*

Sometimes God tests you with suffering to encourage you to obey him.

1 PETER 4:14 | *Be happy when you are insulted for being a Christian, for then the glorious Spirit of God rests upon you.*

Sometimes your suffering comes because you have taken a stand for Jesus.

JAMES 1:3 | *When your faith is tested, your endurance has a chance to grow.*

Sometimes your suffering is designed to help you grow and mature.

2 TIMOTHY 3:12 | *Everyone who wants to live a godly life in Christ Jesus will suffer persecution.*

The world hates Christ, so when you identify with him, you can expect that the world that inflicted suffering on him will also inflict suffering on you.

Can any good come from suffering?

JOB 5:17-18 | *Consider the joy of those corrected by God! Do not despise the discipline of the Almighty when you sin. For though he wounds, he also bandages. He strikes, but his hands also heal.*

Suffering brings great renewal and healing when it drives you to God.

ROMANS 5:3-4 | *We can rejoice, too, when we run into problems and trials, for we know that they help us develop endurance. And endurance develops strength of character.*

2 CORINTHIANS 1:5 | *The more we suffer for Christ, the more God will shower us with his comfort through Christ.*

2 CORINTHIANS 12:10 | *That's why I take pleasure in my weaknesses, and in the insults, hardships, persecutions, and troubles that I suffer for Christ. For when I am weak, then I am strong.*

2 TIMOTHY 2:10 | *I am willing to endure anything if it will bring salvation and eternal glory in Christ Jesus to those God has chosen.*

HEBREWS 12:11 | *No discipline is enjoyable while it is happening—it's painful! But afterward there will be a peaceful harvest of right living for those who are trained in this way.*

JAMES 1:3-4 | *When your faith is tested, your endurance has a chance to grow. So let it grow, for when your endurance is fully developed, you will be perfect and complete, needing nothing.*

You can endure suffering with patience and great hope when you have the perspective that what you are enduring will work for your good, for Christ's glory, or for the building up of his church.

How do I stay close to God in times of suffering?

PSALM 22:24 | *[The Lord] has not ignored or belittled the suffering of the needy. He has not turned his back on them, but has listened to their cries for help.*

Recognize that God has not abandoned you.

PSALM 126:5-6 | *Those who plant in tears will harvest with shouts of joy. They weep as they go to plant their seed, but they sing as they return with the harvest.*

Recognize that suffering is not forever. In the dark hours of the night of suffering, it is hard to think of a morning of joy and gladness. But tears of suffering water the seeds of joy.

LAMENTATIONS 3:32-33 | *Though [the Lord] brings grief, he also shows compassion because of the greatness of his unfailing love. For he does not enjoy hurting people or causing them sorrow.*

Recognize that God is a loving God and does not enjoy the suffering that comes your way. But his compassion and care will see you through your times of discipline and pain.

MATTHEW 17:12 | *Elijah has already come, but he wasn't recognized, and they chose to abuse him. And in the same way they will also make the Son of Man suffer.*

LUKE 24:26 | *Wasn't it clearly predicted that the Messiah would have to suffer all these things before entering his glory?*

JOHN 3:16 | *God loved the world so much that he gave his one and only Son, so that everyone who believes in him will not perish but have eternal life.*

Recognize that Jesus himself suffered for you. He not only suffered the physical agonies of the Cross but also bore the unthinkable weight of the sins of the world.

ROMANS 8:17-18 | *Since we are his children, we are his heirs. In fact, together with Christ we are heirs of God's glory. But if we are to share his glory, we must also share his suffering. Yet what we suffer now is nothing compared to the glory he will reveal to us later.*

HEBREWS 2:18 | *Since [Jesus] himself has gone through suffering and testing, he is able to help us when we are being tested.*

Recognize that suffering is not forever and will end when those who believe in Jesus are welcomed into heaven.

Promise from God 2 CORINTHIANS 1:3-4 | *All praise to God, the Father of our Lord Jesus Christ. God is our merciful Father and the source of all comfort. He comforts us in all our troubles so that we can comfort others. When they are troubled, we will be able to give them the same comfort God has given us.*

TALKING

See **WORDS**.

TEMPTATION

Is temptation sin?

MATTHEW 4:1 | *Jesus was led by the Spirit into the wilderness to be tempted there by the devil.*

HEBREWS 4:15 | *[Jesus] faced all of the same testings we do, yet he did not sin.*

Jesus was severely tempted, yet he never gave in to temptation. Since Jesus was tempted and remained sinless, we know that being tempted is not the same as sinning. You don't have to feel guilty about the temptations you wrestle with. Rather, you can devote yourself to resisting them.

Does temptation ever come from God?

JAMES 1:13 | *When you are being tempted, do not say, "God is tempting me." God is never tempted to do wrong, and he never tempts anyone else.*

Temptation originates not in the mind of God but in the mind of Satan, who plants it in your heart. Victory over

temptation originates in the mind of God and flows to your heart.

JAMES 1:2 | *When troubles come your way, consider it an opportunity for great joy.*

Although God does not send temptation, he brings good from it by helping you grow stronger through it.

Why is temptation so enticing to me?

GENESIS 3:6 | *[The woman] saw that the tree was beautiful and its fruit looked delicious. . . . So she took some of the fruit and ate it.*

Satan's favorite strategy is to make that which is sinful appear to be desirable and good. In contrast, he also tries to make good look evil. If Satan can make evil look good and good look evil, then your giving in to temptation appears right instead of wrong. You must constantly be aware of the confusion he desires to create in you.

1 KINGS 11:1-3 | *Solomon loved many foreign women. . . . The LORD had clearly instructed the people of Israel, "You must not marry them, because they will turn your hearts to their gods.". . . And in fact, they did turn his heart away from the LORD.*

Often, temptation begins in seemingly harmless pleasure, soon gets out of control, and then progresses to full-blown sin. But the reality is that the kind of pleasure that leads to sin is never harmless. Before you give in to something that seems innocent, take a look at God's Word to see what it says. If Solomon had done this, he would have been reminded that his "pleasure" was really sin. Maybe he would have been convicted enough to stop.

How can I resist temptation?

1 TIMOTHY 4:7-8 | *Do not waste time. . . . Instead, train yourself to be godly. "Physical training is good, but training for godliness is much better, promising benefits in this life and in the life to come."*

To overcome temptation, you need to prepare for it before it presses in on you. Train yourself in the quieter times so that you will have the spiritual wisdom, strength, and commitment to honor God in the face of intense desires and temptations when they come.

GENESIS 39:12 | *She came and grabbed him by his cloak, demanding, "Come on, sleep with me!" Joseph tore himself away . . . [and] ran from the house.*

If possible, remove yourself from the tempting situation. Sometimes you must literally flee.

MATTHEW 6:9, 13 | *Pray like this: . . . Don't let us yield to temptation, but rescue us from the evil one.*

Make resisting temptation a constant focus of prayer.

ECCLESIASTES 4:12 | *A person standing alone can be attacked and defeated, but two can stand back-to-back and conquer. Three are even better, for a triple-braided cord is not easily broken.*

Enlisting a Christian friend as an accountability partner will give you far more spiritual strength than you have on your own.

1 JOHN 5:21 | *Keep away from anything that might take God's place in your hearts.*

Avoid tempting situations and people.

JAMES 4:7 | *Resist the devil, and he will flee from you.*

1 PETER 5:8-9 | *Stay alert! Watch out for your great enemy, the devil. He prowls around like a roaring lion, looking for someone to devour. Stand firm against him, and be strong in your faith.*

The devil has less power than you think. He can tempt you, but he cannot coerce you. He can dangle the bait in front of you, but he cannot force you to take it. You can resist the devil as Jesus did: by responding to the lies of the tempter with the truth of God's Word (see Matthew 4:1-11).

Promise from God 1 CORINTHIANS 10:13 | *The temptations in your life are no different from what others experience. And God is faithful. He will not allow the temptation to be more than you can stand. When you are tempted, he will show you a way out so that you can endure.*

TESTING

How is testing different from temptation?

1 PETER 1:7 | *These trials will show that your faith is genuine. It is being tested as fire tests and purifies gold—though your faith is far more precious than mere gold.*

Satan tempts to destroy your faith; God tests to strengthen and purify it.

JAMES 1:3 | *When your faith is tested, your endurance has a chance to grow.*

Temptations try to make you quit. Testing tries to help you endure and not quit.

What good comes out of being tested?

GENESIS 22:1 | *God tested Abraham's faith.*

Out of testing comes a more committed faith. Just as commercial products are tested to strengthen their performance, God tests your faith to strengthen your resolve so you can accomplish all God wants you to.

JEREMIAH 6:27 | *[The Lord said,] "Jeremiah, I have made you a tester of metals, that you may determine the quality of my people."*

Spiritual testing reveals the impurities in your heart. Once you are able to recognize your sins and shortcomings, you can let God forgive and remove them, making you stronger and more pure.

DEUTERONOMY 13:3 | *The LORD your God is testing you to see if you truly love him with all your heart and soul.*

God's testing results in a deepening of your obedience and love for him.

DEUTERONOMY 8:2 | *Remember how the LORD your God led you through the wilderness for these forty years, humbling you and testing you to prove your character.*

Testing develops maturity of character. Character is strengthened not through ease, but through adversity.

JAMES 1:2-4 | *When troubles come your way, consider it an opportunity for great joy. For you know that when your faith is tested, your endurance has a chance to grow. So let it grow, for when your endurance is fully developed, you will be perfect and complete, needing nothing.*

Testing develops endurance. It trains you to persist to the end rather than give up before you get there.

LUKE 8:13 | *The seeds on the rocky soil represent those who hear the message and receive it with joy. But since they don't have deep roots, they believe for a while, then they fall away when they face temptation.*

Testing reveals the strength of your commitment.

Promise from God JAMES 1:12 | *God blesses those who patiently endure testing and temptation. Afterward they will receive the crown of life that God has promised to those who love him.*

THANKFULNESS

Why is it important to have a thankful attitude?

PSALM 50:23 | *[God said,] "Giving thanks is a sacrifice that truly honors me. If you keep to my path, I will reveal to you the salvation of God."*

PSALM 92:1 | *It is good to give thanks to the LORD, to sing praises to the Most High.*

LUKE 17:16 | *He fell to the ground at Jesus' feet, thanking him for what he had done. This man was a Samaritan.*

When you give thanks to God, you honor and praise him for what he has done—in your life, in the lives of others, in the church, and in the world. Similarly, you honor others when you give thanks to them, respecting them for who they are and what they have done. This attitude of gratitude prevents you from expecting others to serve you and allows you to enjoy whatever blessings come your way.

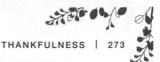

How do I develop an attitude of thanksgiving?

PSALM 9:1 | *I will praise you, LORD, with all my heart; I will tell of all the marvelous things you have done.*

PSALM 92:2 | *It is good to proclaim your unfailing love in the morning, your faithfulness in the evening.*

PHILIPPIANS 1:3 | *Every time I think of you, I give thanks to my God.*

COLOSSIANS 3:15 | *Let the peace that comes from Christ rule in your hearts. For as members of one body you are called to live in peace. And always be thankful.*

1 TIMOTHY 4:4 | *Since everything God created is good, we should not reject any of it but receive it with thanks.*

Cultivate thankfulness by giving thanks regularly—to God and also to others. Set aside time every day to think about things you are thankful for. Make a mental list of all God's blessings in your life and thank him for them. Don't wait to *feel* thankful before giving thanks. Giving thanks will lead you to feel thankful.

How can I express my thankfulness?

1 CHRONICLES 16:7-8 | *David gave to Asaph and his fellow Levites this song of thanksgiving to the LORD: Give thanks to the LORD and proclaim his greatness. Let the whole world know what he has done.*

PSALM 147:7 | *Sing out your thanks to the LORD; sing praises to our God with a harp.*

COLOSSIANS 3:16 | *Sing psalms and hymns and spiritual songs to God with thankful hearts.*

With music and singing.

PSALM 116:17 | *I will offer you a sacrifice of thanksgiving and call on the name of the LORD.*

Through generous giving.

PSALM 111:1-2 | *Praise the LORD! I will thank the LORD with all my heart as I meet with his godly people. How amazing are the deeds of the LORD! All who delight in him should ponder them.*

PSALM 116:17-18 | *I will offer you a sacrifice of thanksgiving and call on the name of the LORD. . . . I will fulfill my vows to the LORD in the presence of all his people.*

Through worship and praise with other believers.

PSALM 119:7 | *As I learn your righteous regulations, I will thank you by living as I should!*

Through obedience and service.

PSALM 9:1 | *I will praise you, LORD, with all my heart.*

COLOSSIANS 4:2 | *Devote yourselves to prayer with an alert mind and a thankful heart.*

Through prayer.

PSALM 100:4 | *Enter his gates with thanksgiving; go into his courts with praise. Give thanks to him and praise his name.*

PSALM 104:1 | *Let all that I am praise the LORD. O LORD my God, how great you are! You are robed with honor and majesty.*

By praising and honoring God.

For what can I always be thankful, regardless of circumstances?

1 CHRONICLES 16:34 | *Give thanks to the LORD, for he is good! His faithful love endures forever.*

PSALM 7:17 | *I will thank the LORD because he is just; I will sing praise to the name of the LORD Most High.*

PSALM 138:2 | *I bow . . . as I worship. I praise your name for your unfailing love and faithfulness; for your promises are backed by all the honor of your name.*

1 CORINTHIANS 15:57 | *Thank God! He gives us victory over sin and death through our Lord Jesus Christ.*

2 CORINTHIANS 9:15 | *Thank God for this gift too wonderful for words!*

EPHESIANS 2:8 | *God saved you by his grace when you believed. . . . It is a gift from God.*

1 THESSALONIANS 5:18 | *Be thankful in all circumstances, for this is God's will for you who belong to Christ Jesus.*

1 TIMOTHY 1:12 | *I thank Christ Jesus our Lord, who has given me strength to do his work. He considered me trustworthy and appointed me to serve him.*

You can thank the Lord for being good and just, and you can thank him for his unchanging, perfect character. You can thank him also for his love for you; for his faithfulness; for sending his Son, Jesus; and for his mercy. And you can thank him for victory over death and for keeping his promises.

Promise from God 1 CHRONICLES 16:34 | *Give thanks to the LORD, for he is good! His faithful love endures forever.*

TIME

See **PRIORITIES.**

TIMING OF GOD

How was God's timing critical in Jesus' life?

JOHN 7:30 | *The leaders tried to arrest [Jesus]; but no one laid a hand on him, because his time had not yet come.*

ROMANS 5:6 | *When we were utterly helpless, Christ came at just the right time and died for us sinners.*

GALATIANS 4:4 | *When the right time came, God sent his Son, born of a woman, subject to the law.*

EPHESIANS 1:10 | *This is the plan: At the right time [God] will bring everything together under the authority of Christ— everything in heaven and on earth.*

1 TIMOTHY 2:6 | *[Christ Jesus] gave his life to purchase freedom for everyone. This is the message God gave to the world at just the right time.*

1 TIMOTHY 6:15 | *At just the right time Christ will be revealed from heaven by the blessed and only almighty God, the King of all kings and Lord of all lords.*

The Hebrew people had been longing for the Messiah for centuries, yet God sent Jesus to Earth at just the right time. You may not fully understand why this was perfect timing until you get to heaven and see God's complete plan, but you can be assured that God sent Jesus at the time when the most people would be reached with the good news of salvation, both present and future.

Can I trust God's timing in my life?

EXODUS 6:1 | *The LORD told Moses, "Now you will see what I will do to Pharaoh. When he feels the force of my strong hand, he will let the people go."*

EXODUS 9:16 | *[The Lord said to Pharaoh,] "I have spared you for a purpose—to show you my power and to spread my fame throughout the earth."*

EXODUS 11:9 | *The LORD had told Moses earlier, "Pharaoh will not listen to you, but then I will do even more mighty miracles in the land of Egypt."*

JOHN 11:1, 3-6, 14-15, 21, 32, 43-45 | *A man named Lazarus was sick. He lived in Bethany with his sisters, Mary and Martha. . . . The two sisters sent a message to Jesus telling him, "Lord, your dear friend is very sick." But when Jesus heard about it he said, "Lazarus's sickness will not end in death. No, it happened for the glory of God so that the Son of God will receive glory from this." So although Jesus loved Martha, Mary, and Lazarus, he stayed where he was for the next two days. . . . [Jesus] told [the disciples] plainly, "Lazarus is dead. And for your sakes, I'm glad I wasn't there, for now you will really believe. Come, let's go see him." . . . Martha said to Jesus, "Lord, if only you had been here, my brother would not have died." . . . When Mary arrived and saw Jesus, she fell at his feet and said, "Lord, if only you had been here, my brother would not have died." . . . Then Jesus shouted, "Lazarus, come out!" And the dead man came out, his hands and feet bound in graveclothes, his face wrapped in a headcloth. Jesus told them, "Unwrap him and let him go!" Many of the people who were with Mary believed in Jesus when they saw this happen.*

Many times God will intervene in your life in a special way, as he has done throughout history. Watch for those times, and then praise God that you can play a part—even if it is a small one—in the movement of God in this world.

PSALM 139:13 | *You made all the delicate, inner parts of my body and knit me together in my mother's womb.*

ISAIAH 25:1 | *O LORD, I will honor and praise your name, for you are my God. You do such wonderful things! You planned them long ago, and now you have accomplished them.*

HABAKKUK 2:3 | *This vision is for a future time. It describes the end, and it will be fulfilled. If it seems slow in coming, wait patiently, for it will surely take place. It will not be delayed.*

God had your whole life planned before you were even born. He knows everything about you and is qualified and can be trusted to intervene on your behalf. His agenda and his timing for you are perfect.

How can I best wait for God's timing?

PSALM 31:5 | *I entrust my spirit into your hand. Rescue me, LORD, for you are a faithful God.*

PSALM 59:9 | *You are my strength; I wait for you to rescue me, for you, O God, are my fortress.*

Remind yourself continually of God's faithfulness. He is actively working in your life to help you become all he made you to be.

PSALM 69:13 | *I keep praying to you, LORD, . . . In your unfailing love, O God, answer my prayer with your sure salvation.*

PSALM 138:3 | *As soon as I pray, you answer me; you encourage me by giving me strength.*

ISAIAH 40:31 | *Those who trust in the LORD will find new strength. They will soar high on wings like eagles. They will run and not grow weary. They will walk and not faint.*

ROMANS 12:12 | *Rejoice in our confident hope. Be patient in trouble, and keep on praying.*

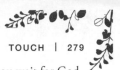

Keep praying, be patient, and stay alert as you wait for God to show you your next assignment.

Promise from God HABAKKUK 2:3 | *This vision is for a future time. It describes the end, and it will be fulfilled. If it seems slow in coming, wait patiently, for it will surely take place. It will not be delayed.*

TOUCH

How did Jesus use physical touch during his time on earth?

MARK 5:28 | *[The woman] thought to herself, "If I can just touch [Jesus'] robe, I will be healed."*

MARK 10:16 | *[Jesus] took the children in his arms and placed his hands on their heads and blessed them.*

LUKE 4:40 | *As the sun went down that evening, people throughout the village brought sick family members to Jesus. No matter what their diseases were, the touch of his hand healed every one.*

JOHN 20:27 | *[Jesus] said to Thomas, "Put your finger here, and look at my hands. Put your hand into the wound in my side. Don't be faithless any longer. Believe!"*

Jesus used touch to comfort, affirm, heal, bless, and encourage.

What are some good purposes of physical touch?

GENESIS 33:4 | *Esau ran to meet [Jacob] and embraced him, threw his arms around his neck, and kissed him.*

GENESIS 45:15 | *Joseph kissed each of his brothers and wept over them, and after that they began talking freely with him.*

LUKE 15:20 | *[The young man] returned home to his father. And while he was still a long way off, his father saw him coming. Filled with love and compassion, he ran to his son, embraced him, and kissed him.*

Touch is used in greetings.

GENESIS 31:28, 55 | *[Laban said to Jacob,] "Why didn't you let me kiss my daughters and grandchildren and tell them good-bye? You have acted very foolishly!" . . . Laban got up early the next morning, and he kissed his grandchildren and his daughters and blessed them. Then he left and returned home.*

1 SAMUEL 20:41 | *David came out from where he had been hiding near the stone pile. Then David bowed three times to Jonathan with his face to the ground. Both of them were in tears as they embraced each other and said good-bye, especially David.*

ACTS 20:37 | *[The elders] all cried as they embraced and kissed [Paul] good-bye.*

Touch is used to say farewell.

LUKE 7:38 | *[A certain immoral woman] knelt behind [Jesus] at his feet, weeping. Her tears fell on his feet, and she wiped them off with her hair. Then she kept kissing his feet and putting perfume on them.*

Touch is used to express gratitude.

EXODUS 17:12 | *Moses' arms soon became so tired he could no longer hold them up. So Aaron and Hur found a stone for him to sit on. Then they stood on each side of Moses, holding up his hands. So his hands held steady until sunset.*

ACTS 9:8-9 | *[Saul's] companions led him by the hand to Damascus. He remained there blind for three days and did not eat or drink.*

Touch is used to help others.

SONG OF SONGS 1:2 | *Kiss me and kiss me again, for your love is sweeter than wine.*

SONG OF SONGS 2:6 | *His left arm is under my head, and his right arm embraces me.*

Touching is part of intimacy.

ACTS 6:6 | *These seven were presented to the apostles, who prayed for them as they laid their hands on them.*

ACTS 8:17 | *Peter and John laid their hands upon these believers, and they received the Holy Spirit.*

1 TIMOTHY 4:14 | *Do not neglect the spiritual gift you received through the prophecy spoken over you when the elders of the church laid their hands on you.*

Touch can be used to heal and minister to others.

What are some dangers and abuses of physical touch?

EXODUS 21:12 | *Anyone who assaults and kills another person must be put to death.*

JOB 31:21-22 | *If I raised my hand against an orphan, knowing the judges would take my side, then let my shoulder be wrenched out of place! Let my arm be torn from its socket!*

JOB 38:15 | *The light disturbs the wicked and stops the arm that is raised in violence.*

JOHN 19:3 | *"Hail! King of the Jews!" they mocked, as they slapped [Jesus] across the face.*

Violence and physical abuse are inappropriate uses of touch.

LUKE 22:47-48 | *Judas walked over to Jesus to greet him with a kiss. But Jesus said, "Judas, would you betray the Son of Man with a kiss?"*

Using touch to deceive is wrong.

GENESIS 20:3-6 | *God came to Abimelech in a dream and told him, "You are a dead man, for that woman you have taken is already married!" But Abimelech had not slept with her yet, so he said, "Lord, will you destroy an innocent nation? Didn't Abraham tell me, 'She is my sister'?" . . . In the dream God responded, "Yes, I know you are innocent. That's why I kept you from sinning against me, and why I did not let you touch her."*

LEVITICUS 18:6 | *You must never have sexual relations with a close relative.*

DEUTERONOMY 27:21 | *Cursed is anyone who has sexual intercourse with an animal.*

PROVERBS 6:29 | *The man who sleeps with another man's wife . . . will not go unpunished.*

ROMANS 1:26-27 | *God abandoned them to their shameful desires. Even the women turned against the natural way to have sex and instead indulged in sex with each other. And the men, instead of having normal sexual relations with women, burned with lust for each other. Men did shameful things with other men, and as a result of this sin, they suffered within themselves the penalty they deserved.*

Sexual abuse of any kind or sexual activity outside of marriage is wrong.

Promise from God MATTHEW 9:28-30 | *Jesus asked [the two blind men], "Do you believe I can make you see?" "Yes, Lord," they told him, "we do." Then he touched their eyes and said, "Because of your faith, it will happen." Then their eyes were opened, and they could see!*

TRUST

What does it mean to trust God?

PSALM 33:21 | *In him our hearts rejoice, for we trust in his holy name.*

REVELATION 4:11 | *You are worthy, O Lord our God, to receive glory and honor and power. For you created all things.*

Trusting God means recognizing that he is worthy of your trust and praise.

GENESIS 6:13-14, 17, 22 | *God said to Noah . . . "Build a large boat. . . . I am about to cover the earth with a flood." . . . So Noah did everything exactly as God had commanded him.*

Trusting God means obeying his commands even when you don't fully understand why.

PSALM 112:1 | *How joyful are those who fear the LORD and delight in obeying his commands.*

Trusting God and obeying him will bring you joy.

JOHN 3:36 | *Anyone who believes in God's Son has eternal life.*

Trusting God means depending on Jesus Christ alone for salvation.

GALATIANS 2:16 | *No one will ever be made right with God by obeying the law.*

Trusting Christ for salvation means ceasing to trust in your own efforts to be righteous.

1 PETER 1:8 | *Though you do not see him now, you trust him; and you rejoice with a glorious, inexpressible joy.*

Trusting God requires faith and produces joy.

Promise from God ISAIAH 26:3 | *You will keep in perfect peace all who trust in you, all whose thoughts are fixed on you!*

TRUTH

How does truth impact my relationship with God?

TITUS 1:2 | *[The] truth gives [those whom God has chosen] confidence that they have eternal life, which God—who does not lie—promised them before the world began.*

You can trust God because he always tells the truth. Nothing he has said in his Word, the Bible, has ever been proven wrong or false. He specifically created you in order to have a relationship with you for all eternity, so if God says he loves you—and he always tells the truth—you can be sure he desires a relationship with you.

PSALM 36:10 | *Pour out your unfailing love on those who love you; give justice to those with honest hearts.*

ISAIAH 33:15-16 | *Those who are honest and fair, who refuse to profit by fraud, who stay far away from bribes, . . . who shut their eyes to all enticement to do wrong—these are the ones who will dwell on high.*

Striving for honesty will help you experience the benefits of God's ultimate justice and protection.

PSALM 37:37 | *Look at those who are honest and good, for a wonderful future awaits those who love peace.*

Striving for honesty helps you enjoy life because you can live at peace with God, with others, and with yourself.

JOHN 14:6 | *Jesus [said], "I am the way, the truth, and the life. No one can come to the Father except through me."*

ROMANS 1:18 | *God shows his anger from heaven against all sinful, wicked people who suppress the truth by their wickedness.*

God wants you to accept the truth that only by following Jesus can you spend eternity with him. He wants to spare you from the terrible consequences of pushing this most important truth away.

Does God really expect me to tell the truth all the time?

EXODUS 20:16 | *You must not testify falsely against your neighbor.*

PROVERBS 6:16-17 | *There are six things the LORD hates— no, seven things he detests: . . . a lying tongue.*

God's law clearly forbids intentional lying.

EPHESIANS 4:15 | *We will speak the truth in love.*

Followers of Jesus are called to speak the truth, in a loving manner.

Why is telling the truth so important?

PROVERBS 12:19 | *Truthful words stand the test of time, but lies are soon exposed.*

LUKE 16:10 | *If you are faithful in little things, you will be faithful in large ones. But if you are dishonest in little things, you won't be honest with greater responsibilities.*

Telling the truth is the litmus test to see if you are trying to model your life after the God of truth. If you are truthful in even small matters, you will gain the reputation of being an honest person.

EPHESIANS 4:25 | *Stop telling lies. Let us tell our neighbors the truth, for we are all parts of the same body.*

Telling the truth promotes good relationships.

MATTHEW 12:33 | *A tree is identified by its fruit. If a tree is good, its fruit will be good. If a tree is bad, its fruit will be bad.*

Honest dealings reveal an honest character. What you do reveals who you are.

PSALM 24:3-5 | *Who may climb the mountain of the LORD? Who may stand in his holy place? Only those whose hands and hearts are pure, who . . . never tell lies. They will receive the LORD's blessing and have a right relationship with God their savior.*

Telling the truth is necessary for a relationship with God.

ROMANS 12:3 | *Be honest in your evaluation of yourselves, measuring yourselves by the faith God has given us.*

Honestly evaluating your walk with the Lord allows you to continue growing in your faith.

1 TIMOTHY 1:19 | *Cling to your faith in Christ, and keep your conscience clear. For some people have deliberately violated their consciences; as a result, their faith has been shipwrecked.*

Always telling the truth keeps your conscience clear.

PROVERBS 11:3 | *Honesty guides good people; dishonesty destroys treacherous people.*

There is freedom in honesty because you never have to worry about getting tripped up. Dishonesty and deception are forms of bondage because you get trapped by your lies.

Promise from God PSALM 119:160 | *The very essence of your words is truth; all your just regulations will stand forever.*

UNITY

What is true unity?

JOHN 10:14, 16 | *[Jesus said,] "I am the good shepherd. . . . I have other sheep, too, that are not in this sheepfold. I must bring them also. They will listen to my voice, and there will be one flock with one shepherd."*

ROMANS 12:4-5 | *Just as our bodies have many parts and each part has a special function, so it is with Christ's body. We are many parts of one body, and we all belong to each other.*

1 CORINTHIANS 12:18-20 | *Our bodies have many parts, and God has put each part just where he wants it. How strange a body would be if it had only one part! Yes, there are many parts, but only one body.*

GALATIANS 3:28 | *There is no longer Jew or Gentile, slave or free, male and female. For you are all one in Christ Jesus.*

Unity is not the same as uniformity. Everyone has unique gifts and personality. It is the celebration and appreciation of these differences to reach the common goal of serving God that is true unity.

Why is unity important?

ACTS 2:42-43 | *All the believers devoted themselves to the apostles' teaching, and to fellowship, and to sharing in meals (including the Lord's Supper), and to prayer. A deep sense of awe came over them all, and the apostles performed many miraculous signs and wonders.*

1 CORINTHIANS 1:10 | *I appeal to you, dear brothers and sisters, by the authority of our Lord Jesus Christ, to live in harmony with*

each other. Let there be no divisions in the church. Rather, be of one mind, united in thought and purpose.

Unity allows you to share a sense of fellowship and devotion and to work together with a common purpose.

PSALM 133:1 | *How wonderful and pleasant it is when brothers live together in harmony!*

ROMANS 15:6 | *All of you can join together with one voice, giving praise and glory to God, the Father of our Lord Jesus Christ.*

Unity creates a more beautiful worship experience.

How can I help achieve unity?

ROMANS 15:5 | *May God, who gives this patience and encouragement, help you live in complete harmony with each other, as is fitting for followers of Christ Jesus.*

By working hard to develop the same kind of attitude Jesus had, one of patience and encouragement, of uniting not dividing.

EPHESIANS 4:12-13 | *Equip God's people to do his work and build up the church, the body of Christ. This will continue until we all come to such unity in our faith and knowledge of God's Son that we will be mature in the Lord, measuring up to the full and complete standard of Christ.*

By exercising your God-given responsibility to build others up.

1 PETER 3:8 | *All of you should be of one mind. Sympathize with each other. Love each other as brothers and sisters. Be tender-hearted, and keep a humble attitude.*

By sympathizing with others.

EPHESIANS 4:2-3 | *Always be humble and gentle. Be patient with each other, making allowance for each other's faults because of your love. Make every effort to keep yourselves united in the Spirit, binding yourselves together with peace.*

By being humble and gentle.

COLOSSIANS 3:13-14 | *Make allowance for each other's faults, and forgive anyone who offends you. Remember, the Lord forgave you, so you must forgive others. Above all, clothe yourselves with love, which binds us all together in perfect harmony.*

By loving and forgiving others.

Promise from God ROMANS 15:6 | *All of you can join together with one voice, giving praise and glory to God, the Father of our Lord Jesus Christ.*

VULNERABILITY

How do I keep myself from being vulnerable to harm?

NUMBERS 14:41-42 | *Moses said, "Why are you now disobeying the LORD's orders to return to the wilderness? It won't work. Do not go up into the land now. You will only be crushed by your enemies because the LORD is not with you."*

DEUTERONOMY 28:48 | *You will serve your enemies whom the LORD will send against you. You will be left hungry, thirsty, naked, and lacking in everything. The LORD will put an iron yoke on your neck, oppressing you harshly until he has destroyed you.*

LAMENTATIONS 1:8 | *Jerusalem has sinned greatly, so she has been tossed away like a filthy rag. All who once honored her now despise her, for they have seen her stripped naked and humiliated. All she can do is groan and hide her face.*

Keep yourself from being vulnerable to harm by obeying God and staying within his plan and revealed will. Shame and humiliation are direct consequences of being disobedient to God.

EZRA 8:22-23 | *We had told the king, "Our God's hand of protection is on all who worship him, but his fierce anger rages against those who abandon him." So we fasted and earnestly prayed that our God would take care of us, and he heard our prayer.*

When you pray to God for his protection and care, he will build a wall of spiritual protection around you.

NEHEMIAH 4:13 | *I placed armed guards behind the lowest parts of the wall in the exposed areas. I stationed the people to stand guard by families, armed with swords, spears, and bows.*

You can keep from being vulnerable by joining together with others and standing together against danger.

REVELATION 16:15 | *Look, I will come as unexpectedly as a thief! Blessed are all who are watching for me, who keep their clothing ready so they will not have to walk around naked and ashamed.*

If you are fully prepared for Christ's coming, you will not be vulnerable to God's wrath on Judgment Day.

Is God vulnerable in any way?

ISAIAH 53:12 | *I will give him the honors of a victorious soldier, because he exposed himself to death. He was counted among the rebels. He bore the sins of many and interceded for rebels.*

God, in Christ, made himself vulnerable to abuse and death at the hands of evil people.

MATTHEW 4:1 | *Jesus was led by the Spirit into the wilderness to be tempted there by the devil.*

Jesus made himself vulnerable to temptation, but he resisted.

Promise from God ROMANS 5:6 | *When we were utterly helpless, Christ came at just the right time and died for us sinners.*

WAITING

See **PATIENCE.**

WEARINESS

Why am I so weary?

JOB 7:1-3 | *Is not all human life a struggle? Our lives are like that of a hired hand, like a worker who longs for the shade, like a servant waiting to be paid. I, too, have been assigned months of futility, long and weary nights of misery.*

You may be weary because of the normal, everyday struggles of life, which can be tiring when they seem relentless and futile.

NEHEMIAH 4:10 | *The people of Judah began to complain, "The workers are getting tired, and there is so much rubble to be moved. We will never be able to build the wall by ourselves."*

You may be tired because there is so much work it is overwhelming.

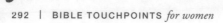

PROVERBS 23:4 | *Don't wear yourself out trying to get rich. Be wise enough to know when to quit.*

You may be tired because you are striving too hard for something that isn't worth it.

2 CORINTHIANS 5:2 | *We grow weary in our present bodies, and we long to put on our heavenly bodies like new clothing.*

You may be tired because of the limitations of your present body.

1 SAMUEL 14:24 | *The men of Israel were pressed to exhaustion that day, because Saul had placed them under an oath, saying, "Let a curse fall on anyone who eats before evening—before I have full revenge on my enemies." So no one ate anything all day.*

You may be tired because you are not eating well.

2 CORINTHIANS 11:27 | *I have worked hard and long, enduring many sleepless nights. I have been hungry and thirsty and have often gone without food. I have shivered in the cold, without enough clothing to keep me warm.*

You may be tired because you lack basic necessities.

MATTHEW 9:20-21 | *A woman who had suffered for twelve years with constant bleeding came up behind [Jesus]. She touched the fringe of his robe, for she thought, "If I can just touch his robe, I will be healed."*

You may be tired because you have a chronic illness.

JOHN 4:6 | *Jacob's well was there; and Jesus, tired from the long walk, sat wearily beside the well about noontime.*

You may be tired from traveling.

ECCLESIASTES 12:12 | *Be careful, for writing books is endless, and much study wears you out.*

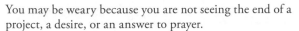

You may be weary because you are not seeing the end of a project, a desire, or an answer to prayer.

PSALM 31:10 | *I am dying from grief; my years are shortened by sadness. Sin has drained my strength; I am wasting away from within.*

LUKE 22:45 | *At last [Jesus] stood up again and returned to the disciples, only to find them asleep, exhausted from grief.*

You may be tired because grief has drained your strength.

What do I have to watch out for when I'm weary?

GALATIANS 6:9 | *Let's not get tired of doing what is good. At just the right time we will reap a harvest of blessing if we don't give up.*

Being tired makes you more susceptible to discouragement, temptation, and sin and causes you to lose hope that things will be better in the future.

PROVERBS 30:1-2 | *I am weary, O God; I am weary and worn out, O God. I am too stupid to be human, and I lack common sense.*

Being tired can cause you to lose perspective. When you're weary, it is not a good time to try to make important decisions.

JOB 10:1 | *I am disgusted with my life. Let me complain freely. My bitter soul must complain.*

Being tired can cause you to say things you may later regret.

ECCLESIASTES 1:8 | *Everything is wearisome beyond description. No matter how much we see, we are never satisfied. No matter how much we hear, we are not content.*

Being weary can cause you to lose your vision and purpose.

PSALM 127:2 | *It is useless for you to work so hard from early morning until late at night . . . for God gives rest to his loved ones.*

Chronic tiredness may mean you are trying to do too much. It may be God's way of telling you to slow down.

2 SAMUEL 17:1-2 | *Ahithophel urged Absalom, "Let me choose 12,000 men to start out after David tonight. I will catch up with him while he is weary and discouraged. He and his troops will panic, and everyone will run away. Then I will kill only [David]."*

Weariness makes you vulnerable to your enemies. When your guard is down, it's easier for you to be attacked.

Who can help me when I am tired?

ISAIAH 40:29-31 | *He gives power to the weak and strength to the powerless. Even youths will become weak and tired, and young men will fall in exhaustion. But those who trust in the LORD will find new strength. They will soar high on wings like eagles. They will run and not grow weary. They will walk and not faint.*

ISAIAH 49:4 | *My work seems so useless! I have spent my strength for nothing and to no purpose. Yet I leave it all in the LORD's hand; I will trust God for my reward.*

JEREMIAH 31:25 | *[The Lord said,] "I have given rest to the weary and joy to the sorrowing."*

HABAKKUK 3:19 | *The Sovereign LORD is my strength! He makes me as surefooted as a deer, able to tread upon the heights.*

MATTHEW 11:28 | *Jesus said, "Come to me, all of you who are weary and carry heavy burdens, and I will give you rest."*

2 CORINTHIANS 12:9 | *[God] said, "My grace is all you need. My power works best in weakness." So now I am glad to boast about my weaknesses, so that the power of Christ can work through me.*

HEBREWS 12:3, 12 | *Think of all the hostility [Jesus] endured from sinful people; then you won't become weary and give up. . . . So take a new grip with your tired hands and strengthen your weak knees.*

The Lord will give you renewed strength when you grow weary. When you come to him in praise, he refreshes your heart. When you come to him in prayer, he refreshes your soul. When you come to him in solitude, he refreshes your mind. When you come to him in need, he refreshes your body. When you come to him with thankfulness, he refreshes your perspective. Coming to God with all your needs releases the burdens of life and you draw strength from God, the source of strength.

Promise from God ISAIAH 40:29-31 | *He gives power to the weak and strength to the powerless. Even youths will become weak and tired, and young men will fall in exhaustion. But those who trust in the LORD will find new strength. They will soar high on wings like eagles. They will run and not grow weary. They will walk and not faint.*

WILL OF GOD

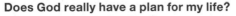

Does God really have a plan for my life?

PSALM 139:3 | *You see me when I travel and when I rest at home. You know everything I do.*

PHILIPPIANS 1:6 | *I am certain that God, who began the good work within you, will continue his work until it is finally finished on the day when Christ Jesus returns.*

God has both a general plan and a specific plan for your life. He wants you to follow a certain path toward his desired purpose for you, but he also cares about the details along the way.

JEREMIAH 29:11 | *"I know the plans I have for you," says the LORD. "They are plans for good and not for disaster, to give you a future and a hope."*

God's plans for you are always good. The unknown can be frightening, but when you belong to God, you can be sure he has good planned for your future.

PSALM 138:8 | *The LORD will work out his plans for my life.*

God's plan for your life is not an unthinking, automated script that you must follow. It is a journey, with various important destinations and appointments but also with a great deal of freedom as to the pace and scope of the travel. God's plan for you will always have a sense of mystery, but you can be certain that he will guide you as long as you rely on his leading.

What can I do to discover God's will for my life?

PROVERBS 2:3-5 | *Cry out for insight, and ask for understanding. Search for them as you would for silver; seek them like hidden treasures. Then you will understand what it means to fear the LORD, and you will gain knowledge of God.*

ISAIAH 2:3 | *Come, let us go up to the mountain of the LORD, to the house of Jacob's God. There he will teach us his ways, and we will walk in his paths.*

You can't sit around waiting for God to reveal his will for you; you must proactively look for it. Actively seek God's will through prayer, reading the Bible, conversation with mature believers and reliable advisers, and discernment of the circumstances around you.

HOSEA 6:3 | *Oh, that we might know the LORD! Let us press on to know him. He will respond to us as surely as the arrival of dawn or the coming of rains in early spring.*

Give yourself completely to knowing his will. Seek God's will passionately, not casually.

PROVERBS 2:6 | *The LORD grants wisdom!*

JAMES 1:5 | *If you need wisdom, ask our generous God, and he will give it to you. He will not rebuke you for asking.*

1 JOHN 5:14 | *We are confident that he hears us whenever we ask for anything that pleases him.*

Pray, asking God to reveal his will to you.

ACTS 21:14 | *When it was clear that we couldn't persuade him, we gave up and said, "The Lord's will be done."*

Sometimes God's will for you becomes evident through circumstances beyond your control. You do the seeking, but you allow God to work out his will in the way he knows is best. You will discover that you are satisfied wherever he takes you.

What are some things I can know are God's will for me?

EXODUS 20:1 | *God gave the people [a list of] instructions.*

God's will is that you obey his laws for living.

PROVERBS 16:3 | *Commit your actions to the LORD, and your plans will succeed.*

God's will is that you do everything as if you were doing it for him. God has not revealed everything to his followers, but he has revealed all you need to know to live for him now.

1 CORINTHIANS 14:1 | *Let love be your highest goal!*

God's will is that you love others.

MARK 10:45 | *Even the Son of Man came not to be served but to serve others and to give his life as a ransom for many.*

God's will is that you serve others, putting them above yourself.

AMOS 5:24 | *[The Lord says,] "I want to see a mighty flood of justice, an endless river of righteous living."*

God's will is that you seek justice at all times and do what is right.

GALATIANS 5:22-23, 25 | *The Holy Spirit produces this kind of fruit in our lives: love, joy, peace, patience, kindness, goodness, faithfulness, gentleness, and self-control. . . . Since we are living by the Spirit, let us follow the Spirit's leading in every part of our lives.*

God's will is that you live by the power and under the guidance of the Holy Spirit.

Promise from God PROVERBS 3:6 | *Seek [God's] will in all you do, and he will show you which path to take.*

WISDOM

How can I obtain wisdom?

JOB 28:28 | *The fear of the Lord is true wisdom; to forsake evil is real understanding.*

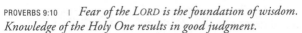

PROVERBS 9:10 | *Fear of the LORD is the foundation of wisdom. Knowledge of the Holy One results in good judgment.*

Giving God first place in your life is a prerequisite for receiving God's wisdom. Asking God for wisdom is a hollow request if you are not willing to let God rule in your heart. Wisdom comes from fearing (honoring, revering, respecting) God.

1 JOHN 2:27 | *You have received the Holy Spirit, and he lives within you, so you don't need anyone to teach you what is true. For the Spirit teaches you everything you need to know, and what he teaches is true—it is not a lie. So just as he has taught you, remain in fellowship with Christ.*

Wisdom comes from the Holy Spirit, who lives in you when you believe in Jesus Christ.

PROVERBS 1:5-6 | *Let the wise listen to these proverbs and become even wiser. Let those with understanding receive guidance by exploring the meaning in these proverbs and parables, the words of the wise and their riddles.*

Obedience to God's Word—his commands, laws, and teachings—will make you wise.

JAMES 1:5 | *If you need wisdom, ask our generous God, and he will give it to you. He will not rebuke you for asking.*

When you need wisdom, ask God, and he will give it.

PSALM 86:11 | *Teach me your ways, O LORD, that I may live according to your truth! Grant me purity of heart, so that I may honor you.*

COLOSSIANS 3:16 | *Let the message about Christ, in all its richness, fill your lives. Teach and counsel each other with all the wisdom he gives.*

Following Christ's teachings and obeying his words will give wisdom.

PROVERBS 8:12, 17 | *I, Wisdom, live together with good judgment. I know where to discover knowledge and discernment. . . . I love all who love me. Those who search will surely find me.*

You find wisdom when you pursue it wholeheartedly.

Promise from God PROVERBS 3:5-6 | *Trust in the LORD with all your heart; do not depend on your own understanding. Seek his will in all you do, and he will show you which path to take.*

WITNESSING

How can I overcome my fear of witnessing?

EXODUS 4:12 | *[The Lord said,] "Now go! I will be with you as you speak, and I will instruct you in what to say."*

LUKE 21:15 | *[Jesus said,] "I will give you the right words and such wisdom that none of your opponents will be able to reply or refute you!"*

Trusting that God will speak through you will help you overcome your fear of witnessing.

2 CORINTHIANS 4:11, 13 | *We live under constant danger of death because we serve Jesus, so that the life of Jesus will be evident in our dying bodies. . . . But we continue to preach because we have the same kind of faith the psalmist had when he said, "I believed in God, so I spoke."*

Even if you face death, faith in God can give you the courage to speak.

PSALM 27:1 | *The LORD is my light and my salvation—so why should I be afraid? The LORD is my fortress, protecting me from danger, so why should I tremble?*

ISAIAH 44:8 | *Do not tremble; do not be afraid. Did I not proclaim my purposes for you long ago? You are my witnesses— is there any other God? No! There is no other Rock—not one!*

ACTS 18:9-10 | *One night the Lord spoke to Paul in a vision and told him, "Don't be afraid! Speak out! Don't be silent! For I am with you."*

Take courage and find strength in God's power, presence, and protection.

EZEKIEL 2:6 | *Son of man, do not fear them or their words. Don't be afraid even though their threats surround you like nettles and briers and stinging scorpions. Do not be dismayed by their dark scowls, even though they are rebels.*

Be strong in God, and realize that rejection just "goes with the territory."

JOHN 12:26 | *Anyone who wants to be my disciple must follow me, because my servants must be where I am. And the Father will honor anyone who serves me.*

ACTS 4:18-20 | *[The religious leaders] called the apostles back in and commanded them never again to speak or teach in the name of Jesus. But Peter and John replied, "Do you think God wants us to obey you rather than him? We cannot stop telling about everything we have seen and heard."*

ACTS 5:40 | *[The members of the high council] called in the apostles and had them flogged. Then they ordered them never again to speak in the name of Jesus, and they let them go.*

Realize that when you witness, you are following in Christ's and the apostles' footsteps.

ACTS 1:8 | *You will receive power when the Holy Spirit comes upon you. And you will be my witnesses, telling people about me everywhere . . . to the ends of the earth.*

Remember that the Holy Spirit will empower you and help you to speak.

1 CORINTHIANS 2:4 | *[Paul said,] "My message and my preaching were very plain. . . . I relied only on the power of the Holy Spirit."*

1 THESSALONIANS 1:5 | *When we brought you the Good News, . . . the Holy Spirit gave you full assurance that what we said was true.*

Go ahead and speak, and the Holy Spirit will work in people's hearts and minds.

1 THESSALONIANS 2:4 | *Our purpose is to please God, not people. He alone examines the motives of our hearts.*

Focus on pleasing God rather than on pleasing people.

What do I do when people aren't interested in hearing about Jesus?

ACTS 17:32-34 | *When they heard Paul speak about the resurrection of the dead, some laughed in contempt, but others said, "We want to hear more about this later." That ended Paul's discussion with them, but some joined him and became believers.*

The majority may seem disinterested or even hostile, but you never know when people will believe—so for their sake, don't give up.

EZEKIEL 2:5, 7-8 | *Whether they listen or refuse to listen—for remember, they are rebels—at least they will know they have had a prophet among them. . . . You must give them my messages*

whether they listen or not. But they won't listen, for they are completely rebellious! . . . Do not join them in their rebellion.

2 TIMOTHY 4:2 | *Preach the word of God. Be prepared, whether the time is favorable or not.*

If circumstances or people's attitudes are not favorable, speak out anyway and tell people what Jesus has done in your life.

LUKE 9:5 | *If a town refuses to welcome you, shake its dust from your feet as you leave to show that you have abandoned those people to their fate.*

If people refuse to accept God's good news after you have shared it, move on—there are many others waiting to hear the gospel.

Promise from God ROMANS 10:15 | *How beautiful are the feet of messengers who bring good news!*

WORDS

What kinds of words should I speak?

GENESIS 50:21 | *He reassured them by speaking kindly to them.*

Speak kind words to others.

PSALM 50:23 | *Giving thanks is a sacrifice that truly honors me.*

ROMANS 15:6 | *All of you can join together with one voice, giving praise and glory to God, the Father of our Lord Jesus Christ.*

Speak words of thanks and praise to God.

EPHESIANS 4:29 | *Let everything you say be good and helpful, so that your words will be an encouragement to those who hear them.*

Use words that encourage and build up others.

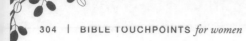

PROVERBS 15:4 | *Gentle words are a tree of life.*

PROVERBS 25:15 | *Patience can persuade a prince, and soft speech can break bones.*

Speak to others with gentleness and patience.

1 PETER 3:9 | *Don't repay evil for evil. Don't retaliate with insults when people insult you. Instead, pay them back with a blessing. That is what God has called you to do, and he will bless you for it.*

Use your words to bless even those who injure you.

ZECHARIAH 8:16 | *Tell the truth to each other. Render verdicts in your courts that are just and that lead to peace.*

Speak truthfully.

What kinds of words should I avoid speaking?

EXODUS 22:28 | *You must not dishonor God or curse any of your rulers.*

Never curse God or anyone in leadership over you.

ECCLESIASTES 10:20 | *Never make light of the king, even in your thoughts. And don't make fun of the powerful, even in your own bedroom. For a little bird might deliver your message and tell them what you said.*

Don't make fun of those in leadership.

PSALM 34:12-13 | *Does anyone want to live a life that is long and prosperous? Then keep your tongue from speaking evil and your lips from telling lies!*

Avoid saying anything that is deceptive or false.

PROVERBS 18:8 | *Rumors are dainty morsels that sink deep into one's heart.*

Avoid slander or spreading gossip about other people.

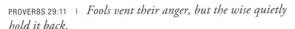

PROVERBS 29:11 | *Fools vent their anger, but the wise quietly hold it back.*

Avoid speaking in the heat of anger; you will usually regret it later.

JAMES 4:11 | *Don't speak evil against each other, dear brothers and sisters. If you criticize and judge each other, then you are criticizing and judging God's law.*

Avoid criticizing other people.

Promise from God PROVERBS 10:11 | *The words of the godly are a life-giving fountain.*

WORRY

How can I worry less?

PSALM 55:4 | *My heart pounds in my chest. The terror of death assaults me.*

Worry and fear are normal responses to threatening situations, but often you imagine far worse scenarios than ever happen. Most of your worries never take place.

EXODUS 14:13 | *Moses told the people, "Don't be afraid. Just stand still and watch the LORD rescue you today."*

Combat worry and anxiety by remembering and trusting what God, in his Word, has already promised to do for you.

PHILIPPIANS 4:6 | *Don't worry about anything; instead, pray about everything.*

Combat worry by placing your cares in Jesus' hands.

PSALM 62:6 | *[God] alone is my rock and my salvation, my fortress where I will not be shaken.*

Remembering that God's love and care for you are as solid as a rock can help keep your worries in perspective. He has everything under control.

MATTHEW 6:27 | *Can all your worries add a single moment to your life?*

Instead of adding more time or a better quality of life, worry affects your health and kills your joy.

When does worry become sin?

MATTHEW 13:22 | *The seed that fell among the thorns represents those who hear God's word, but all too quickly the message is crowded out by the worries of this life and the lure of wealth, so no fruit is produced.*

COLOSSIANS 3:2 | *Think about the things of heaven, not the things of earth.*

Worry is like thorny weeds—left uncontrolled, it crowds out what is good. Worry over the concerns of life becomes sin when it prevents the Word of God from taking root in your life. Worry is the misuse of your God-given imagination.

Promise from God 1 PETER 5:7 | *Give all your worries and cares to God, for he cares about you.*

WORSHIP

How is worship integral to my relationship with God?

1 CHRONICLES 16:29 | *Give to the LORD the glory he deserves! Bring your offering and come into his presence. Worship the LORD in all his holy splendor.*

PSALM 145:3 | *Great is the LORD! He is most worthy of praise! No one can measure his greatness.*

Worship is the recognition of who God is and who you are in relation to him. It is acknowledging his character and his many acts of love toward you. And it is returning love to him.

EXODUS 29:43 | *I will meet the people of Israel there, in the place made holy by my glorious presence.*

God meets with his people in a powerful way when they worship him together.

DEUTERONOMY 31:11 | *Read this Book of Instruction to all the people of Israel when they assemble before the LORD your God at the place he chooses.*

MICAH 4:2 | *Come, let us go up to the mountain of the LORD, to the house of Jacob's God. There he will teach us his ways, and we will walk in his paths.*

Something unique happens when God's people congregate to sing, praise, and listen to his Word, worshiping him together. There is a sense of community and fellowship that can happen only in corporate worship.

PSALM 5:7 | *Because of your unfailing love, I can enter your house; I will worship at your Temple with deepest awe.*

ISAIAH 6:3 | *Holy, holy, holy is the LORD of Heaven's Armies! The whole earth is filled with his glory!*

Worship is a fitting response to God's holiness, power, and grace.

REVELATION 4:9-11 | *Whenever the living beings give glory and honor and thanks to the one sitting on the throne (the one who lives forever and ever), the twenty-four elders fall down and worship. . . . And they lay their crowns before the throne and say, "You are worthy, O Lord our God, to receive glory and honor*

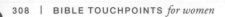

and power. For you created all things, and they exist because you created what you pleased.”

Your worship of God is a foretaste of heaven.

What does worshiping God involve? How should I worship God?

GENESIS 35:2-3 | *Jacob told everyone in his household, “Get rid of all your pagan idols, purify yourselves, and put on clean clothing. We are now going to Bethel, where I will build an altar to the God who answered my prayers when I was in distress. He has been with me wherever I have gone.”*

DEUTERONOMY 11:16 | *Don’t let your heart be deceived so that you turn away from the LORD and serve and worship other gods.*

Worship only God, because he alone is worthy of your utmost devotion.

EXODUS 3:5 | *“Do not come any closer,” the LORD warned. “Take off your sandals, for you are standing on holy ground.”*

Recognize that, wherever you are when you approach God’s presence in worship, you are standing on holy ground.

PSALM 35:18 | *I will thank you in front of the great assembly. I will praise you before all the people.*

Your worship should include praise and thanks to God for what he has done.

1 CHRONICLES 13:8 | *David and all Israel were celebrating before God with all their might, singing songs and playing all kinds of musical instruments—lyres, harps, tambourines, cymbals, and trumpets.*

Worship can take the form of a joyous celebration with instruments of music.

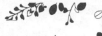
PSALM 95:6 | *Come, let us worship and bow down. Let us kneel before the LORD our maker.*

Kneeling and bowing are two appropriate postures for worship.

HEBREWS 12:28 | *Since we are receiving a Kingdom that is unshakable, let us be thankful and please God by worshiping him with holy fear and awe.*

Respect and awe for what is holy should accompany thanksgiving as appropriate attitudes in worship.

AMOS 5:21 | *I hate all your show and pretense—the hypocrisy of your religious festivals and solemn assemblies.*

Public worship is useless unless it is done with sincerity and with the desire to live wholeheartedly for God.

Promise from God PHILIPPIANS 2:9-11 | *God elevated him to the place of highest honor and gave him the name above all other names, that at the name of Jesus every knee should bow, in heaven and on earth and under the earth, and every tongue confess that Jesus Christ is Lord, to the glory of God the Father.*

WORTH/WORTHINESS

What am I worth—what is my value to God?

GENESIS 1:27 | *God created human beings in his own image. In the image of God he created them; male and female he created them.*

DEUTERONOMY 26:18 | *The LORD has declared today that you are his people, his own special treasure, just as he promised, and that you must obey all his commands.*

PSALM 8:5 | *[The Lord] made [human beings] only a little lower than God and crowned them with glory and honor.*

MATTHEW 16:26 | *What do you benefit if you gain the whole world but lose your own soul? Is anything worth more than your soul?*

EPHESIANS 2:10 | *We are God's masterpiece. He has created us anew in Christ Jesus, so we can do the good things he planned for us long ago.*

God made you in his own image—you are his treasure and masterpiece! You are invaluable to him, which is why he sent his own Son to die for your sins so that you could live in heaven with him forever.

PSALM 139:13 | *You made all the delicate, inner parts of my body and knit me together in my mother's womb.*

JEREMIAH 1:5 | *I knew you before I formed you in your mother's womb. Before you were born I set you apart and appointed you.*

God made you with great skill and crafted you with loving care. He showed how much value he places on you by the way he made you.

PSALM 139:17 | *How precious are your thoughts about me, O God. They cannot be numbered!*

Almighty God thinks wonderful thoughts about you all the time. He looks inside you and sees your real value.

PSALM 139:1-3, 6 | *O LORD, you have examined my heart and know everything about me. You know when I sit down or stand up. You know my thoughts even when I'm far away. You see me when I travel and when I rest at home. You know everything I do. . . . Such knowledge is too wonderful for me, too great for me to understand!*

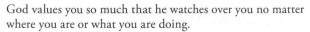

God values you so much that he watches over you no matter where you are or what you are doing.

1 CORINTHIANS 6:19 | *Don't you realize that your body is the temple of the Holy Spirit, who lives in you and was given to you by God?*

God values you so much that he even allows your body to become the temple in which he lives. God does not need to live in you. He can live anywhere. But by choosing to live within you, he declares you his dwelling place.

GALATIANS 3:26 | *You are all children of God through faith in Christ Jesus.*

GALATIANS 4:7 | *You are no longer a slave but God's own child. And since you are his child, God has made you his heir.*

God values you so much that he has adopted you as his child.

MATTHEW 28:20 | *[Jesus said,] "Be sure of this: I am with you always, even to the end of the age."*

God's Son promises to be with you always. Why would he want to be with you if he didn't value you?

What makes me worthy?

GENESIS 1:27 | *God created human beings in his own image. In the image of God he created them; male and female he created them.*

You—and all other human beings—are created in God's image. This means God values you highly.

1 CORINTHIANS 6:20 | *God bought you with a high price. So you must honor God with your body.*

1 CORINTHIANS 7:23 | *God paid a high price for you, so don't be enslaved by the world.*

You are worthy because God paid a high price for you. He loved you enough to die for you.

EPHESIANS 1:4-7 | *Even before he made the world, God loved us and chose us in Christ to be holy and without fault in his eyes. God decided in advance to adopt us into his own family by bringing us to himself through Jesus Christ. This is what he wanted to do, and it gave him great pleasure. So we praise God for the glorious grace he has poured out on us who belong to his dear Son. He is so rich in kindness and grace that he purchased our freedom with the blood of his Son and forgave our sins.*

Before God made the world, he chose you to be born as his unique creation, holy and forgiven.

How can I develop a healthier sense of self-worth?

PSALM 139:17 | *How precious are your thoughts about me, O God. They cannot be numbered!*

ROMANS 12:3 | *Be honest in your evaluation of yourselves, measuring yourselves by the faith God has given us.*

1 PETER 4:10 | *God has given each of you a gift from his great variety of spiritual gifts. Use them well to serve one another.*

Healthy self-esteem comes from an honest appraisal of yourself—not too proud, because your gifts and abilities were given to you by God, yet not so self-effacing that you fail to accept and use your gifts and abilities to their potential. Using your gifts to bless and serve others actually increases your self-worth because it takes the focus off of you and allows God to work more effectively through you.

Promise from God PSALM 8:5 | *[The Lord] made [human beings] only a little lower than God and crowned them with glory and honor.*